PERSPECTIVES IN CALIFORNIA ARCHAEOLOGY

Cotsen Institute of Archaeology
Perspectives in California Archaeology

The volumes in this series cover substantive and theoretical topics focusing on archaeological research in California.

THE ARCHAEOLOGY AND HISTORICAL ECOLOGY OF LATE HOLOCENE SAN MIGUEL ISLAND

BY
TORBEN C. RICK

COTSEN INSTITUTE OF ARCHAEOLOGY
UNIVERSITY OF CALIFORNIA, LOS ANGELES
2007

This book is set in Janson Text.
Copyedited by Rena Copperman
Produced by Leyba Associates
Cover design by William Morosi
Index by Robert and Cynthia Swanson

Library of Congress Cataloging-in-Publication Data

Rick, Torben C.
The archaeology and historical ecology of Late Holocene San
Miguel Island / by Torben C. Rick.
      p. cm. -- (Perspectives in California archaeology ; v. 8)
   Includes bibliographical references and index.
   ISBN 978-1-931745-36-9 (pbk. : alk. paper)
   ISBN 978-1-931745-37-6 (cloth : alk. paper)
   1. Paleo-Indians—California—San Miguel Island. 2. Chumash Indians—California—San Miguel Island—Antiquities. 3. Paleoecology—Holocene. 4. Excavations (Archaeology)—California—San Miguel Island. 5. San Miguel Island (Calif.)—Antiquities.
I. Title. II. Series.
E78.C15R53 2007   979.4'91--dc22
                                        2007000294

Contents

List of Figures

List of Tables

Preface

This book is a revised and expanded version of my University of Oregon Ph.D. dissertation. I have significantly modified sections of the dissertation, including the addition of more detailed analyses of bird and fish remains and soils, and a larger sample of artifacts and faunal remains for some of the sites presented in the original study. I have also updated the references and expanded and refined the book's conclusions. Most significantly, the original dissertation included a lengthy chapter on my research at SRI-2 on Santa Rosa Island. The book presented here focuses on San Miguel Island, and consequently this chapter was omitted, although the data are referred to for comparisons.

This project could never have been completed without the help of a great number of individuals. I thank the members of my Ph.D. committee: Jon Erlandson, Mel Aikens, John Johnson, Douglas Kennett, Madonna Moss, and Cathy Whitlock for providing constructive comments on earlier versions of this document and greatly improving its content. In particular, I thank Jon Erlandson, my friend, mentor, and committee chair for his support and encouragement throughout this project. I thank Jeanne Arnold, Shauna Mecartea, Julia Sanchez, the editorial board of the Cotsen Institute of Archaeology, and the Cotsen Institute publications staff for their help in the revision, editing, and production of this manuscript. I thank Jeanne Arnold and Terry Jones for providing a number of insightful and important comments on an earlier version of this manuscript.

This project was funded by a National Science Foundation Dissertation Improvement Grant (BCS-0201668) awarded to Rick and Erlandson. Portions of this research were also funded by a National Park Service Cooperative Agreement (#1443CA8120–00–007). Steve Schwartz of the Naval Air Weapons Facility, Point Mugu, provided funds for radiocarbon dating and research on San Miguel Island. This research was also supported by the Western National Parks Association and by a dissertation writing fellowship from the University of Oregon.

At Channel Islands National Park, I am indebted to Ann Huston, Don Morris, Georganna Hawley, Kelly Minas, Ian Williams, and Mark Senning for their help and encouragement. Don Morris introduced me to many of the sites I excavated and helped set up the initial cooperative agreement that funded some of this research. Ann Huston has always been supportive of my research and was instrumental in providing funds that helped me conduct this research. I thank Ian Williams for his support, insight on island natural history, and logistical help on San Miguel Island.

I also thank Bob DeLong and Sharon Melin of the National Marine Mammal Laboratory in Seattle for logistical help on San Miguel Island, for fantastic cooking, for help understanding island ecology and history, and for encouraging and supporting my research. Bob also helped identify marine sea mammal remains and graciously provided access to comparative collections in Seattle. Mike Etnier also helped identify some of the collections, provided insight on marine mammal identification, supplied thoughtful comments on marine mammals and ecology in general, and gave me a place to stay in Seattle. I also thank Dan Guthrie and Paul Collins for their help identifying some of the bird remains presented in this study.

A number of graduate and undergraduate students at the University of Oregon and Southern Methodist University helped in the field and laboratory. In particular, I thank René Vellanoweth for being a valued friend and colleague. I also thank Scott Fitzpatrick, Geoffrey Hamilton, Jerry Jacka, Rob Losey, and Todd Braje for their friendship, collegiality, and encouragement of this research. I thank Deana Dartt for making me a more thoughtful and inclusive scholar. Many of the shell midden samples discussed in this book were originally sorted by Jenna Boyle, Jessica Brower, Sara Davis, Erika Dickey, Josh Harris, Twila Lorange, John

Mackey, Angela Maxwell, Melissa Reid, Jennifer Rice, Jason Schroeder, Kelly Shaw, Natalie Smith, Kate Swanger, David Wickham, and Jessica Zehr. Numerous students from Erlandson's *Fundamentals of Archaeology* courses in 2001, 2002, and 2003 also greatly helped in the lab. Julie Bernard, Michael Cruz, Deana Dartt, Jon Erlandson, Julia Knowles, Leah Largaespada, Tony Largaespada, Twila Lorange, Rob Losey, and René Vellanoweth provided invaluable help in the field.

I thank Mike Glassow and Jeanne Arnold for getting me started in the archaeology of California and the Channel Islands, providing thoughtful comments at the start of this project, and continuing to be supportive of my research. A number of people contributed to my research intellectually or otherwise, including Julie Bernard, Paul Collins, Lynn Gamble, Ken Gobalet, Anthony Graesch, Mike Jochim, Terry Jones, Kent Lightfoot, Ann Munns, Anna Noah, Peter Paige, Jennifer Perry, Scott Pletka, Mark Raab, John Ruiz, Bill Smith, John Sharp, Jan Timbrook, and Phil Walker.

Finally, I thank my wife, Kelsey, and daughter, Luella, for their support and encouragement throughout this process. I also thank my parents, Gary and Linda, and sister, Hadley, for their help and support. In particular, my parents graciously provided a place to stay and to store field equipment while I was conducting fieldwork. Ellen Gerhard and Jeff Lychwick were also extremely supportive throughout this project. If there is anyone I have overlooked please accept my thanks.

1

Introduction

The world's coastal regions have long been centers of human settlement, commerce, and interaction. The interface of land and sea, which creates some of the most diverse and productive environments on earth, fostered a variety of unique cultural developments and lifeways. In recent years, the environments and peoples of coastal areas have spurred a series of lively debates, prompting researchers to examine a number of broad anthropological and environmental issues. For example, when and why did people first adopt a coastal lifestyle? What is the role of ancient seacoasts, rivers, lakes, and other aquatic environments in promoting high population densities, sedentism, and cultural elaboration? How have people impacted and altered the various coastal environments they inhabited? In the broader

scheme of human cultural and biological evolution, what is the significance of coastal regions?

In this book, I explore some of these issues by examining social, economic, and ecologic developments among the Chumash and their predecessors of California's northern Channel Islands (Figure 1.1). The Chumash were a coastal hunter-gatherer society that flourished in southern California for millennia. Historically, the Chumash occupied the northern Channel Islands and the adjacent mainland from San Luis Obispo to Malibu, and the archaeological record of the area extends back about 13,000 calendar years. The Chumash and their predecessors have been intensively studied by anthropologists and archaeologists, providing a rich ethnographic and archaeological data set. The archaeology of the

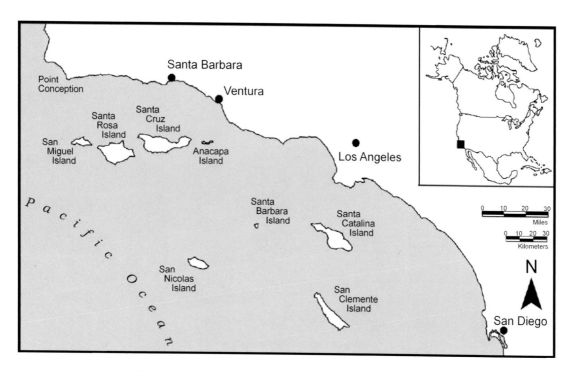

Figure 1.1. The southern California coast and Channel Islands.

1

area has played a pivotal role in studies of the evolution of cultural complexity and the antiquity of maritime adaptations (see Arnold 1996; Arnold, ed. 2001, 2004; Erlandson 1994; Kennett 2005). In recent years, contemporary Chumash people have also been in the midst of a cultural revival, including cross-channel voyages to Santa Cruz Island in a traditional tomol (plank canoe).

Although the Channel Islands have a lengthy and continuous archaeological record, there is a dearth of information for the period between about 3,000 and 1,500 years ago, and numerous spatial gaps, including relatively limited research conducted on the westernmost island of San Miguel. Using archaeological data from five sites on San Miguel Island, I help fill this gap by exploring changes in human daily activities, community dynamics, emergent complexity, and ecology over the last 3,000 years (Figure 1.2). Through the integration of artifact, faunal, and settlement data, I outline the organization and types of activities that people on San Miguel Island conducted at various stages of the Late Holocene. When compared with research elsewhere on the Channel Islands and from Early and Middle Holocene sites, these data provide a

framework for understanding long-term changes in cultural and social evolution. Detailed analysis of faunal remains from these sites also provides an overview of how humans interacted with and impacted Channel Islands environments through time. In this framework, human cultural evolution and ecological changes are inseparably linked (Crumley 2001). Ultimately, these reconstructions of Chumash lifeways provide broad lessons about the diversity and variability of coastal peoples around the world. In the remainder of this chapter, I provide an overview of the research goals and theoretical orientation of the study.

COASTAL ADAPTATIONS

Over the last 25 years, archaeologists and anthropologists have amassed a considerable amount of data on the strategies and lifeways of the world's coastal peoples (see Bailey 2004; Bailey and Milner 2002; Erlandson 2001; Erlandson and Fitzpatrick 2006). These studies have shown that coastal societies hold a distinct place in human history. Native North American coastal peoples, for example, were among the most densely populated hunter-gatherers in the world. Often rivaling the social organiza-

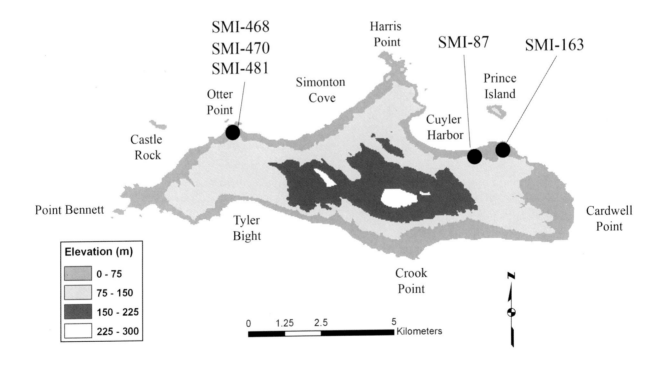

Figure 1.2. San Miguel Island and major archaeological sites and locations discussed in the text.

tion and high population densities of intermediate-scale agriculturalists, the cultural complexity of Northwest Coast or California coastal peoples stands in sharp contrast to the small bands of hunter-gatherers typified by Lee and Devore (1968) and in popular culture.

With the publication of two edited volumes on complex hunter-gatherers in the 1980s, and a series of articles on coastal adaptations more generally, archaeologists and anthropologists took note of the variability of past and present hunter-gatherer societies (Koyama and Thomas 1981; Price and Brown 1985). These and other works began to paint a new picture of coastal regions, including several studies on the productivity of coastal resources and the role of coastal environments in human social and cultural evolution (e.g., Arnold 1992a; Bailey 1975; Erlandson 1988a; Moseley 1975; Osborn 1977; Perlman 1980; Quilter and Stocker 1983; Raymond 1981; Waselkov 1987; Wilson 1981; Yesner 1980). Early research on the world's coastal areas was often highly polarized, with some scholars arguing that coastal regions abounded with food and other resources, while others suggested that coastal areas were inhabited only as a last resort. Erlandson (1994) characterized these opposing views of coastal resources as Garden of Eden vs. Gates of Hell models, concluding that the truth probably lies somewhere in the middle.

Today research on coastal peoples and complex hunter-gatherers is flourishing. Once thought to have been intensively utilized only since the late Upper Paleolithic in the Old World and the Middle Holocene in North America (Yesner 1987:285), the antiquity of coastal adaptations has recently been extended back to our ancient human ancestors (Erlandson 2001; Henshilwood et al. 2001; Klein 1999; Klein et al. 2004; Parkington 2003). Several early sites occupied by *Homo habilis*, *Homo erectus*, and archaic *Homo sapiens* provide tantalizing but speculative associations with aquatic resources (Erlandson 2001; Erlandson and Fitzpatrick 2006). The possibility of *Homo erectus* on an offshore island in Java (Flores Island) suggests that some seafaring capabilities may have existed as much as 800,000 years ago (Morwood et al. 1998, 1999), and much longer voyages by anatomically modern humans contributed to the colonization of Australia and the Bismarck Archipelago during the past 60,000 to 30,000 years (Erlandson 2001). With the appearance of anatomi-

cally modern humans, the number of coastal sites increased in the Old World. Locating such early sites, however, is hindered by destruction or submergence of early sites by rising sea levels, and often dubious associations of marine resources with clear human occupation in early sites (see Bailey 2004; Erlandson 2001; Erlandson and Moss 2001; Rowley-Conwy 2001).

Recent research in the Americas has also emphasized the early origins of coastal settlement and subsistence. Perhaps the most dramatic change in thought has centered around the initial peopling of the Americas. The first Americans were previously believed to have followed an exclusively overland migration across the Bering Land Bridge, but numerous researchers are now emphasizing the possibility of a coastal migration into the New World (Dixon 1999; Erlandson 1994, 2002; Fedje and Christensen 1999; Fedje et al. 2004; Fladmark 1979; Jones et al. 2002). In Peru, the exploitation of coastal resources, including the use of fishnets and unique birding strategies, have been documented by about 12,500 cal BP or earlier (deFrance 2005; Keefer et al. 1998; Sandweiss et al. 1998). The California Channel Islands have also provided evidence of coastal adaptations by about 11,500 cal BP at Daisy Cave on San Miguel Island (Erlandson et al. 1996; Rick et al. 2001a). Redating of the Arlington Springs skeleton on Santa Rosa Island suggests that ancient peoples may have used boats for cross-channel voyages as early as 13,000 cal BP (Johnson et al. 2002). Although still debated, a consensus is emerging that coastal areas played an important role in human biological and cultural evolution and that by the onset of the Holocene, if not earlier, coastal adaptations throughout the world were widespread and diverse.

Paralleling the resurgence in research on the antiquity of aquatic adaptations, studies on the emergence of cultural complexity in coastal areas have also greatly expanded. Archaeologists and anthropologists have demonstrated that coastal regions around the world were centers of ancient cultural complexity, including portions of Florida (Marquardt 1988, 1992a, 2001), the Northwest Coast of North America (Ames 1994, 2003; Ames and Maschner 1999; Matson and Coupland 1995; Moss and Erlandson 1995), coastal Peru (Moseley 1975), Thailand (Higham 1996; Higham and Thosarat 1994), and Japan (Habu 2002, 2004). In some of these areas, evolutionary trajectories led to the development of agriculture (e.g., Peru, Thailand, Japan), while in other regions people subsisted on wild plants and animals (e.g., Northwest Coast, California, and Florida). The recognition of relatively widespread cultural complexity in coastal and other regions has led recent scholars to emphasize the distinct pathways that people in various regions followed toward higher population densities, complex exchange systems, and more rigid social hierarchies (see Arnold 1993, 1996, 2001a, 2001b; Erlandson and Jones 2002; Fitzhugh 2003; Hayden 1995; Kennett 2005; Kennett and Kennett 2000; Prentiss and Kuijt 2004; Sassaman 2004).

RESEARCH ISSUES AND THEORETICAL ORIENTATION

In this book, I use archaeological data to address a number of broad research issues and questions. Specifically, I provide a detailed overview of changes in human daily activities, emergent complexity, and ecology over roughly the last 3,000 years on San Miguel Island. This research represents a baseline for understanding long-term cultural developments among the Chumash and other coastal hunter-gatherers. This study joins recent work by Erlandson and Rick (2002a), Gamble (2005), Gamble and Russell (2002), Gamble et al. (2001), Glassow (2002a), and J. Johnson (2000) on Late Holocene mainland Chumash culture, and research by Arnold (1987, 1991, 1992a, 1992b, 1993, 1994; Arnold, ed. 2001, 2004), Kennett (1998, 2005), Kennett and Conlee (2002), Munns and Arnold (2002), Noah (2005), and Perry (2003, 2004) on Late Holocene Island Chumash cultures. Together these studies supply a rich context for understanding the evolution of Chumash society and among coastal hunter-gatherers more generally.

Through archaeological analysis of five sites on San Miguel Island occupied at various intervals over the last 3,000 years, I examine a variety of economic, cultural, and ecologic developments. These sites were selected for research because they are all large and dense occupational sites that represent a different interval of time during the Late Holocene. The research issues fall under three primary categories: (1) daily activities and community dynamics; (2) complex hunter-gatherers and emergent complexity; and (3) historical ecology and human impacts on ancient environments. Within each of these categories, archaeological data are used to examine a variety of issues. For example, what was the nature of human daily activities and community organization at each site and did these patterns vary through time and space? Is there evidence for changes in social organization through time at these sites, such as heightened cultural elaboration and craft specialization, that suggests a trend toward increasing cultural complexity? If so, what were the scale and pace of these events? Finally, how do human daily activities and changing social landscapes relate to alterations in island environments and historical ecology over the last 3,000 years? A study of this nature is admittedly broad in scope, but through my research I aim to illustrate how daily activities, social organization, and environmental developments are interrelated phenomena.

My research is grounded in cultural ecology and materialism (see Hayden 1998:243), and I use an evolutionary and historical approach to contextualize archaeological data over the entire Holocene rather than looking at a narrow window of time (Ames 1991; Lightfoot 1993; McGuire 1996; Moss and Erlandson 1995). In this approach, material remains represent utilitarian items, as well as the symbolic and social worldviews of individuals and the larger society around them. Likewise, faunal remains not only represent subsistence goods, but are indicative of changes in human health, demography, technology, status, environmental developments, and impacts on local habitats and organisms (Reitz and Wing 1999). Through the careful documentation and analysis of artifacts and ecofacts, we can begin to understand both individual behavior and community organization.

In recent years, a number of theoretical paradigms have been used to explain the evolution of social organization in coastal California. These include models based on Marxism (Arnold 1992a, 1993), resource intensification (Raab 1996; Raab et al. 1995a, 2002), risk management (Scalise 1994), and behavioral ecology (Kennett 2005). In various ways, these models seek to explain the evolution of complexity in California through an understanding and evaluation of individual pursuits, group responses, and ecological changes. I use a multitheoretical approach focused on agency, ecology, and history (see Pauketat 2001). Such an approach is complex, but is valuable for developing a comprehensive picture of cultural development and building bridges across theoretical paradigms (see Pauketat 2001, 2003; Schiffer 2000). According to VanPool and VanPool (2003:2):

> theoretical plurality can and frequently does lead to greater insight than is possible using a single theoretical perspective by itself. In a book that is less widely read in archaeological circles than his *Structures of Scientific Revolutions* titled *The Essential Tension*, Kuhn (1977) made this point as well. He observes that some of the greatest scientific insights are made possible only through the collaboration of and debate among different theoretical perspectives.

My approach echoes these sentiments and bears much similarity to what Hegmon (2003) recently defined as processual-plus archaeology and what Pauketat (2001, 2003) has called historical-processualism.

The integration of daily activities and ecology also draws from aspects of evolutionary and cultural ecology. As Fitzhugh (2003:9) noted, multiple theoretical paradigms (e.g., evolutionary ecology, practice) can be intertwined and interrelated, often emphasizing changes in social dynamics as the accumulation of the long-term actions of people. As archaeological theory has become more fragmented and dispersed over the years (Dunnell 1986), a trend toward eclecticism/plurality, if used in the proper way, may help to unify the theoretical approaches and goals of archaeology.

Daily Activities and Community Dynamics

One of archaeology's greatest strengths is reconstructing aspects of human daily life. Archaeological analysis of midden or trash deposits, architecture, and artifacts provides information on the often mundane activities that people engaged in on a daily basis (Lightfoot et al. 1998). Archaeologists and anthropologists have long emphasized the importance that human daily practice has in building the social, spiritual, political, and symbolic world (see Hegmon 2003; Pauketat 2001). A growing body of archaeological research also illustrates how human daily activities can help reconstruct broader issues of social organization, ritual, and ideology (Hegmon 2003). Some of the most potent studies of human daily practice emerge from re-

search on culture contact in pluralistic settings (e.g., Lightfoot 2005; Lightfoot et al. 1998; Silliman 2001, 2004). Working on the northern California coast, Lightfoot et al. (1998) outlined the study of everyday life as a tool for understanding changes in worldview in the multiethnic community of nineteenth-century Fort Ross. Here the structure and contents of trash middens, architecture, and other aspects of material culture provided the foundation for reconstructing human daily routines. With the addition of new aspects of material culture (e.g., metal tools), we gain insight into how Native peoples and colonists in this pluralistic setting influenced, interacted with, and sculpted the world around them (Lightfoot et al. 1998).

In this study, I use archaeological data, including faunal remains, artifacts, and the structure of Native communities, to reconstruct aspects of everyday life. These activities include the organization and distribution of subsistence pursuits (fishing, hunting, gathering, etc.), bead and other artifact production, exchange, and the formation of social relations. By understanding how these practices vary through time and space we can gain a diachronic perspective of changes in the fabric of Chumash society. One complication in this process is that studying human daily activities necessarily involves reconstructing individual behaviors, including gender, status, and age differences. However, the archaeological record rarely speaks directly to individuals, but rather is a palimpsest of the activities of groups of individuals. Ultimately, I aim to demonstrate how reconstructions of human daily life (even at the group level) provide insight into changing social relations and human–environmental interactions among the Chumash and their predecessors on San Miguel Island. Specifically, the archaeological data on daily life that I gathered include craft and other artifact production, exchange and trade, and subsistence strategies. Through a diachronic investigation of each of these activities, I document patterns of emergent complexity and historical ecology on the Channel Islands.

Complex Hunter-Gatherers and Emergent Complexity

Archaeological research on complex hunter-gatherers and emergent complexity has grown exponentially, including a number of studies from coastal areas (see Ames 1994; Arnold 1996;

Arnold, ed. 2001; Fitzhugh 2003; Habu 2002; Matson and Coupland 1995; Price and Brown 1985; Sassaman 2004). Referencing the Calusa of coastal Florida, groups in the Pacific Northwest, and the Chumash, Arnold (2001a: 2) suggested that:

> the rich and varied wild resources, potentials for storage and control of crucial foods and goods, large semi-sedentary to sedentary populations, and sophisticated technologies of these favorably situated coastal/riverine groups ultimately permitted the same kinds of labor control and political structures to develop as those of intermediate-scale agricultural societies.

Arnold is quick to add that it was not these favorable environmental conditions alone that were the cause of complexity, but it is clear that the productivity of coastal areas often promoted significant cultural elaboration. Patterns of social and political complexity have often waxed and waned through time with no clear directional trend toward complexity or from complex hunter-gatherers to agriculturalists (Rowley-Conwy 2001). Moreover, all human societies are complex to a degree, but clearly the high population densities and elaborate social and political systems of some coastal hunter-gatherers hold a unique place in the human past.

A major issue in the study of complex hunter-gatherers is developing a definition of complexity (Arnold 1996). A number of researchers have emphasized the archaeological correlates of complexity, often relating these to the emergence of a chiefdom level of social organization (e.g., Arnold 1993, 1996, 2001a; Carneiro 1981; Johnson and Earle 1987). Arnold (1996, 2001a) provided perhaps the most detailed definition, aligning complex hunter-gatherers with a simple chiefdom, where hereditary political control extends beyond the level of a household or village. Essential to Arnold's definition is that hereditary leaders have sustained control of non-kin labor. She reserves the term affluent *hunter-gatherers* for those groups that are collectors, but are typified by sequential and situational leadership (Arnold 2001a: 3). Fitzhugh (2003:3) provided a similar definition, suggesting that complex hunter-gatherers are unified by institutionalized inequality and the integration of multiple family units into larger political forms. Erlandson and Rick

(2002a) suggested that defining chiefdom levels of social organization and hereditary leadership in the archaeological record is complicated by a variety of factors (taphonomy, chronological resolution, etc.). I treat cultural complexity as the combination of different elements, including elaboration in material culture, subsistence and economic shifts, institutionalized exchange, household and community organization, and other factors (see Ames 1994, 2003). In this sense, I do not seek to explain the Chumash transition to a chiefdom, but rather I investigate at the variability in Chumash social organization and trends in cultural elaboration and complexity during the Late Holocene.

COMPLEXITY IN MARITIME SOUTHERN CALIFORNIA

Several lively scholarly exchanges in California have involved the nature of Chumash sociopolitical organization and the emergence of cultural complexity (see Chapter 2; Arnold 1992a, 2001a, 2001b, 2004; Arnold and Bernard 2005; Erlandson and Rick 2002a; Gamble 2005; Gamble and Russell 2002; Gamble et al. 2001; J. Johnson 2000; Kennett 2005; Kennett and Conlee 2002; King 1990; Munns and Arnold 2002; Raab 1996; Raab and Bradford 1997; Raab and Larson 1997). The most comprehensive studies of sociopolitical organization on the Channel Islands have been provided by Jeanne Arnold and her colleagues. Arnold's research focuses on the evolution of Chumash cultural complexity using data gathered from Santa Cruz Island (see Arnold 1991, 1992a, 1992b, 1994; 1997, 2001b, 2004; Arnold et al. 1997a, 1997b; Munns and Arnold 2002), with broader theoretical implications described in Arnold (1993, 1996, 2000). Arnold's model draws on Marxist theory complemented by a multitheoretical approach, which looks at aspects of human intentionality, craft specialization, elite control, and responses to environmental shifts (see Arnold 1992a). Arnold (2001b:237) argued that Chumash complexity is not accidental, but rather emerged from a series of human responses to social and environmental variables. Arnold (1992, 2001b) proposed a punctuated model, arguing that between about AD 1150 and 1300 (Middle to Late period transition; referred to hereafter as the Transitional period), people in coastal southern California underwent dramatic political and social reorganization. This punctuated model contrasts with the more gradual model proposed by King (1990) who argued that Chumash complexity may have been in place by about 2,500 years ago. Erlandson and Rick (2002a:182) presented an intermediate view, emphasizing the combination of punctuated and gradual events in changing social dynamics and cultural elaboration.

Recent research by Kennett (2005; Kennett and Conlee 2002; Kennett and Kennett 2000) has examined Island Chumash society across the Holocene. Grounded in behavioral ecology, Kennett's (2005) research emphasizes variability in the regional archaeological record and a host of local responses to a variety of environmental and cultural variables. In his model, Chumash cultural complexity increased between 1,500 and 800 years ago within the context of long-term population growth, climatic instability, resource intensification, and heightened patterns of interpersonal violence. Raab (1996), Raab and Bradford (1997), Raab and Larson (1997), and others have also explored changes in cultural complexity, emphasizing the importance of population growth, resource depression, and other factors in promoting increased social hierarchy. Arnold (1992a) and J. Johnson (2000) have emphasized the importance of intervillage trade in developing political hierarchies. Each of these models documents a series of relatively abrupt changes occurring largely during the Late Holocene and culminating during the Late period.

Data from individual burials and cemeteries have also been used to examine changes in sociopolitical complexity in the region, particularly evidence for hereditary (ascribed) leadership (Gamble et al. 2001; C. King 1990; L. King 1982; Martz 1992). Burial data are often important for interpreting social organization because they can provide perspectives on the status of individuals (Wason 1994). However, the analysis of cemetery data to determine aspects of social organization are complicated by a variety of factors, such as preservation of the site deposits and excavation strategies (see Arnold and Green 2002). King (1990:94–96), relying partly on burial data from SCRI-333 (a.k.a. SCRI-3) on Santa Cruz Island, suggested that Chumash cultural complexity and hereditary status differentiation may have emerged roughly 2,500 years ago or earlier. Martz (1992) examined several cemeteries on the southern California coast and Santa Monica Mountains, comparing patterns of

achieved and ascribed status. To Martz (1992), evidence for ascribed status emerged after about 900 years ago. Munns and Arnold (2002:144–145) recently challenged King's assertions for social ascription around 2,500 years ago, suggesting the data were too limited to propose such an early date (but see Gamble et al. 2001). All of the burial data from the Channel Islands and much of the data from the adjacent mainland come from reanalyses of materials excavated 50 years ago or more by Phil Orr, Ronald Olsen, David Banks Rogers, and other early scholars working in the region. These studies often did not have the tight chronological or stratigraphic control necessary for defining changes in time, making the interpretation of burial data in the region somewhat problematic (Arnold and Green 2002).

Analyses of patterns of health, disease, and violence from human skeletal remains from the Channel Islands and Santa Barbara mainland have also been used to explore the evolution of Chumash society (Hollimon 1990; Lambert 1993, 1994; Lambert and Walker 1991). Lambert (1993) documented a decline in health through time among northern Channel Islanders, particularly during the late Middle period when Channel Islanders became increasingly focused on fishing. These data also show a slight rebound in human health during the Late period (Lambert 1993). Lambert and Walker (1991) indicated increased evidence of lethal conflict between about AD 300 and 1150, but a decrease during the Late period. To Lambert (1993, 1994) and Lambert and Walker (1991), growing population densities and greater circumscription and territoriality promoted declines in health and increased violence. When compounded with environmental perturbations, these events were important causes of cultural change and complexity. Hollimon's (1990) study of gender roles, health, and status of the Santa Barbara mainland and northern Channel Islands confirms many of Arnold's hypotheses about cultural changes during the Transitional period. Hollimon (1990:213–214) indicated that people living during the Transitional period suffered poorer health than people living before or after this time, and that cultural changes were probably instituted to buffer subsistence stress. Kennett (2005:214-215) and Raab and Larson (1997) have also used some of these data to suggest that increased violence, subsistence stress, and other variables beginning after about 1,500 years ago may have promoted instability in the area and led to more competition and greater cultural complexity.

My research into human daily activities and community dynamics on Late Holocene San Miguel Island addresses a variety of issues surrounding changing social organization on the Channel Islands. I contribute to the larger dialogue on emergent complexity on the Channel Islands by presenting primary data focused on craft and other artifact production, exchange, and subsistence from Late Holocene San Miguel Island, which are used to evaluate the role of people on this outer island in the larger Chumash interaction sphere. Through an integrated comparison of changes in craft and other artifact production, I also assess the timing of key patterns of Chumash cultural elaboration.

Historical Ecology

Historical ecology is a broad field of study focused on understanding how people have interacted with and altered the environments they have inhabited through time (see Balée 1998; Crumley 1994; Gragson 2005). Crumley (1994) suggested that historical ecology itself has multiple meanings and probably most simply is the cross-disciplinary integration of ecology and history. According to Crumley (1994:40):

knowledge of the history of natural systems is an indispensable part of their scientific analysis. The structural and functional properties of organisms, communities, and ecosystems must be sought in their history because they are only partly revealed in their extant form.

Historical ecology in this regard provides a framework for investigating long-term environmental and cultural relationships.

Archaeologists have long been interested in reconstructing ancient environments and the place of people within the natural world (e.g., Binford 1968; Butzer 1971, 1982; Dincauze 2000). A number of researchers have recently emphasized that archaeology and other historical disciplines supply a framework for investigating long-term human environmental interactions and the ways these data can elucidate contemporary environmental issues (Fisher and Feinman 2005; Hayashida 2005; Jack-

son et al. 2001; Kay and Simmons 2002; Kirch 1997, 2004; Kirch and Hunt 1997; Kirch et al. 1992; Krech 1999; Lyman and Cannon 2004; Redman 1999; Redman et al. 2004; van der Leeuw and Redman 2002). Van der Leeuw and Redman recently called for greater collaboration among archaeologists and life and natural scientists, suggesting a common approach to understanding past and present environmental issues:

The time is right for archaeology to assume a more central role in understanding human-environmental relations and addressing problems of broad significance to the sustainability of our society. (van der Leeuw and Redman 2002: 603)

Other researchers have demonstrated how archaeological and historical data can be integrated into developing effective ecological remediation, restoration, and management strategies for both terrestrial and marine ecosystems (Egan and Howell 2001; Jackson et al. 2001; Lyman 1996; Lyman and Cannon 2004; Steneck et al. 2002).

Grayson's (2001:46) synthesis of ancient human impact on animals suggests that all people—no matter how dense their populations or culturally complex they were—had some impacts on the environments they inhabited. In a study of faunal remains from the Emeryville Shell Mound in California, Broughton (1994, 1997, 1999, 2002) highlighted the potential of archaeology to reconstruct human impacts on the environment and help shape wilderness policy. Similar research has been conducted by Butler (2000; Butler and Campbell 2004) for the Northwest Coast of North America. A current debate in the Northwest Coast also centers on the role of ancient human use of fire and landscape burning in the promotion of open canopy wilderness (see Boyd 1999a; Whitlock and Knox 2002). Research by Marquardt (1992b, 1994, 1995) and colleagues in south Florida provided insight on the role of archaeology in reconstructing ancient environments and the potential of archaeology for raising contemporary environmental consciousness. Relying on historical photos and other documents, Kay (2002) highlighted the role of ancient environmental change for guiding wilderness policy in Yellowstone National Park. Similar studies have also been conducted in the Old World (Butzer 2005;

Roberts 1998; Simmons 2001). Simmons' (2001) detailed chronicle of environmental history in Great Britain from the late Pleistocene through the modern day is a particularly potent example of how researchers can intertwine history, prehistory, and environmental science.

On the northern Channel Islands, a number of researchers have also initiated long-term investigations of environmental change. Research by Braje et al. (2006a), Erlandson et al. (2004a, 2005a), and Rick et al. (2006a) supplies an overview of ancient and historical human impacts on Channel Islands ecosystems and the regional archaeological record of environmental change and continuity. Kennett (2005) also provided evidence for human impacts on Channel Islands marine resources, especially marine mammals and shellfish. These studies emphasize a variety of issues, including human harvesting of shellfish, hunting of marine mammals, kelp forest ecology, and dune formation (Erlandson et al. 2004a, 2005a, 2005b; Rick et al. 2006a). Walker et al. (2002; see also Kennett 2005) recently initiated a long-term investigation of human impact on a large breeding colony of pinnipeds (seals and sea lions) on San Miguel Island. Porcasi et al. (2000) conducted a similar study on sea mammal frequencies in trans-Holocene deposits on San Clemente Island, one of the southern Channel Islands. A number of archaeologists on the Channel Islands have also used the presence of various shellfish taxa and measurements of stable isotopes from archaeological shells to reconstruct ancient environments and climatic conditions on the Channel Islands (e.g., Arnold and Tissot 1993; Erlandson et al. 2004a; Glassow 1993a, 2002b, 2005a; Glassow et al. 1994; Kennett 1998, 2005; Kennett and Kennett 2000; Rick et al. 2005a; Sharp 2000). These studies have illustrated that the Channel Islands can play a pivotal role in understanding long-term ecological continuity and change and the role of people in influencing and documenting those developments.

I use faunal samples from the five San Miguel Island archaeological sites to reconstruct human subsistence and use of various habitats and organisms over the last 3,000 years. The taxonomic identification and quantification of faunal remains demonstrate the importance of various animals and habitats in human subsistence economies, exchange systems, and village location. These data also supply insight on the possibility of human impacts on local animal populations and ecological communities. Here I address several broad archaeological issues. How did subsistence patterns vary across the Late Holocene? How does the Late Holocene record compare with the Early and Middle Holocene? Specifically, how did the dietary importance of marine mammals, fish, birds, shellfish, and terrestrial foods differ temporally and spatially? Is there evidence for intensification through time, and what measurable impacts, if any, did people have on local environments? How do the impacts of the Chumash and their predecessors on San Miguel Island compare with Euroamerican impacts on the environment?

PREVIOUS RESEARCH ON SAN MIGUEL ISLAND

Currently, there are nearly 700 recorded sites on San Miguel Island. Compared with some of the other Channel Islands, however, San Miguel has received relatively limited attention from researchers. The first archaeological projects were conducted on the island in the late nineteenth century by Dall, Schumacher, Bowers, de Cessac, and others (Baldwin 1996; Glassow 1977). These projects were largely intended to acquire museum specimens, and consequently project records and provenience data are relatively poor. Freer, Glidden, and Woodward also worked on the island in the early twentieth century, and similarly little is known about each of these projects or the specific sites or locations where research was performed. Rogers (1929) also conducted limited research on the island in the early twentieth century. Phil Orr inventoried sites on the island and made some of the first formal site records for island sites in the 1950s. Although his site descriptions are limited, his research ushered in a series of survey and excavation projects during the 1960s and 1970s.

Between 1963 and 1968, Charles Rozaire and George Kritzman systematically surveyed San Miguel Island and excavated three sites (Rozaire 1978:65). They recorded 542 archaeological sites, with the vast majority of these scattered along the island's north coast between Point Bennett and Cuyler Harbor. Rozaire's test excavations at SMI-1, SMI-261 (Daisy Cave), and SMI-525 also yielded a variety of artifacts and faunal remains. Sixty-nine units were excavated at SMI-1, producing a large assemblage of faunal remains and several hundred artifacts. Two 5 × 5-foot pits were excavated at SMI-525, resulting in over 100 artifacts and abundant faunal remains. Twelve 5 × 5-foot pits were excavated at SMI-261. Unfortunately, these excavations were conducted in arbitrary levels, resulting in a mixing of stratigraphic deposits, and primarily ¼-inch mesh screen was used.

In 1977 and again in 1981, Greenwood (1978, 1982) surveyed portions of the island, visiting and updating the status of many of the sites recorded by Rozaire and Kritzman. Working for Channel Islands National Park, Greenwood updated the status of these sites and outlined criteria for park management of some of the island's cultural resources. Glassow (1982) conducted a small survey during 1980, which was followed up by a small-scale excavation project and analysis of human remains by Phil Walker and Pandora Snethkamp in 1982 (Walker and Snethkamp 1984). Limited faunal data and radiocarbon dates from the column samples are available in Walker and Snethkamp (1984).

Jon Erlandson excavated at the trans-Holocene site of Daisy Cave from 1992 to 1998, building on previous work by Rozaire in the 1960s and Snethkamp in 1985 (see Baldwin 1996; Connolly et al. 1995; Erlandson et al. 1996; Rick et al. 2001a). This research has demonstrated that coastal peoples occupied the island for at least 11,500 calendar years with unique maritime adaptations. Erlandson, Braje, and Rick have also recently surveyed the island's northwest and south coasts, identifying a number of early archaeological sites dated to about 10,000 to 8,000 years ago (Braje and Erlandson 2005; Braje et al. 2005a; Erlandson and Rick 2002b; Erlandson et al. 2004a, 2005b). Vellanoweth et al. (2002, 2003) conducted excavations at Cave of the Chimneys (SMI-603) in 1997–1999, providing additional data on Early, Middle, and Late Holocene peoples on the island. Erlandson and Vellanoweth also excavated in Middle Holocene deposits at Otter Cave (SMI-605) and SMI-481, but generally little is known about Middle Holocene cultural developments on the island (Erlandson et al. 2001a, 2005c; Vellanoweth et al. 2005). In a project designed to investigate the impact of human hunting on pinniped populations, Doug Kennett, Phil Walker, Bob DeLong, and Terry Jones excavated at three Middle and Late Holocene sites on the Point Bennett Pinniped rookery (SMI-525, -528, and -602). The results of their work are pending, but a preliminary report was published by Walker et al. (2002).

Despite these research projects, a number of significant gaps remain in our understanding of the ancient occupation of San Miguel Island. This is particularly true of the Middle and Late Holocene. The research presented here represents the first systematic study of Late Holocene peoples on the island and one of the few to provide detailed artifact, faunal, and other archaeological data for any period of the Holocene. One of the primary goals of this book is to bring San Miguel's remarkable archaeological record, particularly the last 3,000 years, into the larger context of Channel Islands and coastal California prehistory.

HERITAGE PRESERVATION

Archaeologists working in North America and beyond have increasingly emphasized the importance of conducting archaeological research in collaboration with the Native peoples they study. All of the research presented in this book was carried out in collaboration with Channel Islands National Park and in consultation with local Chumash representatives. This research, along with excavations at SRI-2 on Santa Rosa Island, was initiated under a cooperative agreement with Channel Islands National Park to investigate a variety of formation processes (i.e., marine erosion, wind deflation, and rodent burrowing) that were impacting and threatening Channel Islands archaeological sites (Rick 2002, 2004a; Rick and Erlandson 2004; Rick et al. 2006b). In keeping with the preservation ethic inherent in National Park Service policy and local Chumash concerns, relatively small samples were excavated, primarily in eroding or threatened areas of sites. This combination of a research-oriented project and cultural resource management (CRM) joins a number of other such projects in California (e.g., Erlandson 1994; Glassow 1996; Jones 2003; Jones and Waugh 1995). These studies demonstrate the importance of integrating preservation- and conservation-oriented archaeology with broad research goals and issues. The information presented in this book is a testament to the rich cultural traditions and histories of the Chumash and other Native peoples of the California coast.

OVERVIEW

In the next several chapters, I explore cultural and ecological issues using a variety of archaeological data sets. Each chapter provides a different view of Late Holocene human occupation of San Miguel, offering reconstructions of human activities throughout the last 3,000 years in a variety of island contexts. This information supplies insight on long-term changes in Island Chumash lifeways and ecology during the Late Holocene.

In Chapter 2, I present an environmental and cultural overview of the Santa Barbara Channel region and northern Channel Islands. I begin by describing contemporary environmental and climatic regimes in the area and then explore environmental changes across the terminal Pleistocene and Holocene. I then provide a trans-Holocene overview of human cultural developments in the area, placing people within the context of the environments of the Channel Islands and southern California coast. In Chapter 3, I build on this environmental and cultural overview by presenting the methods and procedures used during my field and laboratory research. In this chapter, I explain how I collected, analyzed, and interpreted the data and ultimately derived inferences on human daily activities, emergent complexity, and historical ecology.

Chapter 4 begins the data section of this book which also includes Chapters 5 and 6. These chapters are organized chronologically, beginning with the oldest site I analyzed and concluding with the Historic period occupation of the island. In Chapter 4, I present the results of excavation and surface collection at SMI-87, one of the largest sites on San Miguel with a series of occupations dated between about 4,500 and 2,500 years ago on eastern Cuyler Harbor. I focus on faunal and artifact data from the most substantial occupation of the site which occurred between about 3,000 and 2,500 years ago. Relatively few sites of this age have been excavated or reported on the northern Channel Islands, making this research important for understanding human cultural developments at the beginning of the Late Holocene.

In Chapter 5, I continue exploration of Late Holocene human occupation of San Miguel Island by presenting the results of excavation, mapping,

and surface collection at SMI-481 and SMI-468 located near Otter Point and Simonton Cove on the northwest coast of the island. SMI-481 is also one of the largest sites on the island and contains a roughly 30-m-high dune with a series of shell middens located at various heights and spanning much of the last 7,300 years. My focus is on faunal and artifact data from a roughly 1,400- to 1,200-year-old component. I then present the results of excavation at SMI-468, a village located about 500 m from SMI-481 that contains occupations dated to between about 1,300 and 400 years ago. My research at this site is focused on two components dated to roughly 1,200 to 800 years ago during the late Middle and Transitional periods (see Arnold 1992a).

In Chapter 6, I provide the results of excavation, surface collection, and mapping at SMI-163, the Chumash village of *Tuqan*, one of only two historic Chumash villages documented in ethnohistoric records on San Miguel (J. Johnson 1999a; Kennett 2005). I also present the results of mapping, ^{14}C dating, and limited testing at SMI-470, the probable village of *Niwoyomi*. My research at SMI-163 and SMI-470 provides the first detailed artifact and faunal data from Historic period sites on San Miguel Island. This is surprising since San Miguel has long been of interest to historians and other researchers because of the possibility that Juan Rodríguez Cabrillo, the first well-documented European to voyage into the Chumash area, may have wintered on the island and may even be buried there (Erlandson and Bartoy 1995; Erlandson et al. 2001b; Kelsey 1986; Wagner 1929). I also summarize the location and chronology of several other sites on San Miguel Island that have Protohistoric or Historic occupations. Collectively, the data from these sites provide an archaeological overview of Chumash occupation of San Miguel Island during the Historic and Protohistoric periods. These findings expand our knowledge of landscape use during this significant period of rapid cultural change.

Finally, comparisons of the artifacts and faunal remains from each of the five major archaeological sites are presented in Chapter 7. This comparative analysis documents developments in Chumash society and ecology on San Miguel Island and places the data within the context of the research issues outlined in this chapter.

2

Environments and Peoples
of the Channel Islands

The Channel Islands were separated from the mainland throughout the Quaternary and have long attracted the attention of researchers and the general public. This isolation promoted some of the most distinct terrestrial and marine environments along the North American Pacific Coast, including a number of island endemic and relict species, and breeding habitats for numerous marine mammals and sea birds. The Channel Islands have also been inhabited by people for at least 13,000 calendar years, providing a continuous record of Native American occupation through the early nineteenth century. Although the rough configuration of island environments was probably in place for most of the Holocene, a number of significant environmental changes occurred during the time of human occupation, often triggering changes in subsistence strategies and social organization. Because of their unique setting and long archaeological record, the Channel Islands provide an important perspective on human use of island and coastal environments.

In this chapter, I present a brief environmental and cultural overview of the southern California coast. My emphasis is on the northern Channel Islands and Santa Barbara Channel region, especially San Miguel Island. I begin by describing modern environmental conditions and broad environmental changes over the last 13,000 years. I then describe the trans-Holocene human cultural history in the area, placing people within the context of these unique marine and terrestrial environments. As Kennett (2005), Engle (1993), and others noted, there is considerable variability in the distribution and abundance of terrestrial and marine resources across the Channel Islands. This variability fostered distinct local human foraging strategies and exchange systems, a pattern that is reiterated throughout this book. These data provide the backdrop for the archaeological, historical, and ecological analyses of Late Holocene San Miguel Island presented in later chapters.

GEOGRAPHY, SETTING, AND CONTEXT

The Santa Barbara Channel region contains a great deal of topographic and environmental diversity, with a series of four offshore islands, steep mountainous slopes, foothills, and coastal plains. This interface of environmental conditions promotes a distinct terrestrial flora and fauna and a diverse array of animals and plants (Schoenherr 1992). The Santa Barbara Channel region's mountains generally trend east–west and are part of the larger Transverse Ranges geological province.

The eight Channel Islands, located offshore between Point Conception and San Diego, are divided into northern (Anacapa, Santa Cruz, Santa Rosa, and San Miguel) and southern chains (San Clemente, Santa Catalina, San Nicolas, and Santa Barbara) and are owned and managed by a variety of federal and private agencies. The northern Channel Islands and Santa Barbara Island form Channel Islands National Park, with the western portion of Santa Cruz owned by the Nature Conservancy and San Miguel owned by the U.S. Navy. San Nicolas and San Clemente are both administered by the U.S. Navy and contain naval installations. Santa Catalina is privately owned and contains the only formal city on the islands (Avalon). Other than these relatively small settlements and a long history of ranching, the islands remain largely undeveloped.

During the Historic period, the southern islands were inhabited by Tongva (Gabrielino) peoples who spoke a Uto-Aztecan language, while the northern islands were inhabited by the Chumash. The Tongva and Chumash exchanged a variety of goods with one another and are somewhat similar socially, politically, and culturally (see Gamble and Russell 2002; McCawley 1996). While my focus is on the northern Channel Islands, my data also relate to the southern chain, and comparisons between the two island groups are made throughout this book.

Southern California is characterized by a Mediterranean climate, with cool, wet winters and warm, dry summers. Temperatures in the area tend to become more extreme as one moves into the interior. The northern Channel Islands also have a mild and maritime climate, with an average of about 14° C in temperature and 356 mm of rain annually on San Miguel Island (Schoenherr et al. 1999:263). Ranging in size from about 2.9 to 249 km^2, the northern islands are between about 20 and 44 km from the mainland coast and form a roughly east–west trending line along the Santa Barbara Channel (Table 2.1). San Miguel sits about 42 km off the mainland coast and is the westernmost of the northern Channel Islands. The island has a maximum elevation of 253 m and is bisected by numerous ravines, gullies, and dune sheets that cover roughly 37 km^2 in area.

During the late Pleistocene and Early Holocene, sea level was considerably lower, making the islands larger in area and somewhat closer to the mainland coast (see D. Johnson 1983; Porcasi et al. 1999). At the height of the last glacial period, around 18,000 years ago, the northern islands formed one large island land mass (Santarosae), with the islands reaching their rough configuration shortly after the onset of the Holocene. A number of additional islets were also located throughout the area, most of which are now submerged (Porcasi et al. 1999). A series of small passages (~5 to 9 km wide) currently separates each of the northern islands.

The northern Channel Islands are a geological extension of the Santa Monica Mountains on the mainland (Weaver 1969:9). A variety of volcanic and sedimentary rocks found on the islands was used by people as raw materials for tool manufacture. Among the richest raw materials are Monterey chert deposits found on eastern Santa Cruz Island (Arnold 1987) and the Cico chert deposit found on eastern San Miguel Island (Erlandson et al. 1997). Metavolcanic and sandstone rocks found across the islands were also used for tool manufacture, particularly expedient tools and ground-stone bowls (Conlee 2000; Delaney-Rivera 2001). Asphaltum (bitumen) seeps occur just offshore of some of the islands and occasionally send large accumulations of tar onshore (see Roberts 1991:14), supplying a source of glue or sealant used in a variety of manufacturing and maintenance activities.

TERRESTRIAL ENVIRONMENT

Modern vegetation communities in southern coastal California are composed of coastal sage scrub, coastal strand, coastal oak woodland, chaparral, grassland, and other habitats (Schoenherr 1992; Smith 1998). Within these vegetation communities, a number of terrestrial resources are available, including acorns, pine nuts, chia seeds (Timbrook 1990), deer, birds, rabbits, and other mammals. Vegetation communities in the Santa Barbara region contain primarily dissected and transitional plant communities, with roughly 1,500 native species of plants and more than 140 endemics (Smith 1998:15). During the Historic and Protohistoric periods, and perhaps much earlier, Native people burned portions of the landscape to increase the productivity of some of these resources (Timbrook et al. 1982). Although only limited data are available, the Chumash also appear to have burned portions of the Channel Islands (Timbrook 1993).

Table 2.1. General Attributes of the Northern Channel Islands.

Island	Area (km^2)	Maximum Elevation (m)	Distance from Mainland (km)	# of Land Mammals	Native Plant Taxa
Anacapa	2.9	283	20	2	190
Santa Cruz	249	753	30	12	480
Santa Rosa	217	484	44	4	387
San Miguel	37	253	42	3	198

Note: Based on Power (1980) and Schoenherr et al. (1999:7).

Figure 2.1. Aerial photographs of San Miguel Island. (*Left*) 1978 photo showing substantial sand and vegetation clearing. (*Right*) 1994 photo illustrating substantial vegetation and landscape stabilization. Note disappearance of spit at Cardwell Point (far right of photo) following vegetation recovery.

The northern Channel Islands contain vegetation communities similar to those of the mainland, but they support a more impoverished terrestrial flora and fauna, including more relicts and endemics. The larger and more topographically diverse islands (i.e., Santa Rosa and Santa Cruz) have greater plant and animal diversity than the outer islands (see Table 2.1). Santa Cruz Island, for example, contains roughly 480 native plant taxa compared with just 198 for San Miguel Island.

A few studies have examined Channel Islands terrestrial flora (e.g., Junak et al. 1995), with recent emphasis on restoring and stabilizing native ecosystems that have been devastated by historical overgrazing from non-native livestock and introduced plants (Halvorson 1994). Historical overgrazing had a profound effect on Channel Islands environments, resulting in considerable erosion and deflation (D. Johnson 1972, 1980). Under National Park Service management, these environments have gradually been stabilizing and rejuvenating (Figure 2.1).

Anacapa Island contains primarily coastal sage scrub and chaparral, and Santa Cruz and Santa Rosa also support pines, oaks, freshwater marshes, and a large marsh and Torrey pine grove on Santa Rosa (see Schoenherr et al. 1999; Smith 1998:18; Figures 2.2, 2.3). San Miguel Island, composed largely of sand dunes, raised marine terraces, and tablelands, has unique dune ecosystems that have been stabilizing over the last few decades (Figure 2.4). The island also contains an abundance of caliche (calcium carbonate) plant casts which demonstrate that island vegetation has changed significantly in the past and is heavily influenced by the movement of dune sand (Figure 2.5). Each of the northern Channel Islands

has considerable variability in the distribution of terrestrial resources. Although some oaks are present on Santa Cruz and Santa Rosa, the islands generally lack the rich acorn resources and other plants that were widely available on the mainland. Timbrook (1993) suggested that the general dearth or patchiness of edible terrestrial plants on the islands promoted several distinct strategies, including trading for, substituting, or going without many of the mainland plant staples. Currently, the only systematic study of Late Holocene island paleobotanical remains is by Martin and Popper (2001), who identified a variety of fruits, seeds, nuts, and other plant materials that came from the islands and mainland in Santa Cruz Island sites. Paleoecological studies by Anderson (2002) and Cole and Liu (1994) (see below) also provide important details on island vegetation history.

Other than humans, the largest post-Pleistocene land mammals present on the Channel Islands were domesticated dogs (*Canis familiaris*), the island fox (*Urocyon littoralis*), and spotted skunk (*Spilogale gracile*). The island fox and spotted skunk are each about the size of a house cat; foxes were found on San Miguel, Santa Rosa, and Santa Cruz islands, and the skunk on Santa Rosa and Santa Cruz. Island fox populations have recently declined dramatically and are undergoing captive breeding. During the Pleistocene, pygmy mammoths (*Mammuthus exilis*) lived on the northern Channel Islands (Agenbroad 1998; Agenbroad et al. 2005), but until the Historic period the islands were devoid of most of the herbivores, carnivores, and rodents that dominated the mainland coast. This includes a number of burrowing animals (gophers, badgers, etc.) that

Figure 2.2. Marsh at the mouth of Old Ranch House Canyon, Santa Rosa Island, with peaks of Santa Cruz Island visible in the distance. A section of this marsh complex was cored for paleoecological research.

Figure 2.3. Torrey pine grove on eastern Santa Rosa Island. Torrey pines are found only in a small area of San Diego and on Santa Rosa Island. Stands of pine and oak are primarily confined to the larger islands of Santa Cruz and Santa Rosa.

Figure 2.4. Large dunes on Cuyler Harbor, San Miguel Island.

Figure 2.5. Caliche forest on San Miguel Island showing calcified plant casts.

have bioturbated mainland archaeological sites for millennia (Erlandson 1984; D. Johnson 1989). The island deer mouse (*Peromyscus maniculatus*) is currently the only native rodent known to occur on all the northern Channel Islands; the harvest mouse (*Reithrodontomys megalotis santacruzae*) is also found on Santa Cruz (Schoenherr et al. 1999).

Numerous sea and land birds occupy the islands, and the remains of a variety of birds have

been identified in Channel Islands sites (Bleitz 1993; Guthrie 1980; 1993a), including gulls (*Larus* spp.), cormorants (*Phalacrocorax* spp.), osprey (*Pandion haliaetus*), eagles (Accipitridae), auklets (Alcidae), and others. A limited number of reptiles and amphibians also occurs on the northern islands, including the southern alligator lizard (*Elgaria multicarinatus*), the island western fence lizard (*Sceloporus occidentalis becki*), the Pacific tree

Figure 2.6. Freshwater spring at Running Springs, San Miguel Island, with large sand dune in background.

frog (*Hyla regilla*), and the Channel Islands slender salamander (*Batrachoseps pacificus*). The only snakes on the northern islands are the island gopher snake (*Pituophis melanoleucus pumilis*), the racer (*Coluber constrictor mormon*), and the spotted night snake (*Hypsiglena torquata*), occurring only on Santa Cruz or Santa Rosa (Schoenherr et al. 1999:250–251). Except for some caves and rock shelters, the remains of reptiles and amphibians are relatively rare in Channel Islands archaeological sites.

Freshwater has often been cited as a limiting factor for sustained human occupation of the Channel Islands. Several freshwater streams and creeks flow year round on Santa Rosa and Santa Cruz, however, and several seeps and springs on San Miguel Island also produce relatively reliable freshwater. Many freshwater sources appear to be regenerating in the absence of overgrazing and with the stabilization of the landscape (Figure 2.6). Clustered around many of the reliable freshwater sources are large and dense archaeological sites.

MARINE ENVIRONMENT

Unlike most of the California coast, which trends north–south and is exposed to prevailing winds and heavy surf, the Santa Barbara Channel and portions of the Los Angeles Basin are relatively sheltered, containing numerous stretches of protected coastline that trend east–west. The marine environment of the Channel Islands—and the California coast in general—is exceptionally productive, with an abundance of kelp forest, rocky nearshore, and sandy nearshore habitats (Dailey et al. 1993; Glassow and Wilcoxon 1988; Landberg 1975). Upwelling and nutrient-rich currents support dense and diverse populations of marine mammals, fish, sea and shorebirds, and shellfish. The Channel Islands are located on an interface between colder currents to the north and warmer currents to the south, providing a mix of cold and warm water marine fauna (Figure 2.7).

The region is home to over 900 species of marine fishes (Love 1996), with a wide diversity of taxa inhabiting environments around the Channel Islands (Engle 1993). People have taken advantage of

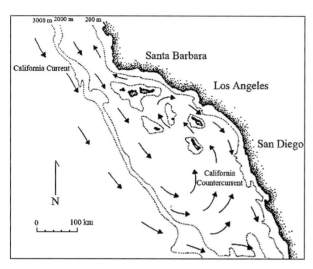

Figure 2.7 Surface circulation of major currents along the southern California coast (adapted from Dailey et al. 1993:9).

these diverse marine fishes and other resources in a variety of marine habitats throughout the Holocene. Fishes from rocky shore and kelp forest habitats are particularly abundant and are generally among the most common fishes found in Channel Islands archaeological sites, including rockfish (*Sebastes* spp.), surfperch (Embiotocidae), sculpins (Cottidae), and California sheephead (*Semicossyphus pulcher*) (Bowser 1993; Colten 2001; Noah 2005;

Paige 2000; Pletka 2001a; Rick et al. 2001a; Salls 1998; see also Engle 1993). Sharks and sandy bottom taxa are also identified in Channel Islands sites.

Pinniped (seals and sea lions) and cetacean (dolphins, whales, etc.) populations around the Channel Islands are highly productive (Figure 2.8). The greatest abundance of seals and sea lions is currently found on San Miguel Island, where well over 100,000 animals use the island to breed or haul out (DeLong and Melin 2002; Figure 2.9). This includes at least six pinniped species: northern fur seal (*Callorhinus ursinus*), Guadalupe fur seal (*Arctocephalus townsendi*), California sea lion (*Zalophus californianus*), Steller sea lion (*Eumetopias jubatus*), harbor seal (*Phoca vitulina*), and elephant seal (*Mirounga angustirostris*). Pinnipeds also haul out on portions of Santa Rosa and Santa Cruz islands, but their abundance decreases dramatically away from San Miguel. Sea otters (*Enhydra lutris*), before being driven to local extinction, were another important marine mammal found around the Channel Islands (Erlandson et al. 2005a). Pinnipeds and sea otters have been identified in numerous Channel Islands sites and were important sources of meat, fat, and oil, but their bones were also used in tool production (see Colten 2002; Hildebrandt and Jones 1992; Noah 2005). A variety of dolphins, porpoises, and whales also inhabit the waters of the

Figure 2.8. Seals and sea lions hauled out on Otter Point, San Miguel Island.

Figure 2.9. Point Bennett pinniped rookery on western San Miguel Island.

Santa Barbara Channel. Whales occasionally beach on the shores of the Channel Islands, and the remains of whales and other cetaceans (e.g., dolphins) occur in many Channel Islands sites (see Glassow 2005b; Porcasi and Fujita 2000).

Sea birds are also abundant on the islands, including a number of breeding species. Gulls (*Larus* spp.), cormorants (*Phalacrocorax* spp.), auklets (Alcidae), and brown pelicans (*Pelecanus occidentalis*) are among the most common birds around the Channel Islands. On San Miguel Island, sea birds and pinnipeds are known to breed on the offshore rocks, Prince Island and Castle Rock (Figures 2.10, 2.11). The remains of a variety of birds were identified in paleontological and archaeological deposits on San Miguel Island (Guthrie 1980, 1993a, 1993b) and in Late Holocene archaeological deposits on Santa Cruz and Santa Rosa islands (Colten 2001; Noah 2005; Rick 2004b). Bird bones were often used to make tools, such as gorges, pins, and awls (Wake 2001). Numerous bone fishing gorges dated to the Early Holocene at Daisy Cave, for example, are made of bird bone (Rick et al. 2001a).

Rocky intertidal habitats on the Channel Islands are rich and productive (Figure 2.12). Research in Channel Islands shell middens demonstrates that shellfish from rocky intertidal environments are the dominant taxa in middens across the Holocene, suggesting a fair amount of continuity and stability in these environments for at least the last 10,000 years (see Erlandson et al. 1999; Erlandson et al. 2004a; Rick et al. 2006a). Rocky intertidal shellfish, such as California and platform mussels (*Mytilus californianus* and *Septifer bifurcatus*), black and red abalone (*Haliotis cracherodii* and *H. rufescens*), owl limpets (*Lottia gigantea*), and black and brown turbans (*Tegula funebralis* and *T. brunnea*), are among the most common taxa in Channel Islands archaeological sites. *Olivella biplicata* (purple olive), red abalone, California mussel, and numerous other shell types were important for making beads, ornaments, fishhooks, and other artifacts. Sea grass (*Phyllospadix* spp.) occurring in and around rocky intertidal regions was also an important raw material for making cordage, baskets, and other items on the Channel Islands (Connolly et al.

Figure 2.10. Prince Island located on the north end of Cuyler Harbor, San Miguel Island, as seen from the island campground.

Figure 2.11. Castle Rock located on the western portion of San Miguel Island is an important area for breeding sea birds and pinnipeds.

Figure 2.12. Rocky intertidal and kelp beds at Otter Point, San Miguel Island.

1995; Martin and Popper 2001; Vellanoweth et al. 2003). The presence of estuarine shellfish (*Chione undatella*, *Ostrea lurida*, etc.) in Early and Middle Holocene sites on Santa Rosa Island suggests a large estuary was once present near the mouth of Old Ranch Canyon (Rick et al. 2005a). Pismo clams (*Tivela stultorum*) and other surf-swept, sandy-bottom-dwelling taxa are sometimes present (and occasionally abundant) in Channel Islands sites, generally depending on local availability (Arnold and Graesch 2001:97). Collectively, Channel Islands marine environments are among the most productive in North America and provide a variety of resources for people to exploit. There is, however, considerable spatial and temporal variability in the distribution of resources related to a variety of environmental factors. This variability and its relationship with human cultural developments is the subject of the chapters that follow.

LATE PLEISTOCENE/HOLOCENE ENVIRONMENTAL CHANGE

Terminal Pleistocene/Early Holocene Environments (13,000 to 7,500 Years Ago)

Although plant communities similar to those of the present day appear to have been extant since the Early Holocene, the productivity and distribution of these communities varied considerably through time (Erlandson 1994:30). Between about 10,000 and 8,000 years ago, the climate was fairly cool and moist, with temperature and aridity increasing around 8,000 years ago (Carbone 1991; Erlandson 1994:31; Glassow et al. 1988; Heusser 1978; Kennett 2005:69). A decline in pollen richness and an abundance of coyote brush at Soledad Pond on Santa Rosa Island also suggest relatively arid conditions on the Channel Islands during portions of the Early Holocene (Anderson 2002:10–11).

During the Early Holocene, sea levels were rising and flooding many former coastal lowlands and canyons, leading to the formation of numerous estuarine embayments (Erlandson 1985, 1994; Inman 1983). This forced a reorganization of many biotic communities, greatly reducing coastal plain habitats in some areas. These embayments became centers of human settlement and subsistence along the mainland coast (Erlandson 1994). Data from Early Holocene shell middens on the Channel Islands suggest that by the onset of the Holocene, and possibly earlier, rocky intertidal and kelp forest habitats were the dominant marine environment available and were used by people on the islands (Erlandson et al. 1999). Large estuaries were absent from the

Channel Islands, except for one near the mouth of Old Ranch Canyon on Santa Rosa Island. Between about 8,000 and 5,000 years ago, several sites on eastern Santa Rosa Island contained Venus clams (*Chione* spp.), oysters (*Ostrea lurida*), and other estuarine taxa that were probably obtained from the Abalone Rocks Estuary, which is now a marsh (Rick et al. 2005a). The available data suggest, however, that rocky intertidal taxa were dominant at most sites.

Kinlan et al. (2005) have recently analyzed changes in glacial versus interglacial marine productivity on the Channel Islands associated with rising sea levels and changing reef mass in the nearshore environment. They noted that during the terminal Pleistocene and Early Holocene, reef mass was considerably larger than later in time, including increased kelp forests. Graham et al. (2003) also suggested that the ecological productivity of the marine environment declined in southern California following the close of the Pleistocene. These and other data demonstrate that early people on the Channel Islands were living in rapidly changing environments, a pattern that continues during the Middle Holocene.

Middle Holocene Environments (7,500 to 3,500 years ago)

A number of significant environmental changes characterize the Middle Holocene from about 7,500 to 3,500 years ago. Consequently, several theories relate Middle Holocene cultural developments with changes in climatic and environmental conditions of this time period (e.g., Glassow 1993a; Glassow et al. 1988, 1994). Portions of the Middle Holocene appear to have been relatively warm and dry (Glassow et al. 1988; Kennett 2005:69–70). A pollen record from the Abalone Rocks Marsh on Santa Rosa Island suggests vegetation changes indicative of greater aridity between about 5200 and 3250 RYBP (Cole and Liu 1994:332). Data from Soledad Pond and the Abalone Rocks Marsh also indicate a higher frequency of fire events after 5,000 years ago (Anderson 2002).

Many estuaries persisted along the mainland coast through the early portions of the Middle Holocene, but as sea level began to stabilize between about 6,000 and 5,000 years ago (Inman 1983), most of the smaller estuaries filled with sediment (Erlandson 1997). Large embayments like the Goleta Slough, however, persisted into the historic period as enclosed bays with surrounding mudflats (Glassow 1997). Similar to other periods, Middle Holocene archaeological deposits on the Channel Islands are generally dominated by rocky intertidal and kelp forest marine fauna.

An apparent increase in interior sites on the Channel Islands and high frequencies of dental caries rates during the Middle Holocene may reflect an intensified reliance on terrestrial plants (Kennett 2005; Walker and Erlandson 1986). Paleoclimatic reconstructions based on marine records indicate that sea-surface temperatures were relatively warm during most of the Middle Holocene, but also include periods of cooler temperatures (Friddell et al 2003; Glassow et al. 1988:71; Kennett 2005:65). Stable isotope analysis of marine shells from a Santa Cruz Island red abalone midden (SCRI-333)—a distinct island archaeological site type with a high proportion of red abalone shells—suggests that marine sea-surface temperatures may have been cool during portions of the Middle Holocene, possibly resulting in the cool water red abalone moving closer to shore (Glassow 1993a, 2002b, 2005a; Glassow et al. 1994). Sharp's (2000) analysis of another Santa Cruz Island red abalone midden (SCRI-109, Punta Arena), however, indicates that a wide variety of shellfish were found in some Middle Holocene sites, including pink abalones (*Haliotis corrugata*) which may indicate warm sea-surface temperatures, suggesting warm and cold sea-surface temperatures during this time (see also Kennett 2005).

Glassow's (2005a, 2005b) and Sharp's (2000) recent analysis of Punta Arena and several other Middle Holocene sites on western Santa Cruz Island documents a focus on California mussel, red abalone, and other shellfish, as well as the capture of nearshore marine fishes, dolphins, and other resources. A variety of rocky intertidal shellfish species have also been identified in Middle Holocene archaeological deposits on San Miguel Island (Erlandson et al. 2005c; Vellanoweth et al. 2006). Ongoing research in these and other site types should provide important details on the character and structure of Middle Holocene environments on the Channel Islands. What seems clear from the available data is that the Middle Holocene was a period of dynamic environmental change that spurred several unique cultural developments.

Late Holocene Environments (3,500 Years Ago to Present)

During the Late Holocene, environmental conditions were roughly comparable with those of the present day, but in the last 3,500 years climatic variability was exceptionally high, and this also appears to have been on average one of the coldest, most unstable marine climatic intervals of the last 10,000 years (Kennett and Kennett 2000). The climatic instability of the last 3,000 years indicates general episodes of marine cooling that may coincide primarily with cool and dry terrestrial conditions. Many early environmental reconstructions were based on data presented by Pisias (1978). Recent analysis of a 200-m-long core obtained from the Santa Barbara Basin (see Kennett and Ingram 1995) illustrates several potential problems with such reconstructions (Kennett and Kennett 2000). Figure 2.13 presents data adapted from Kennett and Kennett (2000) that illustrate different Late Holocene climatic schemes for the California coast, including records of sea-surface temperature, marine productivity, and precipitation. These schemes suggest that climatic conditions were highly variable and unstable over the last 3,000

years. In particular, between about 1,500 and 500 years ago, sea-surface temperatures appear to have been extremely cold, correlating with increased aridity, but there were also warmer intervals.

Pollen data from Soledad Pond on Santa Rosa Island show an increase in plants characteristic of coastal sage scrub and grassland communities, as well as increases in wetland plants about 4000 RYBP (Anderson 2002:11–12). Martin and Popper's (2001) analysis of paleobotanical remains from Late Holocene Santa Cruz Island archaeological sites illustrates the use of plant remains from both mainland and island flora during the last 1,500 years. Sea level had also stabilized throughout the region by the Late Holocene, resulting in a similar coastal setting as the present. The available data from Channel Islands archaeological sites again emphasize the overwhelming importance of rocky intertidal and kelp forest habitats.

A number of scholars have debated the effects of climatic events during the Transitional period between AD 1150 and 1300 (Arnold 1992a; Arnold et al. 1997a; Gamble 2005) and in the Medieval Climatic Anomaly between AD 800 and 1350 (Jones et al. 1999; Kennett and Kennett 2000; Raab and Lar-

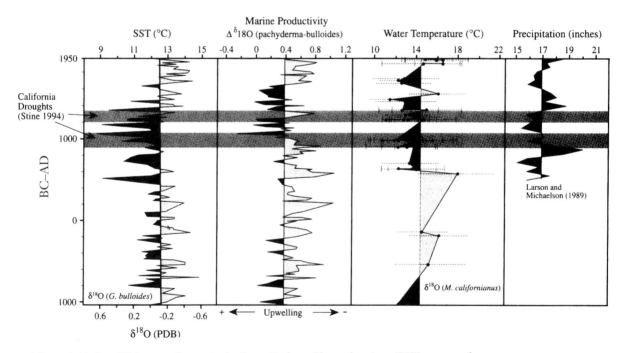

Figure 2.13. Late Holocene climate in the Santa Barbara Channel region. (SST = sea-surface temperature, marineproductivity based on upwelling record, water temperature based on oxygen isotopic data, and precipitation record based on tree rings for the southern California coast). Adapted from Kennett and Kennett (2000).

son 1997), focusing on the possible effects of drought and decreases in marine resource productivity. During the last 10,000 years, people responded to numerous climatic changes and perturbations on a variety of different scales. The effects of these environmental disturbances, however, may have been most pronounced during the last 3,000 years, when Chumash populations appear to have reached their height and people became increasingly sedentary and territorial (Erlandson and Rick 2002a; Kennett 2005).

THE ISLAND CHUMASH AND THEIR PREDECESSORS

The southern California coast has one of the earliest and most extensive records of maritime adaptations in the Americas (Erlandson 1994; Erlandson and Moss 1996; Erlandson et al. 2006; Jones 1991). Due to the great time depth and diverse archaeological record of coastal California, numerous researchers have developed cultural sequences for the Santa Barbara Channel and the California coast (Chartkoff and Chartkoff 1984; Harrison 1964; Harrison and Harrison 1966; King 1990; Moratto 1984; Olson 1930; Rogers 1929; Wallace 1955; Warren 1968; and others). These schemes often show considerable overlap, generally relying on a similar suite of cultural changes evident in the archaeological record. These cultural chronologies are often related to local and regional environmental changes.

King (1990) developed the most detailed and widely used cultural sequence for the southern California coast. He defined three broad periods, Early, Middle, and Late, which were each subdivided into phases based on a number of radiocarbon dates (Table 2.2). King's chronology describes a variety of temporally diagnostic artifacts that are widely used today for building site chronologies. As several scholars have noted, one problem with King's sequence is that it is based largely on uncorrected and uncalibrated radiocarbon dates, making it different from calendar years (Kennett 2005:82). Arnold (1992a) expanded on King's sequence by adding two periods (see Table 2.2). First, she added the Transitional period between roughly AD 1150 and 1300; then she also added the Early Holocene. The King and Arnold chronologies remain the most widely used today.

Although important for delineating cultural patterns, the proliferation of chronologies is sometimes confusing and hinders comparisons among various regions. For example, several sequences contain phases or other time periods that are defined for one region but not another. It also becomes difficult to compare cultural developments in California with other areas of North America that do not employ these cultural chronologies (see Ames and Maschner 1999; Moratto 1984). To avoid such problems, I employ general geological time periods, including terminal Pleistocene, and Early, Middle, and Late Holocene, and refer to most cultural developments in calendar years. Where necessary, I draw on the more specific chronological sequences established by King (1990) and Arnold (1992a).

Terminal Pleistocene/Early Holocene

In recent years, the number of Early Holocene sites on the southern California coast has grown substantially to include well over 100 sites in excess of 7,000 years old, including at least 42 sites on the northern Channel Islands (Erlandson 1994; Erlandson et al. 2006; Rick et al. 2005b). Consequently, our understanding of the culture history and lifeways of early Native Americans has also improved. The evidence for terminal Pleistocene occupation of the California coast, however, remains limited. Fluted point fragments from the mainland coast (Erlandson et al. 1987, 2006), human bones on Santa Rosa Island (Johnson et al. 2002; Orr 1968), and a low-density shell midden at Daisy Cave on San Miguel Island dated to ca. 11,500 cal BP (Erlandson et al. 1996) are currently the most widely accepted evidence for terminal Pleistocene occupation of the southern California coast.

Along the mainland coast, Early Holocene artifact assemblages are dominated by manos and metates (milling stones), which appear to have been used primarily to grind seeds (Erlandson 1991a, 1994; Moriarty 1967; Warren 1967). However, milling stones are rare or absent from Early Holocene Channel Islands sites. Formal chipped-stone tools are also relatively rare, composed largely of projectile points, knives, and drills (Erlandson 1994). Recent evidence from Daisy Cave, SMI-522, and SMI-608 on San Miguel Island indicates that bone gorges were an important early fishing technology (Erlandson and Rick 2002b; Erlandson et al. 2005d; Rick et al. 2001a). A rich assemblage of sea

Table 2.2. Major Chronological Schemes for the Santa Barbara Channel and Northern Channel Islands.

Geologic Time	Cultural Period	King (1990)	Arnold (1992a)
Early Holocene (10,000–7500 cal BP)	Early Holocene	—	8000–6120 BC (9950–8060 cal BP)
	Early period (All phases)	6120–490 BC (8060–2440 cal BP)	6120–490 BC (8060–2440 cal BP)
Middle Holocene (7500–3500 cal BP)	Early period (Phase Ex)	6120–4650 BC (8060–6600 cal BP)	—
	Early period (Phase Eyb)	4650–3590 BC (6600–5540 cal BP)	—
	Early period (Phase Eya)	3590–970 BC (5540–2920 cal BP)	—
Late Holocene (3500 cal BP–present)	Early period (Phase Ez)	970–490 BC (2920–2440 cal BP)	—
	Middle period (All phases)	490 BC–AD1380 (2440–570 cal BP)	490 BC–AD 1150 (2440–800 cal BP)
	Middle period (Phase M1)	490 BC–AD 170 (2440–1790 cal BP)	—
	Middle period (Phase M2)	AD 170–660 (1790–1290 cal BP)	—
	Middle period (Phase M3)	AD 660–980 (1290–970 cal BP)	—
	Middle period (Phase M4)	AD 980–1170 (970–780 cal BP)	—
	Middle period (Phase M5)	AD 1170–1380 (780–570 cal BP)	—
	Transitional period	—	AD 1150–1300 (800–650 cal BP)
	Late period (All phases)	AD 1380–1804 (570–146)	AD 1300–1782 (650–168 cal BP)
	Late period (Phase L1)	AD 1380–1670 (570–280 cal BP)	—
	Late period (Phase L2)	AD 1670–1782 (280–168 cal BP)	—
	Late/Historic period (Phase L3)	AD 1782–1804 (168–146 cal BP)	AD 1782–1830 (168–120 cal BP)

Note: The dates presented here are calibrated age ranges based on King's (1990:28) original uncalibrated scheme. All calibrations follow Kennett (2005:83).

grass cordage and knots from Daisy Cave and Cave of the Chimneys, which may have been used in fishing activities, also illustrates the variability of early coastal technologies (Connolly et al. 1995; Vellanoweth et al. 2003). Ornamental objects are relatively rare in Early Holocene deposits, but *Olivella* spire ground beads have been found in a number of early island sites (Erlandson 1994; Erlandson et al. 2005d; Vellanoweth et al. 2003).

Early Holocene subsistence practices on the northern Channel Islands appear to be focused on rocky intertidal shellfish, such as California mussels, owl limpets, and abalones, supplemented by fish, mammal, and bird remains (Erlandson 1994; Erlandson et al. 1999, 2005d). At Daisy Cave, Early Holocene dietary reconstructions suggest that fish were the most important part of the diet, emphasizing variability in human subsistence strategies by this early date (Rick et al. 2001a). The use of the Abalone Rocks estuary on eastern Santa Rosa Island also illustrates the diversity of early human subsistence and settlement strategies on the islands (Rick et al. 2005a).

Middle Holocene

For the most part, the archaeology of the Middle Holocene has received less attention than both earlier and later time periods (Erlandson and Glassow 1997). Based on an increase in radiocarbon date frequencies, Channel Islands populations appear to have grown after roughly 5,000 to 4,000 years ago (Glassow 1997:84–85). Large and dense village sites, such as the Aerophysics site (SBA-53) on the mainland, suggest that sedentism also increased in some areas during the Middle Holocene. For the most part, however, Middle Holocene populations appear to have been fairly mobile (Erlandson 1997; Glassow 1997; Kennett 2005).

Artifact assemblages of the Middle Holocene are comparable with earlier assemblages, but a number of changes in artifact forms, such as the first appearance of the mortar and pestle and the use of composite bone fishhooks and side-notched projectile points, characterize this time period (see Erlandson 1997; Glassow 1997; King 1990). The variety and type of shell beads also increase during the Middle Holocene, including an emphasis on rectangular forms. *Olivella* grooved rectangle beads appear to occur almost exclusively during the Middle Holocene throughout the southern Channel Islands, Los Angeles Basin, and in Nevada and Oregon (Jenkins and Erlandson 1996; Raab and Howard 2002; Vellanoweth 2001). However, no *Olivella* grooved rectangle beads have been identified on the northern Channel Islands, and few are known from the Chumash area. These artifact elaborations are part of a broader Holocene trend where ornamental and stylized forms increase by the end of the Middle Holocene.

Faunal assemblages from Middle Holocene sites on the southern Channel Islands comprise a variety of animals, such as giant ocean sunfish (*Mola mola*), dolphin (Delphinidae), seals and sea lions, and albatross (*Diomedea* spp.), suggesting complex and diverse foraging strategies by this early date (Porcasi 1999; Porcasi and Andrews 2001; Porcasi and Fujita 2000; Porcasi et al. 2000). Less is known about Middle Holocene human subsistence on the

northern Channel Islands, but dolphins occur in some northern Channel Islands sites (Glassow 2005b), as do a variety of shellfish and fishes (Erlandson et al. 2005c; Glassow 2005a; Sharp 2000; Vellanoweth et al. 2002, 2005). Shellfish, including California mussel, red and black abalones, turbans, and other species appear to be the most important dietary constituent at most Middle Holocene sites on the northern islands.

Late Holocene/Historic

Many of the cultural hallmarks of Chumash society first appeared in the Late Holocene. The circular shell fishhook, plank canoe, *Olivella* cup beads, bow and arrow, and harpoons accompany significant social changes during the last 3,000 years (Arnold 1995; Erlandson and Rick 2002a; Gamble 2002; Glassow 1996; King 1990; Koerper et al. 1995; Rick et al. 2002). Unfortunately, the first appearance of some of these technologies (e.g., harpoons) is poorly known.

Most archaeological research in California, particularly on the northern Channel Islands, has focused on the last 1,500 years, with comparatively little work done on the earlier part of the Late Holocene (see Arnold 1991, 1992a, 1993; Arnold et al. 1997a; Colten 1993; Larson et al. 1994; Noah 2005; Raab and Larson 1997). The Transitional period (Arnold 1992a; AD 1150 to 1300) or Medieval Climatic Anomaly (Jones et al. 1999; Raab and Larson 1997; Yatsko 2000; AD 800 to 1350) has received the most attention from recent scholars, although sites from this time period are generally limited. Arnold (1992a, 1992b, 2001b, 2004; Arnold et al. 1997a), Colten (1993), and others argue for a major cultural reorganization of Chumash society during the Transitional period, sparked by a period of drought and possibly elevated sea-surface temperatures. Scholars have argued that this period marks a dramatic change in traditional Chumash society, including greater sociopolitical complexity, increased craft production and trade, and changes in human subsistence. The scale of these changes, however, is currently difficult to ascertain because of limited data from the previous 1,500 years, as well as a dearth of data from San Miguel and adjacent Santa Rosa Island.

By the time of European contact, the Chumash occupied much of the coastline between Malibu and Morro Bay (see Landberg 1965). Villages were situated at the mouths of most of the larger coastal

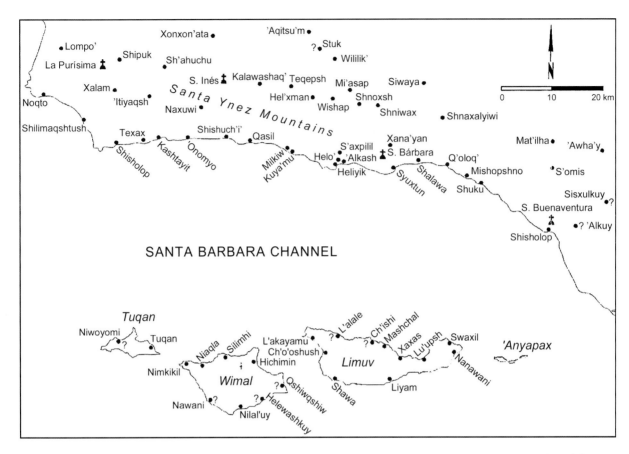

Figure 2.14. Chumash towns in the Santa Barbara Channel region at the time of European settlement (adapted from Johnson and McLendon 1999a:31).

canyons with perennial streams (Figure 2.14; Johnson and McLendon 1999a: 31). Villages of well-defined houses, sweat lodges, dance floors, and other structures (Gamble 1995) were governed largely by hereditary chiefs or captains (Arnold 1992a; J. Johnson 1988; King 1971). Ethnohistoric accounts of mainland Chumash villages suggest that they typically contained houses and a sweat lodge, and many contained menstrual houses, windbreaks, dance areas, a cemetery, structures for storage and food preparation, and sacred areas (see Gamble 1991:48–71). According to Gamble (1995:56), ethnohistoric and ethnographic accounts suggest that Chumash houses were usually dome-shaped, about 4 to 16 m in diameter, posts were arranged around the perimeter and covered in thatch, and a hearth was often located in the center.

Late Holocene subsistence practices on the islands were largely focused on kelp forest and rocky nearshore habitats, but people may have begun tak-ing a wider range of resources from increasingly more costly habitats (e.g., offshore). A general trend appears to be a focus on fish during the Late Holocene, with shellfish, marine mammals, and birds largely occurring as supplementary resources, with some variability (see Colten and Arnold 1998; Glassow 1993b; Kennett and Conlee 2002; Lambert 1993; Noah 2005; Rick 2004a, 2004b).

Ultimately, the Late Holocene ushered in a period of important social and political changes, including hierarchical social organization, the development of large multifamily sedentary communities, massive craft production (e.g., shell beads), and sophisticated exchange networks. The Late Holocene also marks the end of the Chumash occupation of the northern Channel Islands. The first contact between the Island Chumash and Europeans occurred in the sixteenth century, and most islanders were removed to mainland missions by about AD 1822.

DEMOGRAPHIC TRENDS ON THE NORTHERN CHANNEL ISLANDS

Chumash populations varied considerably through time, and it is difficult to estimate how many people lived in the region prior to contact and before the devastating effects of introduced diseases (Brown 1967; Erlandson and Bartoy 1995; Erlandson et al. 2001b; J. Johnson 1999a). J. Johnson (1999b) presented an updated and detailed review of Chumash population estimates based on mission records and reports from early Spanish expeditions, suggesting there may have been between about 8,000 (Kroeber 1925) and 25,000 (Cook 1976) Chumash living throughout the Santa Barbara Channel region and adjacent areas before contact. These estimates vary considerably because the precise timing of the dramatic declines in population from introduced diseases remains unknown. About 1,270 Island Chumash are known to have been baptized at the Santa Barbara and Ventura area missions (J. Johnson 1999a: 53), suggesting that precontact Island Chumash populations probably numbered a few thousand people (J. Johnson 1982:114).

A number of scholars have explored demographic trends and population fluctuations for the Channel Islands and southern California coast over roughly the last 10,000 years (Erlandson, et al. 2001b; Glassow 1999, 2002a; Tainter 1977). These estimates have been based largely on the frequencies of radiocarbon-dated components from archaeological sites in the region. These plots are subject to a number of biases, including the large number of undated sites, differences in individual research interests, an inadequate number of dates for most sites, difficulty in locating early sites, and variations in the number of people occupying a site. However, they provide a means of examining general frequencies through time in the number of sites occupied, and may be loosely correlated with the number of people occupying a given area (Glassow 1999; Rick 1987).

The radiocarbon distributions for mainland coastal southern California suggest a general increase in human population over the last 10,000 years (Glassow 1999). Early Holocene populations appear to be fairly low, with increases beginning around 5,000 years ago. The most pronounced population growth occurred during the Late Holocene. Erlandson et al. (2001b) presented a plot of 215 calibrated ^{14}C dates from distinct components on the Channel Islands for the last 2,000 years. Their preliminary data show a general increase in the number

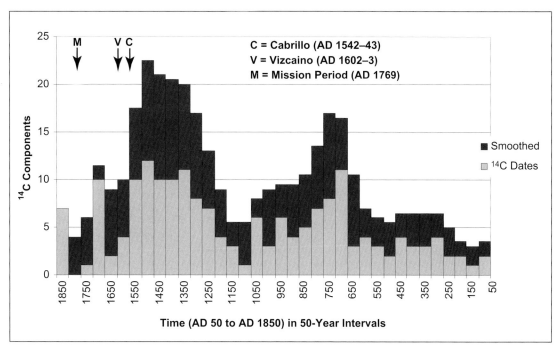

Figure 2.15. Distribution of radiocarbon dates from northern Channel Island sites over the last 2,000 years (50-year intervals; Erlandson et al. 2001b).

of dated site components and two significant declines (Figure 2.15). The first dramatic decline in ^{14}C dates (84 percent) occurs between about AD 750 to 1149 and suggests population declines associated with the Medieval Climatic Anomaly and Transitional period. The other dramatic decline (76 percent) takes place about AD 1550 and may be associated with Protohistoric disease epidemics following initial contact with Europeans, but this proposition remains speculative. The highest number of ^{14}C dates occurs during the late Middle and Late periods.

SUMMARY

In coastal southern California, a variety of terrestrial and marine resources promoted the development of dense populations, large villages, and complex social networks. Terrestrial plant and animal communities on the Channel Islands are relatively impoverished. This resulted in human communities that were considerably more dependent on marine resources and often supplemented their resource limitations through exchange with mainlanders and other islanders (King 1971). The distribution of marine and terrestrial resources varies across the islands, with the greatest abundance of terrestrial resources available on the larger, more topographically diverse islands of Santa Cruz and Santa Rosa, but with rich and varied marine habitats surrounding all of the islands. This variability in the distribution of resources promoted unique human cultural adaptations to island and coastal settings.

The islands were inhabited by the Chumash and their predecessors for about 13,000 calendar years. During this time, people were faced with, and transcended, numerous environmental changes. The rich cultural histories and lifeways of the Chumash and their predecessors were integrally tied to the marine and terrestrial environments of the northern Channel Islands. The chapters that follow present details on local environments and the role of people in influencing or adapting to those changes over the last 3,000 years on San Miguel Island.

3

Project Methods

Reconstructing human daily activities, subsistence, and historical ecology is a multidisciplinary endeavor, drawing on archaeology, biology, paleoecology, and other fields. This study relies on a variety of methods and techniques, integrating archaeological mapping, surface collection, and excavation with detailed faunal and artifact analyses. In this chapter, I briefly outline the methods and analytical procedures employed during field and laboratory work. The information provided here is designed to highlight the decisions made during the course of this research and to help place it in the context of other studies in the region.

EXCAVATION, SURFACE COLLECTION, AND MAPPING

To aid in comparative analysis, all fieldwork was conducted using standard archaeological procedures and methods generally consistent with work by Arnold (1992a; 2001c), Erlandson et al. (1996), Glassow (1996), and Kennett (2005). Field and laboratory research was carried out in collaboration with Channel Islands National Park staff and in consultation with local Native American representatives. Fieldwork was conducted at five primary archaeological sites on San Miguel Island between June 2000 and October 2002, with initial site visits in 1997, 1998, and 1999. These sites include SMI-87, a 3,000- to 2,500-year-old site on Cuyler Harbor; SMI-481, a dense multicomponent shell midden at Otter Point; SMI-468, a Middle, Transitional, and Late period site near Otter Harbor; SMI-163, a Late and Historic period village near Cuyler Harbor; and SMI-470, a Late and Historic period village near Otter Point.

Nine test units, primarily 0.5 × 1 m and 0.5 × 0.5 m wide, were excavated at these sites (Table 3.1). Each site contains dense shell midden deposits,

some of which are over 1 m deep. Due to logistical problems involved in fieldwork on the Channel Islands and following the preservation ethic inherent in National Park Service policy, only relatively small samples were excavated. Although the excavated volume is small, these excavations produced very large faunal and artifact samples comparable with other studies on the Channel Islands and larger than any previously reported for Late Holocene San Miguel Island (see Chapters 4 to 6).

The units were excavated by hand with trowel, generally following natural stratigraphy (Figure 3.1). Several of the units contained materials that were deposited relatively rapidly, and stratigraphic distinctions were minimal. In these instances, the units were excavated in arbitrary 5- or 10-cm levels. All of the archaeological sediments were screened through a combination of 1/8- and 1/16-inch mesh, and volume (liters) was estimated using measured buckets. Most of the deposits were screened over 1/16-inch mesh to maximize the collection of small beads, other artifacts, small fish bones, and additional faunal remains not captured in larger mesh sizes.

To complement the excavation units, 22 auger holes were excavated at SMI-163 and -468. Auger holes (3-inch diameter) were used to determine the depth of site deposits in unexcavated areas, to identify the location of house floors and other subsurface features, to obtain in situ ^{14}C samples from unexcavated houses, and to establish site boundaries. All augers were marked on the site maps and filled with sterile dune sand. The sediments excavated from auger holes were screened over 1/8- or 1/16-inch mesh, and in some cases yielded artifacts not recovered during excavation of the units.

Controlled surface collections and screening of rodent tailings from individual houses at SMI-163 were used to help document differences in the

Table 3.1. Excavation Unit Summary Data.

Site	Unit Designation	Dimensions (meters)	Mesh Size (inches)	Volume[*] (m³)	Comment
SMI-87	West Unit	0.5 × 1.0	1/16 & 1/8	0.240	Excavated as 2 contiguous 0.5 × 0.5 m units
	East Unit	0.5 × 1.0	1/16 & 1/8	0.193	Excavated as 2 contiguous 0.5 × 0.5 m units
Total	—	—	—	0.433	—
SMI-163	Unit 1	0.5 × 1.0	1/16	0.186	Excavated in arbitrary 5-cm levels
	Unit 2	0.5 × 0.5	1/16	0.269	Excavated in arbitrary 10-cm levels to 100 cm deep.
	Unit 3	0.5 × 0.5	1/16	0.131	Excavated in arbitrary 10-cm levels
Total	—	—	—	0.586	—
SMI-468	Unit 1	0.5 × 0.5	1/16	0.236	Excavated in arbitrary 10-cm levels
	Unit 2	0.5 × 0.5	1/16	0.208	Excavated in arbitrary 10-cm levels
Total	—	—	—	0.444	—
SMI-470	Bulk Sample 1	—	1/16	0.032	Excavated from a 40-cm-deep exposure in two 20-cm levels
SMI-481	Unit 1	0.4 × 0.8	1/16 & 1/8	0.157	Excavated as 2 contiguous 0.4 × 0.4 m units

[*] Volume for SMI-87 and SMI-481 is for both contiguous units.

Figure 3.1. Julia Knowles, Leah Largaespada, and Tony Largaespada excavating at SMI-163.

density and distribution of artifacts. At SMI-481 and SMI-87, surface collection of marine mammal bones and artifacts yielded faunal and artifact assemblages that complement the data obtained from the excavation units. These two sites are situated in badly eroding dunes with large, dense surface exposures from relatively well-defined areas.

These surface exposures provided good visibility for the collection of artifacts and mammal remains from discrete areas. The position of these materials on the surface was recorded, and artifacts were collected for analysis. Additional descriptions of the surface collection procedures are described in the individual chapters for these sites.

Sites SMI-163, SMI-468, and SMI-470 were mapped using a laser transit. Topographic data, house depression location and size, site boundaries, and the location of additional features, artifacts, and excavation units were all recorded. The data obtained from mapping were entered into the computer program, Surfer, to draft the maps. The mapping of these three villages is an important aspect of the study, forming the basis for interpreting broader patterns of community organization and layout (Kolb and Snead 1997). Because of the fragile nature of the site deposits at SMI-481 and SMI-87, maps were not created for these two sites. Both of these sites are located in mostly unvegetated dunes that are heavily eroding, and the traffic required to obtain detailed maps would have heavily exacerbated eolian erosion.

Figure 3.2. The author augering at SMI-468 on San Miguel Island, with Julia Knowles and Leah Largaespada excavating in the background.

LABORATORY METHODS

To standardize the data and increase its comparability, laboratory methods also generally follow those of Arnold (1992a, 2001c), Erlandson et al. (1996), Glassow (1996), and Kennett (2005). All excavated materials were returned to the laboratory for analysis. These samples were wet screened and then processed into general faunal and artifact categories. Due to the labor-intensive nature of processing samples from shell middens, numerous undergraduate and graduate students from the University of Oregon and Southern Methodist University helped sort and process the materials excavated during this study. All materials ultimately were checked by senior personnel with experience in sorting and identifying constituents from California shell middens.

Artifact Analysis

A wide variety of artifacts, including shell beads, bone and chipped-stone tools, and other artifacts were recovered. Artifacts were photographed using 35 mm and digital photography. The analysis of artifacts and consideration of their spatial and tempo-ral distribution are instrumental in documenting changes in social organization, exchange, and community dynamics. The spatial and temporal distribution of various artifacts may represent differential access to resources, the presence of wealth and status, and patterns of exchange (Arnold and Green 2002; Gamble et al. 2001; Wason 1994).

As in most Channel Islands archaeological sites, chipped-stone artifacts, except for microliths, are relatively rare. Microlithic (i.e., microblades and microcores) artifacts were the most common chipped-stone artifacts recovered; these were analyzed following Arnold (1987), Arnold et al. (2001), and Preziosi (2001). Non-microlithic debitage has not yet been analyzed. All material types were identified following descriptions by Arnold (1987), Erlandson (1994), Erlandson et al. (1997), Glassow (1996), Pletka (2001b:194–195), and other researchers. Because of macroscopic similarities between Cico chert found on San Miguel Island and Island Monterey chert found on Santa Cruz Island, particularly in small microblades, I only distinguished between these two stone materials in relatively large specimens. One obsidian flake recovered from SMI-163, along with additional specimens housed in southern California museums, were geochemically analyzed by Craig Skinner of the Northwest Obsidian Research Studies Laboratory to determine the source location of the raw material used to make these artifacts (Rick et al. 2001b). This geochemical provenance study helps reconstruct exchange and production patterns in the Santa Barbara Channel region (and beyond) during the Late Holocene.

Researchers working on the Channel Islands have devoted considerable attention to describing and documenting the abundance of shell artifacts, particularly beads found in coastal sites. Shell beads and ornaments were the most abundant artifacts recovered during my research. Beads were described and documented in detail following methods described by Arnold and Graesch (2001), Bennyhoff and Hughes (1987), Gibson (1992), Gifford (1947), King (1990), and others. Evidence for *Olivella* and red abalone bead production was also identified. All bead production sequences follow Arnold and Graesch (2001). Needle-drilled *Olivella* beads were present at SMI-163. Because needles are rarely found in archaeological contexts, needle-drilled beads were determined by measuring the dorsal and ventral dimensions of the drilled hole. If the perforations were less than or equal to 1.1 mm and similar on both the dorsal and ventral sides (i.e., bevel less than 0.3 mm), the bead was considered to be drilled by a needle (see Graesch 2001:279–281).

Researchers working on the California Channel Islands have given bone tools considerably less attention than shell artifacts. Wake (2001), using materials excavated by Arnold on Santa Cruz Island, provided the most current and detailed study of bone artifacts conducted on the Channel Islands. Bone tools in my study were generally analyzed following Wake (2001) and occasionally in reference to Gifford (1940).

FAUNAL REMAINS

Many coastal shell middens are extremely rich in faunal remains, and even the excavation of relatively small samples can result in large quantities of material. Because of the density of faunal remains in the deposits, various subsampling techniques were employed. Faunal remains were analyzed from 1/8-inch and larger screen residuals. A number of researchers have noted that using 1/16-inch mesh can greatly improve recovery of the remains of small fish and other organisms (e.g., Bowser 1993; Erlandson 1994; Pletka 2001a; Rick and Erlandson 2000; Zohar and Belmaker 2005). Pletka (2001a: 233), relying on Santa Cruz Island samples, demonstrated that very small fishes (sardines, etc.) were underrepresented by 14 percent when only 1/8-inch residuals were used. While some small fishes and other animals may be underrepresented, the use of 1/8-inch mesh provides data suitable for Channel Islands archaeological sites where faunal remains are generally well preserved and fragmentation of bone is low.

In the following sections, I highlight aspects of my decision making during faunal analysis and indicate the location of the comparative collections used for each faunal class. These descriptions are crucial for enhancing the comparability of my data with other research on the Channel Islands and beyond (see Driver 1991; Gobalet 2001; Lyman 2002). As Driver (1991:35) noted:

> zooarchaeologists should consider their identification systems more carefully in order to increase the degree of standardization of data presentation and reduce the possibility of interpretive error resulting from misapplication of identification methods.

Recent "blind tests" on fish remains from the California coast have also highlighted the need for greater explication of the methods and choices made during faunal analysis (Gobalet 2001). "Identifications by association" (see Driver 1991: 44) were not made during this study, and most identifications were conservative and relied on multiple comparative specimens.

The analysis of faunal remains is crucial for understanding the structure of local habitats, economy, seasonality, technology, health, and cultural evolution (Brewer 1992; Reitz and Wing 1999). Comparative analysis of various faunal materials can also demonstrate human impacts on local environments, technological capabilities, and aspects of social organization, such as division of labor. Taxonomic identification of faunal remains were used to reconstruct changes in prehistoric environments through time, human exploitation of the various habitats from which these taxa were obtained, and the technologies used to capture specific fauna. This research is part of a larger effort to build a 10,000-year sequence of such developments on San Miguel Island (Braje et al. 2006a; Erlandson et al. 2004a, 2005a, 2005b; Rick and Erlandson 2003; Rick et al. 2006a).

Shellfish and Invertebrates

Shellfish and other invertebrate remains were identified using collections housed at the University of Oregon and Santa Barbara Museum of Natural History. Identification and nomenclature for shellfish remains follow Morris (1974), Morris et al. (1980), and Ricketts et al. (1985). Archaeologists have used numerous techniques for sampling archaeological shell middens (see Claassen 1998). Following Moss (1989:134–135; see also Kennett 1998:185-186), all of the shellfish remains from 1/4-inch and larger screens were sorted, while the fraction from 1/8-inch mesh are based on projections of 25 percent subsamples that were completely processed. Although it is possible that this subsampling may under- or overrepresent the importance of various shell taxa, Moss (1989) indicated that for Northwest Coast shell middens, projections from small samples (10 percent) were generally comparable with the values for the entire sample. Kennett (1998) documented similar patterns for the Channel Islands, suggesting that this subsampling technique for shellfish is valid. To minimize the impact that subsampling had on certain taxa, all *Olivella biplicata*, *Haliotis rufescens*, and other taxa that were used to make artifacts or that may represent environmental shifts (e.g., small gastropods) were sorted from the entire sample. As part of a trans-Holocene study on human impacts on shellfish populations on San Miguel Island (Braje et al. 2006b; Erlandson et al. 2004a; Rick et al. 2006a), the length of the complete California mussel and red and black abalone shells from the five sites were measured using calipers. Because of the excellent preservation of the assemblages, scores of shellfish from a range of shell sizes were measured, providing a good estimate of the average size of each shell class.

Vertebrate Remains

Vertebrate remains, including bone, teeth, and fish scales, were completely sorted from the entire 1/8-inch screen sample. Vertebrate remains were first divided into major taxonomic categories including fish, marine mammal, land mammal, bird, reptile/amphibian, and undifferentiated bone. Because of the excellent preservation of archaeological sites on the Channel Islands, generally less than 10 percent of the bone NISP was classified as undifferentiated bone. As on most Channel Islands sites, bird and land mammal bone were relatively limited in the deposits, although both were used for making bone tools.

MARINE FISHES

The majority of the bones recovered during excavation were from marine fishes, primarily rocky intertidal and kelp forest taxa (rockfish, California sheephead, cabezon, surfperch, etc.). The fish remains were identified to the most specific taxon possible, including identifications to order, family, genus, and species, following the nomenclature, seasonality, and habitat information of Eschmeyer et al. (1983), Love (1996), and Miller and Lea (1972). All fish remains were analyzed using comparative collections from the University of Oregon, University of California, Santa Barbara, Santa Barbara Museum of Natural History, and the California Academy of Sciences. Following Gobalet (1997:320, 2001), my approach to the identification process was conservative, with most identifications made to family or genus. Numerous elements were analyzed, but dense bones, including the angular, dentary, maxilla, parasphenoid, premaxilla, quadrate, teeth, vertebra, and vomer, were among the most commonly identified (see Casteel 1976; Colley 1990; Rick et al. 2001a; Wheeler and Jones 1989). Many of the fragmentary specimens could be typed by element but had features indicative of two or sometimes three different fish taxa, often from entirely different families. Taking a conservative approach, these ambiguous elements were identified as undifferentiated teleost or elasmobranch and excluded from further identification. Many of the problems encountered during analysis stem from a lack of multiple comparative specimens, or ambiguities associated with the preservation of some archaeological specimens. Identifications beyond family or genus were not performed except when a perfect match could be made. Dr. Ken Gobalet of CSU Bakersfield helped identify a few of the more difficult specimens from SMI-163.

MAMMALS

Most of the mammal remains collected during this project were from marine mammals, reflecting the limited terrestrial fauna of the Channel Islands. A small number of dog, fox, deer, and rodent bones were also recovered. An important debate on the Channel Islands and California coast has centered on the importance of marine mammals in ancient subsistence economies (Colten 2002; Colten and Arnold 1998; Erlandson et al. 1998, 2004a; Hildebrandt and Jones 1992; Jones and Hildebrandt 1995; Lyman 1995; Porcasi and Fujita 2000; Porcasi et al. 2000; Walker et al. 2002; and others). Hildebrandt and Jones (1992; see also Jones and Hildebrandt 1995; Porcasi et al. 2000) have proposed a "tragedy of the commons," arguing for significant early declines in migratory/terrestrial breeders (California and Steller sea lions, and Guadalupe, elephant, and northern fur seals) that drove people to pursue more costly resident/aquatic breeders (harbor seals and sea otters). Colten and Arnold (1998) challenged aspects of this model, noting a general dearth of predicted mammal remains in Late Holocene Santa Cruz Island middens. A variety of marine mammal bones was recovered from each of the five sites (e.g., pinniped and small cetacean bones), providing an opportunity to examine ancient human interactions with marine mammal populations. Mammal bones were identified to the most specific taxon possible, using primarily long bones and cranial elements for identification. Marine mammal bones were identified using collections housed at the National Marine Mammal Laboratory (NMML) in Seattle, the Department of Anthropology at the University of Oregon, and the Santa Barbara Museum of Natural History. Nomenclature and habitat information for marine mammals follow Delong and Melin (2002), Le Boeuf and Bonnell (1980), and Riedman (1990).

At least six species of seals and sea lions are found on the Channel Islands today (see Chapter 2). When a perfect match could not be made to species, specimens were identified as Otariidae or Phocidae, undifferentiated pinniped, or simply as marine mammals. Pinniped cranial remains, teeth, and long bones identified to species were aged and sexed using reference materials and with the assistance of Drs. Bob Delong and Mike Etnier at the NMML Laboratory.

A number of dolphins, porpoises, and whales also occurs around the Channel Islands. Cetacean remains are difficult to identify to species unless certain cranial remains (mandibles, auditory bones, teeth, etc.) are recovered. Most cetacean remains were classified either as small cetacean (dolphins or porpoises) or large cetaceans (blue whales, orcas, etc.), unless bones sufficient for making a more specific identification were recovered. Bones from large whales were used by the Chumash for a variety of technological purposes and are generally not considered to represent food remains, although the Chumash sometimes consumed beached whales.

BIRDS

As stated previously, relatively few bird bones were recovered from the five archaeological sites. Bird remains from all of the sites were analyzed using comparative collections at the University of Oregon, Santa Barbara Museum of Natural History, and the Natural History Museum of Los Angeles. Bird descriptions, nomenclature, and habitat information follow Alsop (2001). Bird bones were identified to the most specific taxon possible, using a suite of bones (carpometacarpus, coracoid, cranium, furcula, humerus, femur, fibula, mandible, phalanx, radius, scapula, sternum, synsacrum, tarsometatarsus, tibiotarsus, and ulna). A sample of bird remains was analyzed by Dr. Dan Guthrie, who helped confirm and clarify a number of the identifications. Most of the birds identified were marine birds and are common on the Channel Islands today.

QUANTIFYING FAUNAL REMAINS

To quantify the various faunal taxa, a variety of zooarchaeological measures were used, including number of identified specimens (NISP), minimum number of individuals (MNI), and bone weights. Each of these measures poses some problems (see Casteel 1976, 1978; Grayson 1984; Klein and Cruz-Uribe 1984; Rietz and Wing 1999), but together they offer a variety of measures of the relative importance of faunal classes. NISP is the count of whole and fragmentary elements for each individual taxon. MNI values are an estimate of the lowest possible number of individuals present in the sample and are usually derived from the frequency of nonrepetitive elements (see Grayson 1984; Reitz and Wing 1999; Wheeler and Jones 1989). Due to the excellent preservation of the faunal assemblages and the relatively large size of the samples, a variety of elements could be used in calculating MNI for vertebrates (e.g., long bones, cranial elements, etc.). All elements were separated into right and left sides, and fragments were separated from complete or nearly complete bones to produce a more accurate MNI. For shellfish, weight and MNI were used to quantify the importance of various taxa. MNI for shellfish was calculated using nonrepetitive elements for the major taxa (i.e., sided hinges for bivalves and spires for gastropods). Determining MNI for some marine invertebrates (e.g., sea urchins, small barnacles, tube worms) was hindered by a number of factors (e.g., a dearth of nonrepetitive elements) and consequently, MNI estimates were not determined for these organisms.

Using MNI, NISP, and weight values together, I attempted to provide the most thorough estimate possible of the abundance of various faunal remains at the five sites. To compare the general dietary significance of marine fish versus other faunal classes, I also used the weight method to estimate the approximate meat yields represented by the faunal remains recovered in each stratum (Table 3.2). While the weight method suffers from a variety of analytical problems (see Casteel 1978; Erlandson 1994; Glassow 2000; Mason et al. 1998), these are minimized at Channel Islands sites where stratigraphic integrity and faunal preservation are exceptional. Numerous studies from the Santa Barbara Channel and broader Pacific Coast region have also used such measures to provide

valuable comparative data (see Colten 1993; Erlandson 1994; Glassow and Wilcoxon 1988; Kennett 2005; Moss 1989; Noah 2005; Rick 2004a; Sharp 2000; Vellanoweth and Erlandson 1999). These meat weight estimates should be treated as general approximations which, when used in concert with other zooarchaeological measures (i.e., NISP, MNI, etc.), offer another analytical tool for understanding the economic importance of various fauna. I also present standardized density values for both weight and NISP to complement dietary reconstructions based on the weight method.

SOILS ANALYSIS

Soils were analyzed by John Robbins of the Department of Geological Sciences at Southern Methodist University. The results presented here are refinements on original field data presented by Rick (2004a). Soil texture was determined based on the percentage of sand, silt, and clay, using water to separate the sand from the silt and clay and then using a centrifuge to separate the silt and clay. These three particle sizes were then dried and weighed separately, and soils were classified based on the percentage of each particle according to the Soil Survey Staff (2003). Soil pH was determined using an Orion Smart CheK meter, and all soils were alkaline (pH values from all deposits range from 8.3 to 10) and conducive to good archaeological preservation.

Table 3.2. Multipliers Used in Dietary Reconstructions.

Faunal Taxon	Meat Multiplier	Reference or Comments
Black abalone (*Haliotis cracherodii*)	0.944	Vellanoweth et al. 2002
Red abalone (*Haliotis rufescens*)	1.360	Koloseike 1969
Abalone	1.150	Black and red abalone average
California mussel (*Mytilus californianus*)	0.298	Erlandson 1994:59
Chiton (*Nuttallina californica*)	1.150	Erlandson 1994:59
Owl limpet (*Lottia gigantea*)	1.360	Tartaglia 1976
Platform mussel (*Septifer bifurcatus*)	0.364	Erlandson 1994:59
Sea urchin (*Strongylocentrotus* spp.)	0.583	Moss 1989
Turbans (*Tegula* spp.)	0.365	Erlandson 1994:59
Other shell	0.724	Average of abalone and mussel
Fish	27.700	Tartaglia 1976
Bird	15.000	Ziegler 1975
Sea mammal	24.200	Glassow and Wilcoxon 1988

Soil colors (dry) were determined by comparison with Munsell soil color charts.

RADIOCARBON DATING

Radiocarbon dating was used as the primary means of determining the age of deposits and establishing relative estimates of population and its variation through time. A total of 68 radiocarbon (^{14}C) dates on marine shell and charcoal were obtained from the five archaeological sites. Numerous additional dates were also obtained on materials from adjacent sites that help better understand the context of the five primary research areas. ^{14}C samples were collected from the excavated strata of each site, from auger units and sea-cliff profiles, and were dated using a combination of conventional ^{14}C techniques and AMS dating. AMS dates were also obtained from Historic and Protohistoric components at SMI-163 and -470 to produce a higher-resolution chronology for these sites. A few individual artifacts (fishhooks and red abalone beads) were also directly AMS dated to more precisely trace the chronology and evolution of these artifact types. I primarily dated marine shells (California mussel and black abalone) to avoid potential complications from dating old wood (Schiffer 1986). Although some scholars have suggested that marine shells are less reliable for ^{14}C dating than small twigs or charcoal (see Erlandson 1988b), ^{14}C dates obtained from marine shells on the Channel Islands have been shown to be highly reliable (Erlandson et al. 1996; Kennett et al. 1997). Care was taken to ensure that marine shell samples for AMS dating were taken along portions of the shell that contained multiple growth lines (Culleton et al. 2006).

To provide a calendar-age estimate for each of the radiocarbon dates, all dates were calibrated with CALIB 4.3 (Stuiver and Reimer 1993, 2000), using a marine reservoir correction of 225 ± 35 years (see Kennett et al. 1997). ^{13}C/^{12}C corrections were either determined by the radiocarbon labs or an average of +430 years was applied (Erlandson 1988b). Unless otherwise noted, all dates presented in this book are given in calibrated calendar years (cal BP). For the Historic and later sites, I also include calibrated years in AD/BC to help with comparisons to known historical events. To aid in the regional comparisons provided in Chapter 7, I also rely mostly on calibrated AD/BC dates in this chapter. For

brevity, I often refer to dated assemblages by their calibrated intercept, recognizing that these dates should be treated as approximations of the age of each assemblage rather than an exact date.

TAPHONOMY

Research on taphonomy, formation processes, and site disturbances has dramatically improved the ways archaeologists reconstruct the past (see Dincauze 2000; Lyman 1994; Reitz and Wing 1999; Schiffer 1987; Stein 2001; Stiner 1994). Several studies have explored the taphonomic or formation histories of faunal remains (Butler 1993, 1996; Erlandson and Moss 2001; Lyman 1994; Claassen 1998; Reitz and Wing 1999), floral remains (Dincauze 2000:332–338; Pearsall 2000), artifacts (Villa 1982), and site deposits (Stein and Farrand 2001; Wood and Johnson 1978), resulting in a thorough body of literature and several syntheses (e.g., Lyman 1994; Schiffer 1987). With a general dearth of burrowing rodents (gophers, badgers, etc.) and relative lack of recent human development, the Channel Islands have long been argued to contain one of the best-preserved records of coastal hunter-gatherers in North America (see Arnold 1992a; Erlandson et al. 1996; Kennett 2005; Vellanoweth et al. 2002). The high-resolution record of the Channel Islands contrasts with that of the coastal mainland where sites are often badly bioturbated (Erlandson 1984; D. Johnson 1989) and have been ravaged by more than 150 years of historical development. These disturbances often result in mainland archaeological sites with heavily fragmented contents and multiple components mixed together (Erlandson and Rockwell 1987). Because the Channel Islands lack intensive historic development and most burrowing animals, they contain an archaeological record largely devoid of many of the disturbances plaguing the coastal mainland.

Despite the relatively well-preserved archaeological record of California's Channel Islands, numerous taphonomic agents are actively altering the region's archaeological record, including marine erosion, bioturbation, and historical activities (Table 3.3). A major component of this project was assessing the impact of various processes on the archaeology of each site. All five sites are threatened by a variety of agents, mainly

Table 3.3. Major Taphonomic Processes Operating on the Channel Islands.

Process	Description	Impact on Archaeology
NATURAL PROCESSES		
Animal transporters	Deposition or removal of materials in a site by animals	Introduce noncultural materials, remove some cultural materials
Argilliturbation	Shrinking and swelling of clay soils	Mixing of constituents
Eolian processes	Erosion and deposition of materials by wind, abrasion, and production of ventifacts	Deflation/destruction of sites, deposition of "new" sites
Faunalturbation	Burrowing and mixing of deposits by animals	Mixing, fragmentation, erosion
Floralturbation	Disturbance and mixing of deposits by plants	Mixing, fragmentation, erosion
Fluvial processes	Erosion and deposition of archaeological deposits by stream, creek, or other freshwater runoff	Destruction of sites, introduction of materials from other areas
Marine processes	Erosion and deposition of archaeological deposits by tidal surges and wave action	Destruction of sites, scouring of light fraction, introduce materials
Mass wasting/gravity	Landslides, cliffing, etc.	Erosion, redeposition, and burial of archaeological record
CULTURAL PROCESSES		
Prehistoric human activities	Construction, cleaning, trampling, cooking, etc.; excavation of houses, storage, burial pits, etc.	Mixing, fragmentation, and destruction of archaeological record
Historical impacts	Building or road construction, agriculture, bombing, looting, etc.	Movement, fragmentation, and destruction of archaeological record
Introduction of exotic animals	Overgrazing, stripping of vegetation and soils, trampling, burrowing, rooting, etc.	Fragmentation, mixing, deflation/ erosion

Note: Adapted from Rick et al. 2006b.

marine erosion, wind deflation, and burrowing from small animals. Because taphonomic agents have a significant impact on the interpretation and reconstruction of the archaeological record, analysis of formation processes plays an important role in my study.

SUMMARY

Relying on archaeological and ecological data, I aim to reconstruct human subsistence strategies, ecology, and social organization. Surface collection, mapping, and excavation were conducted at five Late Holocene archaeological sites on San Miguel Island. Large faunal and artifact assemblages were recovered, and surface collections supplement excavated artifacts and large mammal remains. For more than a century, archaeologists have recognized that the southern California coast contains an extensive and diverse archaeological record of maritime peoples. Through the integration of faunal and artifact data, this book documents aspects of the lifeways of the people who left this remarkable record behind.

4

An Early Late Holocene Settlement on Cuyler Harbor

Several archaeologists have noted the dearth of research on Channel Islands sites dated to between 5,000 and 2,000 years ago, often citing the importance of this time period for understanding later cultural developments (e.g., Kennett 2005; Kennett and Conlee 2002; Munns and Arnold 2002). A number of studies have emphasized Early Holocene (e.g., Erlandson 1994) and Late period or Historic developments (see Arnold, ed. 2001, 2004), and although not as well represented as the former two, research at sites dated to around 6,000 to 5,000 years ago has also increased (e.g., Erlandson et al. 2005c; Glassow 2002b, 2005a; Sharp 2000; Vellanoweth 2001; Vellanoweth et al. 2002, 2005). The period of time between about 5,000 and 2,000 cal BP is arguably the biggest gap in the archaeological record of the Channel Islands. Several factors hinder research on this time period. For example, sites of this age generally contain fewer diagnostic artifacts (i.e., shell beads) than later sites, making them more difficult to identify without radiocarbon dating. On portions of the islands, dune building has deeply buried many of these sites. Late period sites are often located on top of earlier sites, which also adds to the difficulty of defining early village and other site types. Radiocarbon dating on San Miguel Island, however, has shown that 23 of 78 ^{14}C dated sites (30 percent) have components that date between about 4000 and 2000 cal BP (unpublished Radiocarbon Database on file at the Department of Anthropology, University of Oregon, 2006). Santa Rosa and Santa Cruz islands also have a number of sites dating to this interval, but many are buried below thick Late period deposits, and relatively few of these sites have been excavated or reported on (Kennett and Conlee 2002; Munns and Arnold 2002).

Elsewhere in North America, numerous important cultural changes happened between about 4,000 and 2,000 years ago. According to Matson and Coupland (1995:303–305), for example, along the Northwest Coast of North America between about 3,000 and 1,500 years ago, numerous hallmarks of the Northwest Coast cultures first appeared. These include such important developments as the appearance of large plank-house villages, storage of salmon, and social inequality. Erlandson and Rick (2002a:181) suggested that on the Santa Barbara mainland coast, several cultural characteristics of the Chumash appear between about 4,000 and 1,500 years ago, including large multihouse villages, social inequality, and elaborate material culture and personal adornment. Many of these patterns are also apparent on the Channel Islands. Sites on the northwest coast of Santa Rosa Island (SRI-3, -4, -5, and -41) investigated by Phil Orr (1968) roughly 50 years ago, for instance, suggest the presence of large residential sites with cemeteries dated to this interval or earlier. The excavation of these sites, however, was often too crude to determine the scale and timing of important cultural changes. It is clear that the Channel Islands underwent significant changes between about 4,000 and 2,000 years ago, but the current dearth of data from this time period makes it difficult to ascertain the scope and scale of these changes.

In this chapter, I present the results of surface collection, excavation, and ^{14}C dating at SMI-87, one of the largest sites on San Miguel Island (170 × 270 m). This large, multicomponent site dates exclusively to the interval between about 4500 and 2500 cal BP, making it an ideal candidate for elucidating cultural developments of this poorly understood time period. Located in sand dunes on the east side of Cuyler Harbor, much of this site is unvegetated and has been significantly impacted by wind erosion. Fieldwork was conducted at SMI-87 during the summers of 1999 and 2000, followed by brief site visits in summer 2001 and 2002. I focus primarily on data from two 1 × 0.5 m units (West Unit and East Unit) excavated in the dense, eroding shell midden exposures on top of the two main dunes (West and East Dunes), supplemented by a systematic surface collection. These data expand on an earlier taphonomic study at SMI-87 (Rick 2002) by presenting the complete analysis of artifacts and faunal remains from surface collection and excavation.

My synthesis of the archaeology and historical ecology of SMI-87 provides important details about human cultural developments during the beginning of the Late Holocene. These data supply the framework for understanding the layout, chronology, and human activities represented at this important site. They also form the baseline for comparing human cultural developments during this time period with later cultural developments. For example, what do the human activities conducted at SMI-87 suggest about human social organization, exchange, and subsistence activities? How does this reconstruction compare with cultural patterns of the Late or Historic period? How do the data from SMI-87 articulate with those of Early or Middle Holocene sites? I use the SMI-87 case study as a starting point for building a long-term reconstruction of human activities over the last 3,000 years.

SITE SETTING

SMI-87 is situated along the shoreline on the eastern edge of Cuyler Harbor. The site has a prominent location with commanding views of Cuyler Harbor and Prince Island. A spring that is intermittently covered with beach sand is located directly in front of the site and probably provided freshwater to the site occupants. SMI-87 is also located at the beginning of the "wind tunnel" (D. Johnson 1972; Rick 2002), a large deflated area caused primarily by historical overgrazing. The wind tunnel starts along the beach on Cuyler Harbor located adjacent to SMI-87 and contains a series of linear dunes that extend across the island all the way to Cardwell Point. Wind, primarily out of the northwest, has had a heavy impact on the site deposits and has sig-

nificantly altered the landscape since the time SMI-87 was occupied. This factor makes it more difficult to reconstruct the layout of this site compared with later villages that contain clear surface house depressions.

SMI-87 is situated in a series of linear dunes located perpendicular to the shoreline and smaller intermediate dunes around the site perimeter (Figure 4.1). Radiocarbon dates from the basal archaeological deposits underlying the dunes suggest that this dune formation roughly coincides with the stabilization of sea level in the region approximately 6,000 to 5,000 years ago (Erlandson et al. 2005b; Inman 1983). The archaeological deposits at the site consist of several discontinuous shell midden strata built in paleosols that are between about 10 and 50 cm thick, separated by several meters of sterile dune sand and capped by dense shell midden deposits. The dunes at the site are roughly 20 m high, but they have been heavily eroded, and buried deposits are easily accessed through erosional exposures.

Vegetation on the site surface is minimal, consisting primarily of a sparse cover of introduced ice plant and other low-lying dune vegetation located primarily on the eastern site margin. Consequently, much of the surface archaeological material is heavily deflated, with obvious lag deposits of sand-blasted mammal bones, stone tools, and highly fragmented shellfish. Prior to excavation, several areas of the site appeared to have intact archaeological deposits, including remnants of several Middle Holocene paleosols containing red abalone (*Haliotis rufescens*) shells and extensive Late Holocene shell midden deposits up to 50 cm deep that cap the dunes. Numerous eroding exposures indicate a reliance on abalone and California mussel, while abundant marine mammal bones scattered across the surface also illustrate the use of seals, sea lions, and small cetaceans. In one of these erosional exposures, an asphaltum basketry impression dated to about 4100 cal BP was carefully excavated and represents one of the earliest such objects in coastal California. A portion of a human cranium was observed on the site in 2000, indicating that human burials or possibly a cemetery are present. Since so much of this site is exposed by the wind, the dearth of human bone suggests that the number of burials or the size of this cemetery may be relatively small.

Large pavements of fractured rock are located on top of the two main dune ridges and appear to be

Figure 4.1. Site setting of SMI-87 showing location of West and East units.

the remains of hearths, living floors, or other features, but further excavation is necessary to determine their function (Figure 4.2). Some of these features contained charcoal, suggesting that they may have been large hearths. A radiocarbon date obtained from a charred twig from one of these platforms on the eastern dune produced a calibrated intercept of 2610 cal BP (OS-27236), suggesting that this platform corresponds with the Late Holocene site occupation. These rock features appear to have stabilized portions of the site, but because of the gradual winnowing of sediments and downslope movement, much of the site is quickly eroding.

There are a number of additional sites in the vicinity of SMI-87, most of which have never been excavated or radiocarbon dated. SMI-152 is located about 1 km east of SMI-87 on a large dune complex overlooking Cuyler Harbor. An abalone shell fishhook, similar to a specimen recovered from SMI-87, was recently AMS dated to 2650 cal BP (3060 ± 80 RYBP; OS-37145). A red abalone shell from near the base of a 40-cm-thick deposit at SMI-152 also produced a date of 2300 cal BP (2830 ± 80 RYBP; Beta-181390), suggesting that portions of this site are contemporaneous with SMI-87. SMI-150, a nearby dune site, yielded a Late period date of 640 cal BP (1300 ±

Figure 4.2. Rock platform on West Dune (note rocks eroding downslope in background).

60 RYBP; Beta-180926). SMI-153, another nearby dune site, was dated to 4350 cal BP (4460 ± 70 RYBP; Beta-181391), a date contemporary with portions of the lower SMI-87 deposits. The complex of sites that make up SMI-161, located about 0.5 km from SMI-87, produced dates of 1350 cal BP (2050 ± 50 RYBP; OS-37139), 4390 cal BP (4490 ± 35 RYBP; OS-51579), and 5860 cal BP (5680 ± 45 RYBP; OS-51581), suggesting earlier, later, and contemporaneous occupations with SMI-87. Collectively, these

sites suggest a relatively intensive human occupation of the Cuyler Harbor area between about 4,500 and 2,000 years ago.

Field Research and Stratigraphy

Two excavation units were placed in areas of the site that appeared to be relatively intact. The units were excavated in natural levels ranging between 4 and 10 cm thick; volume (liters) was determined using measured buckets. Each unit was excavated as two contiguous 0.5 × 0.5 m subunits. The first two units were screened over 1/16-inch mesh (West Unit 1 and East Unit 1), and all screen residuals were retained. The other 0.5 × 0.5 m units were screened over 1/8-inch mesh, and only vertebrate remains, whole shell valves, and artifacts were collected (West Unit 2 and East Unit 2). A total volume of 0.240 m³ was excavated in the West Unit (West Unit 1 = 0.141 m³ and West Unit 2 = 0.099 m³), and 0.193 m³ was in the East Unit (East Unit 1 = 0.096 m³ and East Unit 2 = 0.097 m³).

For both units, I distinguish between the upper deposits (Strata 1A, 1B, and 1C) from roughly 0 to 20 cm deep and the lower deposits (Strata 1D and 1E/F) from about 20 to 45 cm deep. The deposits in Strata 1A, 1B, and 1C of the West Unit are a dark gray (7.5YR4/1) sandy loam (Figure 4.3). The lower deposits are a grayish brown (10YR5/2) sandy clay loam. The island's dunes are composed primarily of calcareous sands, which are generally alkaline and conducive to good preservation of most archaeological constituents (D. Johnson 1972; Chapter 3). The presence of caliche ($CaCO_3$) distributed fairly evenly throughout the deposits also indicates a depositional environment favorable to the preservation of archaeological constituents.

The deposits in the West Unit were not capped by vegetation but, beyond slight surface deflation, appeared to be largely intact. The upper 20 cm of the deposit contained air pockets within a soil cemented together with shellfish and other constituents. Between roughly 15 and 20 cm in depth, the sediments became less cemented, and no air pockets were present. It is in these lower, buried portions of the site that preservation was good and fragmentation was low.

The deposits in the East Unit were roughly similar to those in the West Unit (Figure 4.4). Here the upper deposits range from a grayish brown (10YR5/2) sand to dark gray (10YR4/1) loamy sand. The lower deposits range from a light brownish

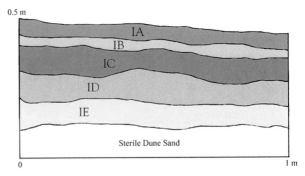

0.5 m

IA Dark gray (7.5YR4/1) sandy loam with dense shellfish, and some air pockets

IB Dark gray (7.5YR4/1) sandy loam with shellfish and some small airpockets

IC Dark gray (7.5YR4/1) sandy loam with dense shellfish

ID Grayish brown (10YR5/2) sandy clay loam with whole shell valves and bone

IE Grayish brown (10YR5/2) sandy clay loam with whole shell valves and bone

Figure 4.3. Stratigraphic profile from West Unit, south wall at SMI-87.

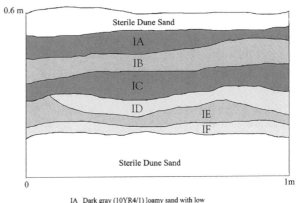

0.6 m

IA Dark gray (10YR4/1) loamy sand with low density shell, bone, and abundant rock accumulations

IB Grayish brown (10YR5/2) sand with shell and scattered bone

IC Grayish brown (10YR5/2) sand with shell and bone

ID Grayish brown (10YR5/2) sand with shell and high density of bone and some charcoal

IE Light brownish gray (10YR6/2) sand with whole shell valves and fairly dense bone

IF Light brownish gray (10YR6/2) sand with whole shell valves and fairly dense bone

Figure 4.4. Stratigraphic profile from East Unit, south wall at SMI-87.

gray (10YR6/2) to grayish brown (10YR5/2) sand. In contrast to the West Unit, the East Unit was capped by roughly 10 cm of recently deposited dune sand and a light cover of ice plant. This unit was also excavated on the edge of one of the site's rock platforms, and consequently the upper 10 cm of the deposit contained a dense concentration of rock. Along with the vegetation and sand cover, these rocks provided additional protection to the deposits. Small air pockets were also present in portions of the upper deposits in the East Unit but were considerably less pervasive than in the West Unit.

After excavation, all of the materials were returned to the archaeology laboratory at the University of Oregon where detailed taxonomic identification of the faunal remains was conducted. Faunal remains from the 1/8-inch midden samples of the West and East units were sorted and identified using procedures described in Chapter 3. Because the surface of SMI-87 is largely unvegetated, surface collections across the site yielded a diverse artifact assemblage and marine mammal bones that complement the comparatively small samples recovered in the units. While data from surface surveys lack the volumetric, spatial, and temporal control inherent in excavated samples, the surface

materials from a site like SMI-87 provide data on the broader range of site constituents. Most of the artifact and vertebrate faunal data presented in this chapter were identified in areas of the site that suggested they had eroded from the uppermost site deposits. While it is possible that a few of these materials may have come from the smaller and discontinuous 4,500- to 4,000-year-old deposits, an age of roughly 3,100 to 2,500 years ago is the best estimate for these materials.

Chronology

Thirteen radiocarbon dates from the deepest site strata, the intermediate strata, and the uppermost deposits suggest that SMI-87 was probably abandoned shortly after 2500 cal BP (550 BC), with most of the site occupation occurring between roughly 4000 and 2500 cal BP (2050 to 550 BC; Table 4.1). The earliest documented occupation of the site occurred at about 4500 cal BP (2550 BC) and roughly

Table 4.1. Radiocarbon Dates from SMI-87.

Sample #	Provenience	Material	Uncorrected ^{14}C Age	^{13}C/^{12}C Adjusted Age	Calendar Age Range (cal BP), 1 sigma	Calendar Age Range (BC/AD), 1 sigma
Beta-146120	East Unit top	Black abalone	2530 ± 60	2960 ± 60	2540 (2420) 2340	590 (470) 390 BC
OS-26071	East Dune surface	Abalone hook	—	2980 ± 35	2540 (2450) 2350	590 (500) 400 BC
OS-27236	East Dune rock feature	Charred twig	2510 ± 55	—	2740 (2610) 2470	790 (660) 520 BC *
Beta-134832	East Dune top	California mussel	2660 ± 70	3090 ± 70	2730 (2690) 2490	780 (740) 540 BC
Beta-145425	East Unit bottom	Black abalone	2830 ± 60	3260 ± 60	2860 (2780) 2740	910 (830) 790 BC
Beta-134831	West Dune tar feature	California mussel	2990 ± 80	3420 ± 80	3130 (2980) 2860	1180 (1030) 910 BC
Beta-146121	West Unit top	California mussel	3000 ± 90	3430 ± 90	3150 (2990) 2860	1200 (1040) 910 BC
Beta-145426	Uppermost West Dune	California mussel	3030 ± 60	3460 ± 60	3160 (3050) 2940	1210 (1100) 990 BC
Beta-145427	West Unit bottom	Black abalone	3070 ± 50	3500 ± 50	3200 (3110) 3000	1250 (1160) 1050 BC
Beta-134835	West red ab. midden	Red abalone	3760 ± 90	4190 ± 90	4090 (3960) 3830	2140 (2010) 1880 BC
Beta-134833	Central swale, basketry	California mussel	3920 ± 60	4350 ± 60	4280 (4160) 4080	2330 (2210) 2130 BC
Beta-134834	West Dune basal swale	Red abalone	4140 ± 60	4570 ± 60	4550 (4460) 4400	2600 (2510) 2450 BC *
OS-37144	Basal Dune	Black abalone	—	4650 ± 110	4790 (4560) 4420	2840 (2620) 2470 BC

Note: All dates were calibrated using Calib 4.3 (Stuiver and Reimer 1993, 2000), and applying a ΔR of 225 ± 35 years for all shell samples (see Kennett et al. 1997). ^{13}C/^{12}C ratios were determined by the radiocarbon labs or an average of +430 years was applied (Erlandson 1988b).

* Denotes samples with multiple intercepts, average is provided.

corresponds with the beginning of major dune building at the site (Erlandson et al. 2005b). *Olivella* barrel beads and large projectile points, described below, were recovered from the site and corroborate the radiocarbon chronology (King 1990). No evidence for later occupations has been identified among a large assemblage of artifacts collected or observed on the site surface. Radiocarbon dates from the top and bottom of the two excavation units suggest they date to a relatively narrow window of time. The West Unit dates between 3110 and 2990 cal BP (1160 to 1040 BC), while the East Unit dates between 2780 and 2420 cal BP (830 to 470 BC). These samples provide an opportunity to document human cultural developments during a relatively discrete occupation, which does not appear to be mixed with materials from other time periods.

FORMATION PROCESSES AND TAPHONOMY

The effects of wind and other formation processes on the SMI-87 deposits are complex and posed some problems that appear to have been minimal at the other excavated sites. Some of the most obvious effects of wind are present on the shellfish assemblage, which is dominated by California mussel (*Mytilus californianus*) and limited amounts of platform mussel (*Septifer bifurcatus*) and black and red abalone (*Haliotis cracherodii* and *H. rufescens*). Because other shellfish taxa are only present in small amounts, I focus on the impact of wind on the most abundant shellfish species (California mussel). The weight and percentage of California mussel shells demonstrate significant differences between the upper and lower deposits. Almost 90 percent of the total shellfish assemblage by weight is located in the upper deposits (1A, 1B, and 1C), compared with just over 10 percent located in the lower deposits (1D and 1E). Because the excavated volume of the upper and lower samples of West Unit 1 (.075 m^3 in the upper and.066 m^3 in the lower) and in East Unit 1 (.043 m^3 in the upper and.053 m^3 in the lower) are relatively comparable, we may assume that these are not purely a result of different sample sizes.

Several lines of evidence suggest that the higher density of shellfish in the upper strata is probably the result of deflation, suggesting that these deposits were at one time considerably thicker. Numerous air pockets in the upper strata probably skewed the volume from these levels and consequently inflated the density of shellfish for the upper strata. Shellfish in the upper deposits are also considerably more fragmented than in the lower deposits, probably from trampling by humans and other animals, battering by eolian particles, and other processes. Many of the California mussel shells in the upper deposits are also clearly ventifacts (although primarily of cultural origin) that have been sand blasted by windblown particles (see Rick 2002). These shells contain faceted and polished surfaces primarily on the side of the shell that was exposed to the wind, suggesting they are the result of wind abrasion rather than fluvial or other processes (Claassen 1998:58–59; Lyman 1994:382). These shell ventifacts are visible across the site surface, and in the units to a depth of about 20 cm. Preliminary observations of the East Unit suggest the presence of only trace amounts of abraded shell, probably due to greater vegetation and rock cover over this unit.

In the field and lab, it was noted that most of the stone tools and shell beads from the site surface contained a patina or sheen caused by sand blasting. Many of the bone tools and unmodified bones from the site surface are also etched by windblown particles. In contrast to a pattern noted by Brain (1967:99), some of the large pieces of bone also appear to be slightly polished by windblown particles (see also Littleton 1999:73). Most of the bones from the excavation units are fragmentary fish bones. The majority of the mammal bones from the units are also small fragments of cancellous or cortical bone and teeth that are probably from marine mammals. A small portion of the bones (about 10 percent) are from birds.

In West Unit 2, roughly 65 percent of the fish bones by count and weight came from the lower deposits. In the upper half of the deposits, however, Strata 1A and 1B combine to account for only about 15 to 20 percent of the total fish bone by count and weight. Stratum 1C also contains a relatively small proportion of fish bone, constituting another 15 to 20 percent of the total count and weight. The large mammal bones, although present in much lower densities, are more evenly distributed throughout West Unit 2. Despite the relatively low count for mammal bones, these remains are fairly heavy, providing more than 45 percent of the total weight of bones from West Unit 2, but just 10 percent of the total count. In contrast, fish bones account for 90 percent of the total bone count, but less than 55 percent of the weight. Although the mammal bones are also fairly evenly distributed through West Unit 2, some of the highest values occur in the upper deposits. Because the excavated volume for these strata are comparable, these differences are not just a result of sampling bias.

Similar results for the vertebrate remains were present in East Unit 2 where there is a much higher frequency of fish bone in the lower deposits (roughly 80 percent by count and weight) than in the upper deposits (approximately 20 percent by count and weight). The mammal bone is again relatively evenly distributed throughout the unit, with some of the highest values in the upper strata. The data from these two units illustrate the differential effects of wind on various faunal classes (shellfish, fish bone, mammal bone, etc.), demonstrating that shellfish and heavy bones tend to become concentrated, while smaller and lighter bones become more dispersed.

Other light materials such as charcoal are also differentially preserved at SMI-87 and corroborate the findings for the faunal remains. The vast majority (99 percent) of charcoal in West Unit 1 is found in the lower deposits. Although projectile points, bifaces, and retouched flakes were found on the site surface, relatively few stone tools or lithic debitage were recovered during excavation. The small amount of debitage (primarily flakes, cores, and chunks of chert or metavolcanic debris) found in West Unit 1 is concentrated in the upper deposits (roughly 90 percent by weight). Again this higher value is similar to the findings for the shellfish and heavy mammal bones, lending further support to the fact that the upper levels are a partially deflated lag deposit. These factors are taken into account when interpreting the data from SMI-87. Because of these disturbances, the best estimates of the relative abundance of various taxa generally come from the lower, buried strata.

ARTIFACTS

A variety of shell, chipped-stone, ground-stone, and bone artifacts were recovered from SMI-87. Similar to other sites dated to this time period, however, artifact densities are considerably lower at SMI-87 than at Late or Historic period sites (Kennett and Conlee 2002). The artifact diversity and densities for SMI-87, for instance, are considerably

lower than those from the units excavated at SMI-163 (see Chapter 6). Nonetheless, a variety of artifacts was recovered, representing hunting and fishing gear, other utilitarian objects, and ornamental items. Many of the artifacts show evidence of polishing or battering by windblown particles, suggesting that some artifacts (e.g., small bone tools) have been damaged or destroyed by this process.

Sixteen shell, bone, and stone artifacts were collected in the excavation units, but most of the assemblage was identified during surface collection. The surface artifacts were assigned provenience based on the general locations where they were recovered: (1) West Dune; (2) East Dune; and (3) North Dune. Based on their stratigraphic position, most of the artifacts probably came from the densest site deposits capping the dunes, suggesting an age of 3200 to 2300 cal BP. Artifacts from the East Unit date between about 2780 to 2420 cal BP and those from the West Unit between 3110 to 2990 cal BP.

The SMI-87 artifact assemblage is described in detail below under four headings: shell artifacts, chipped-stone artifacts, bone artifacts, and other artifacts. As stated previously, the artifact assemblage validates the radiocarbon chronology for the site, as no hallmarks (*Olivella* cup and wall beads, arrow points, etc.) of a later occupation were found. These factors make the surface artifacts a relatively reliable indicator of the types of activities that took place at SMI-87.

Shell Artifacts

Only 20 shell artifacts were recovered from the surface and excavation units at SMI-87 (Table 4.2). While the total number is small, 10 of these came from the test units, the largest of any of the artifact classes. Most of the shell artifacts fall into King's (1990) Middle period. The most common shell artifacts were *Olivella* barrel (n = 6) and spire-lopped (n = 8) beads (Figure 4.5). Most of these were from the surface, but two barrel beads were from the West Unit, and two barrel and five spire-lopped beads were from the East Unit. Four clam disk beads were from the surface and a *Trivia californiana* bead was found in West Unit 1.

A J-shaped fishhook made from abalone nacre was recovered from the surface of the East Dune. This shell fishhook, the only one obtained from the site, was directly AMS dated to roughly 2450 cal BP, making it, along with a specimen from nearby

Table 4.2. Shell Artifacts from SMI-87.

Artifact Type	West Dune	East Dune	North Dune	West Unit 1	West Unit 2	East Unit 2	Total
Clam disk bead	3	—	—	—	—	—	3
Clam disk bead fragment	—	1	—	—	—	—	1
Haliotis J-shaped fishhook	—	1	—	—	—	—	1
Olivella barrel bead	—	1	1	1	1	2	6
Olivella spire-lopped bead	1	2	—	—	—	5	8
Trivia californiana bead	—	—	—	1	—	—	1
Total	4	5	1	2	1	7	20

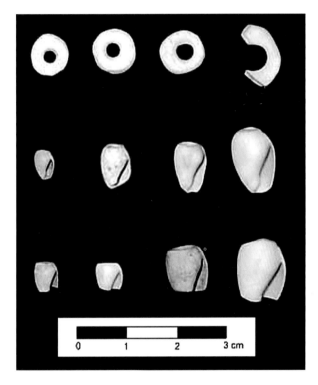

Figure 4.5. Shell beads from SMI-87. Clam disk beads *(top)*, *Olivella* spire-lopped beads *(middle)*, and *Olivella* barrel beads *(bottom)*.

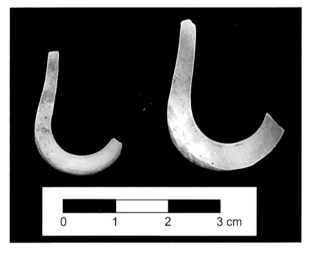

Figure 4.6. Single-piece abalone shell fishhooks from SMI-87 *(left)*, and SMI-152 *(right)*; both specimens have been directly AMS dated to ca. 2500 cal BP.

SMI-152, one of the oldest directly dated shell fishhooks on the California coast (Rick et al. 2002; Figure 4.6).

Olivella shells and shell fragments were also recovered from the units. Considerably less is known about bead making during the early Middle period than at later sites where clear bead blanks, beads in production, and detritus were recovered (see Arnold and Graesch 2001), but these broken *Olivella* fragments probably represent bead making. *Olivella*

densities were 75 g/m^3 for West Unit 1 and 94 g/m^3 for East Unit 1. These densities are much lower than in later sites where values approach 10,000 to 20,000 g/m^3, but are similar to other densities reported for sites of this age (Arnold and Graesch, 2001; Arnold and Munns 1994; Kennett and Conlee 2002; Rick 2004a).

Chipped-Stone Artifacts

The most common artifacts recovered from SMI-87 were chipped-stone tools. Thirty-one chipped-stone tools were collected from the surface of the site, where thousands of flakes, debitage, and expedient tools were also noted (Table 4.3). Only one formal chipped-stone artifact was recovered from the East Unit, but debitage was recovered throughout the two units. Of these artifacts, 21 were found

Table 4.3. Chipped-Stone Artifacts from SMI-87.

Artifact Description	Material[a]	West Dune	Northern Dune	East Dune	East Unit 1, Stratum 1a	Total
Biface or biface fragment	Monterey chert	5	—	1	—	7
Crude biface	Cico chert	1	—	2	—	3
Crude biface	Monterey chert	2	—	—	—	1
Biface fragment	Chert endive.	1	—	—	—	1
Drill	Monterey chert	1	—	1	—	2
Drill	Cico chert	1	—	—	—	1
Drill preform?	Monterey chert	—	—	1	—	1
Gouge/pick	Siliceous shale	1	—	—	1	2
Projectile point (leaf shaped)	Monterey chert	3	2	—	—	5
Projectile point (leaf shaped)	Chert endive.	—	—	1	—	1
Projectile point (contracting stem)	Chert endive.	1	1	—	—	2
Projectile point (small stem?)	Monterey chert	1	—	—	—	1
Retouched or utilized flake	Monterey chert	4	—	—	—	4
Total	—	21	3	6	1	31

Note: For measurements, additional descriptions, and a list of ambiguities associated with some identifications see Rick (2004a: 106).

[a]"Monterey chert" specimens are banded Monterey chert, some of which were probably obtained from the mainland coast.

on the West Dune, six on the East Dune, three on the Northern Dune, and one from the East Unit.

Twenty-one of these artifacts are made of banded Monterey chert (68 percent), some of which may come from the mainland; four are from Cico chert (13 percent) probably obtained on eastern San Miguel Island (Erlandson et al. 1997); four more are made of unidentified cherts (13 percent); and two gouges or picks (see Conlee 2000:382) were made from a siliceous shale (7 percent) probably obtained on the island. Two chipped-stone trifacial macrodrills were also recovered. Another artifact is finely flaked and may be a drill, but could also be a point, and another artifact may be a drill preform (Rick 2004a). Four retouched and/or utilized Monterey chert flakes with at least one modified edge were recovered from the West Dune.

Nine projectile points and two probable point base fragments (bifaces) were recovered from the site (Figure 4.7). Projectile points are relatively rare in Channel Islands sites when compared with the adjacent mainland coast, and their abundance at SMI-87 suggests a relatively specialized hunting strategy or other activity. Eight of these are made of Monterey chert, while the other three are of an un-

Figure 4.7. Projectile points from SMI-87.

differentiated chert. These relatively large projectile points fit into Justice's (2002:242–263) Coastal Contracting Stem Cluster. Two of the specimens are contracting stem points, and most of the others appear to be leaf shaped. A few of the points have small breaks near the base or tip, making it difficult to determine if they are leaf shaped or if they had small stems. Three of the points are relatively short and broad, similar to harpoon points described for the area by Hudson and Blackburn (1982). A number of mammal bone barbs (see below) suggest that these points may have been hafted with the barbs to form a simple harpoon or thrusting spear.

As Glassow (2002c) noted, it is often difficult to determine if projectile points and bone barbs represent harpoon, compound fishhook, or other technologies, including complete museum specimens collected by antiquarians. Harpoons are generally thought to appear in the Santa Barbara Channel region about 1,500 years ago, but other forms may have been used around 2,500 years ago or earlier (see Glassow 1996:20, 134). If the SMI-87 specimens are from harpoons, they are among the oldest well-documented specimens in the region. Elsewhere on the Channel Islands, clear technology for hunting marine mammals is quite rare, with researchers speculating that these animals were harpooned, clubbed, and scavenged and were taken by boat and on land.

Ten bifaces or biface fragments were also recovered from the site, most of which are Monterey chert. Two additional biface fragments appear to be projectile point base fragments, but because of their small size have been called bifaces. These biface fragments were either too small to speculate on function or may be fragments of knives or cutting tools. Some of the bifaces appear to be unfinished, suggesting that some chipped-stone tools were being made on site. One flaked siliceous shale cobble recovered from the East Unit and another from the West Dune appear to be large picks or gouges probably used in the manufacture of stone bowls or other ground-stone tools. Several other picks and broken stone bowls were observed on the site surface.

Bone Artifacts

Bone artifacts are the second most common artifact type found in the SMI-87 assemblage, with 24 specimens made from mammal and bird bones (Table 4.4). As stated in Chapter 3, my analysis generally follows methods described by Wake (2001), but some categories deserve further explanation. Seven artifacts made from mammal bone are classified as worked bone fragments. These are small specimens that are ground or polished, but were too small to determine an artifact type. Two of the artifacts are awls, including one made from a probable island fox ulna. Three marine mammal bone pry bars and one pry bar fragment were recovered from the West Dune. Two artifacts classified as pointed bone objects are broken tip fragments that may be portions of awls or barbs. One artifact classified as a knife or applicator is a roughly 10-cm-long blunt/burned piece of marine mammal bone. Two artifacts are gorges or small

Table 4.4. Bone Artifacts from SMI-87.

Artifact	Material	West Unit 1	West Dune Surface	East Unit 1	East Unit 2	East Dune Surface	Total
Awl	Island fox?	—	—	—	—	1	1
Awl fragment	Mammal	—	1	—	—	—	1
Gorge/small barb	Bird	1	1	—	—	—	2
Knife/applicator	Mammal	—	1	—	—	—	1
Medium barb	Mammal	1	4	1	—	—	6
Pointed object	Bird	—	1	—	—	—	1
Pointed object	Mammal	—	—	—	—	1	1
Pry bar	Mammal	—	4	—	—	—	4
Worked bone	Mammal	2	2	—	1	2	7
Total	—	4	14	1	1	4	24

Note: For measurements and additional artifact descriptions see Rick (2004a: 106).

barbs made of bird bone, with one containing asphaltum smeared on the center of the gorge. Two of the specimens classified as worked bone may be gorge fragments, but are too small to be certain. All of these specimens are similar to fishing gorges used in the Santa Barbara Channel region throughout the Holocene (Rick et al. 2001a).

Finally, four artifacts recovered from the surface, one from Stratum 1C of the West Unit and one from Stratum 1E of the East Unit, were classified as medium bone barbs (Figure 4.8). These have a slight curve and are made of mammal bone. As discussed earlier, these specimens may be the remains of harpoon barbs. Their shape and size closely resemble several Channel Islands harpoon barbs described by Bennyhoff (1950:337; see g, h, and i). Because it is difficult to distinguish between barbs used for harpoons and those used in compound fishhooks—even in hafted specimens (see Glassow 2002c)—some of these may be from compound fishhooks. Wake (2001:185) also noted considerable similarity in artifacts described as compound fishhooks and harpoon barbs by some researchers, making it difficult to determine the precise function of these artifacts. Unfortunately, most of the SMI-87 specimens are from the surface and have been wind abraded, so no signs of asphaltum or other hafting elements, except for asphaltum on a gorge identified in the West Unit, were identified. The association of these barbs with

abundant projectile points and marine mammal bones suggests that the bone barbs and points were probably used to hunt marine mammals and possibly fishes. If so, they represent some of the earliest well-defined hunting technology from the Channel Islands.

Other Artifacts

Several ground-stone artifacts were also collected or observed on the site surface. These include two donut stones or digging stick weights and a notched cobble that may have served as a net weight. Several bowl fragments and a few pestles made of sandstone and metavolcanic materials were also noted on the site surface. The only other artifacts recovered from SMI-87 were artifacts made of asphaltum. Twenty-four fragments (51 g) of asphaltum with basketry impressions were found in situ in Stratum 1D of the East Unit, suggesting that people used asphaltum to waterproof perishable vessels. A number of small, undifferentiated clumps of asphaltum were also identified in the East Unit, and a series of small "tarring pebble features," recently eroded accumulations of tarring pebbles, were noted on the site surface. Collectively, the artifacts from SMI-87 represent a wide variety of activities, including hunting, fishing, plant processing, shellfish collecting, and the possible transport of finished tools or raw materials from the mainland.

SUBSISTENCE STRATEGIES

The most common materials recovered from SMI-87 were faunal remains, including shellfish, fish, mammal, and bird remains. All of the faunal remains described below are from 1/8-inch residuals of the excavated units or from surface collections. Because of the relatively short period of time represented by the deposits, the significance of each faunal category is presented as a total for all strata from each unit. The breakdown of each individual stratum is presented in Rick (2004a).

Shellfish and Invertebrates

WEST UNIT

Over 19 kg of shell, from a minimum of 5,275 individuals, were analyzed from 1/8-inch residuals in West Unit 1 (Table 4.5). At least 29 different taxa were identified in the assemblage, including

Figure 4.8. *(Left)* Two bone gorges; *(right)* four barbs; all from SMI-87.

Table 4.5. Shellfish and Invertebrate Remains from West Unit at SMI-87.

Taxon	Wt.	% Wt.	MNI	% MNI
Barnacle undif.	813.4	4.2	—	—
Calliostoma spp. (top snail)	3.1	< 0.1	19	0.4
Chiton undif.	260.3	1.3	—	—
Clam undif.	2.7	< 0.1	11	0.2
Collisella pelta (shield limpet)	24.8	0.1	18	0.3
Conus californicus (California cone)	0.5	< 0.1	1	<0.1
Corallina spp. (coralline algae)	0.9	< 0.1	—	—
Crab undif.	114.5	0.6	—	—
Crepidula spp. (slipper shells)	21.3	0.1	185	3.5
Cryptochiton stelleri (gumboot chiton)	94.2	0.5	—	—
Fissurella volcano (volcano limpet)	4.4	< 0.1	13	0.2
Gastropod undif.	9.2	< 0.1	60	1.1
Glans subquadrata (eccentric ribbed clam)	0.4	< 0.1	8	0.2
Haliotis cracherodii (black abalone)	424.5	2.2	40	0.8
Haliotis rufescens (red abalone)	195.0	1.0	26	0.5
Haliotis spp. (abalone undif.)	51.9	0.3	—	—
Hormomya adamsiana (Stearns' mussel)	8.6	< 0.1	16	0.3
Land snail	152.1	0.8	196	3.7
Limpet undif.	37.5	0.2	457	8.7
Lottia gigantea (owl limpet)	2.3	< 0.1	3	0.1
Megathura crenulata (giant keyhole limpet)	4.1	< 0.1	2	<0.1
Mytilus californianus (California mussel)	13,480.1	69.7	2561	48.5
Nacre undif.	296.1	1.5	—	—
Olivella biplicata (purple olive)	10.6	0.1	—	—
Pelecypod	1.3	< 0.1	2	<0.1
Pollicipes polymerus (gooseneck barnacle)	281.7	1.5	—	—
Protothaca staminea (Pacific littleneck)	1.4	< 0.1	10	0.2
Septifer bifurcatus (platform mussel)	1165.4	6.0	1352	25.6
Serpulorbis squamigerus (scaled worm snail)	2.3	< 0.1	—	—
Strongylocentrotus spp. (sea urchins)	580.2	3.0	—	—
Tegula brunnea (brown turban)	157.4	0.8	33	0.6
Tegula funebralis (black turban)	784.8	4.1	175	3.3
Tegula spp. (turban undif.)	263.6	1.4	87	1.6
Undif. shell	75.9	0.4	—	—
Total	19,326.5	—	5275	—

Note: Based on 1/8-inch recovery and all weights in grams. Volume = 0.141 m^3.

California mussels, platform mussels, black and red abalones, turban shells, sea urchins, limpets, and chitons. As is true of most Channel Islands shellfish assemblages, the West Unit is dominated by California mussels, which constitutes roughly 70 percent of the total weight and about 49 percent of the total MNI. The second most abundant taxon is platform mussel, making up about 6 percent of the weight and 26 percent of the MNI. Black turban make up about 4 percent of the weight and 3 percent of the MNI, with sea urchins also constituting about 3 percent of the total weight of shell, and black and red abalone combining for only about 3 percent of the weight of shell. All other taxa generally make up only trace amounts of the shellfish sample and appear to have been of minor significance. Many of the shells in the West Unit were probably introduced into the assemblage as incidental byproducts of collecting other shellfish or kelp. These include gooseneck and small, undifferentiated barnacles, which combine for over 5 percent of the total shell weight, and smaller limpets, gastropods, and tube worms. Land snail remains were probably introduced to the site naturally.

Variation in the importance of different shellfish taxa between the five strata is minimal, resulting largely from the short amount of time that elapsed between the accumulation of the lower deposits and the accumulation of the upper strata. As stated previously, there are considerable differences in the density and preservation of food remains between the upper and lower strata that are probably the result of wind disturbances to the upper deposits. California mussels are the dominant taxa in all of the strata, followed by platform mussels with generally only minor changes in the distribution of each shell category (Rick 2004a). The only difference between the strata is the amount of shellfish remains present. The upper strata contain about 15,850.8 g of shell, whereas the lower strata contain only about 3475.6 g. This higher density in the upper strata is probably the result of wind-related disturbances, where the upper deposits have been partially deflated and contain a higher density of shells, rocks, flakes, and other heavy constituents, with a dearth of lighter constituents such as fish bone (Rick 2002). The lower strata are also considerably better preserved, including whole shell fragments.

EAST UNIT

Almost 17.5 kg of shell, from a minimum of 6,447 individuals and representing at least 30 different shellfish taxa, were recovered and analyzed from East Unit 1 (Table 4.6). The major shellfish taxa are very similar to those in West Unit 1, with California mussels constituting roughly 65 percent of the total shell weight and about 36 percent of the MNI. Platform mussels are the second most abundant taxon, accounting for about 8 percent of the weight, but nearly 47 percent of the MNI. Black turbans again make up about 3 percent of the total weight and MNI, sea urchins about 5 percent of the total weight, and black and red abalones combined for almost 4 percent of the total weight. Gooseneck and acorn barnacles account for almost 7 percent of the shell weight, with other incidental species such as small limpets and gastropods contributing only trace amounts of shell.

As in the West Unit, there are generally minimal differences in the percentages of shellfish identified in each of the strata. California mussels and platform mussels dominate all strata, with generally minor changes in the distribution of various taxa. A few small changes were identified. For example, sea urchins make up about 10 percent of the total shell weight in Stratum 1C compared with about 5 percent in most other strata; and black abalones make up about 13 percent of the total weight in Stratum 1B compared with about 3 percent in most other strata. There are also larger amounts of platform mussels in the lower deposits. These relatively minor differences are likely the result of variability in the location of shellfish collecting, changes in the places that materials were deposited, or other minor shifts that do not alter the overall importance of major shellfish taxa. Again, this similarity is likely the result of the short amount of time represented by the sample, resulting from one occupation or a series of short-term occupations over a relatively brief period of time. Unlike in the West Unit, the upper deposits in the East Unit contain 7762.2 g of shell, with 9776.5 g of shell in the lower strata. The similar amount of shell recovered in the upper and lower strata of the East Unit is likely the result of slightly better preservation in this unit, which was capped by sterile dune sand, some rocks, and a light vegetation cover that provided a setting less susceptible to deflation than the exposed deposits of the West Unit (Rick 2002).

Table 4.6. Shellfish and Invertebrate Remains from East Unit at SMI-87.

Taxon	Wt.	% Wt.	MNI	% MNI
Barnacle undif.	864.0	4.9	—	—
Chiton undif.	142.3	0.8	—	—
Clam undif.	1.1	< 0.1	2	< 0.1
Corallina spp. (coralline algae)	7.0	< 0.1	—	—
Crab undif.	115.5	0.7	—	—
Crepidula spp. (slipper shells)	7.1	< 0.1	59	0.9
Cryptochiton stelleri (gumboot chiton)	269.0	1.5	—	—
Dendraster excentricus (sand dollar)	0.3	< 0.1	—	—
Fissurella volcano (volcano limpet)	1.9	< 0.1	25	0.4
Gastropod undif.	3.2	< 0.1	33	0.5
Glans subquadrata (eccentric ribbed clam)	0.2	< 0.1	1	< 0.1
Haliotis cracherodii (black abalone)	482.8	2.8	44	0.7
Haliotis rufescens (red abalone)	194.8	1.1	37	0.6
Hiatella arctica (Arctic rock borer)	0.2	< 0.1	4	0.1
Kelletia kelleti (Kellet's whelk)	0.8	< 0.1	1	< 0.1
Land snail	20.0	0.1	42	0.7
Limpet undif.	45.8	0.3	510	7.9
Lottia gigantea (owl limpet)	7.2	< 0.1	4	0.1
Margarites succinctus (tucked margarite)	0.4	< 0.1	4	0.1
Mytilus californianus (California mussel)	11,423.9	65.3	2333	36.2
Nacre undif.	388.2	2.2	—	—
Nucella spp. (dogwinkles)	9.0	0.1	8	0.1
Olivella biplicata (purple olive)	9.0	0.1	2	< 0.1
Pectinidae (scallops)	0.1	< 0.1	1	< 0.1
Pollicipes polymerus (gooseneck barnacle)	308.3	1.8	—	—
Protothaca staminea (Pacific littleneck)	2.0	< 0.1	4	0.1
Septifer bifurcatus (platform mussel)	1347.2	7.7	3025	46.9
Serpulorbis squamigerus (scaled worm snail)	6.9	< 0.1	—	—
Strongylocentrotus spp. (sea urchins)	885.5	5.1	—	—
Tegula brunnea (brown turban)	266.5	1.5	57	0.9
Tegula funebralis (black turban)	578.7	3.3	217	3.4
Tegula spp. (turban undif.)	79.0	0.5	34	0.5
Undif. shell	24.9	0.1	—	—
Total	17,492.8	—	6447	—

Note: Based on 1/8-inch recovery and all weights in grams. Volume = 0.096 m^3.

Fish

WEST UNIT

Almost 70 g of fish bone, 982 bones, and a minimum of 28 fishes were identified in West Unit 2 (Table 4.7). Of these, 191 bones (20 percent) weighing almost 35 g (50 percent) were identified to family, genus, or species. At least 10 teleost taxa were identified in the sample, including cabezon, sheephead, rockfish, lingcod, perch, and mackerel. The few fish bones that were recovered lack clear signs of modification, except for burning on a small number (< 10 percent) of bones, making it difficult to determine natural vs. cultural deposition of faunal remains. However, the similarity of the taxa to other Channel Islands assemblages (see Bowser 1993; Rick et al. 2001a) and the presence of fishing technology at the site suggest that most of the fish bones were deposited by cultural activities rather than natural processes. All of the taxa could have been caught in rocky shore or kelp forest habitats using relatively simple technology such as hook or gorge and line, spears, or nets. The presence of bone gorges, one shell fishhook, and a probable net weight suggests a variety of methods were used to catch fish. The possible harpoons described earlier also may have been used to catch some fish.

Rockfish are the most abundant taxon, making up about 65 percent of the weight, 59 percent of the NISP, and 32 percent of the total MNI of the identified fish. Perch are the next most abundant taxon, making up about 7 percent of the weight, 21 percent of the NISP, and 14 percent of the MNI. Cabezon follow closely behind with about 7 percent of the weight, 6 percent of the NISP, and 11 percent of the MNI. All other taxa appear to make up only minor amounts of the total fish sample. Similar to the shellfish sample, the importance of various fishes in the individual strata is comparable to the total for the unit as a whole. However, the upper strata contain significantly smaller amounts of bone (16 g) than the lower strata (54 g). This appears to be largely the result of wind deflation in the upper strata, which may have removed much of the light

Table 4.7. Fish Remains from West Unit 2 at SMI-87.

Taxon	Wt.	% Wt.[a]	NISP	% NISP	MNI	% MNI
Teleost						
Cottidae (sculpin)	0.1	0.3	1	0.5	1	3.6
Scorpaenichthys marmoratus (cabezon)	2.4	6.9	11	5.8	3	10.7
Embiotocidae (surfperch)	2.6	7.4	40	20.9	4	14.3
Hexagrammidae (greenling)	< 0.1	0.3	1	0.5	1	3.6
Ophiodon elongatus (lingcod)	1.1	3.2	5	2.6	1	3.6
Labridae (senorita or wrasse)	0.3	0.9	15	7.9	4	14.3
Semicossyphus pulcher (California sheephead)	4.9	14.0	2	1.1	2	7.1
Mackerel undif.	0.3	0.9	2	1.1	2	7.1
Malacanthidae						
Caulolatilus princeps (ocean whitefish)?	0.3	0.9	1	0.5	1	3.6
Scorpaenidae						
Sebastes spp. (rockfish)	22.8	65.3	113	59.2	9	32.1
Teleost undif.	34.9	—	791	—	—	—
Total	69.8	—	982	—	28	—

Note: Based on 1/8-inch recovery and all weights given in grams. Volume = 0.099 m³. Any specimen noted with a ? is a preliminary identification.

[a] Percentages for fish bones are based on specimens identified to family, genus, and species.

fraction, rather than a decline in the importance of fishing through time.

EAST UNIT

As in the West Unit, all of the fish bones from East Unit 2 were completely analyzed and identified to the most specific taxon possible. I identified 17 g of fish bone, 422 bones, and a minimum of 14 individual fishes from 1/8-inch residuals of East Unit 2 (Table 4.8). These are slightly lower amounts than were obtained from the West Unit. Of these, 80 bones (19 percent) weighing 6.1 g (35 percent) were identified to family, genus, or species. At least six teleost taxa and one unidentified elasmobranch were identified in the sample, including perch, rockfish, cabezon, and kelpfish. A single billfish vertebra was recovered from the surface of the East Dune. As in the West Unit, however, most of the taxa could be obtained from rocky nearshore or kelp forest habitats, using hook/gorge and line, nets, and spears. The fish also show little sign of modification, but appear to be largely the result of cultural rather than natural processes.

The fish sample is dominated by perch (about 60 percent of NISP and weight), followed by rockfish (19 percent of weight and 14 percent of NISP). Cabezon make up about 14 percent of the weight and 5 percent of the NISP, with all other taxa being

only minor contributors. As in the West Unit, most of the bones are concentrated in the lower strata (15 g), with about 2.8 g in the upper strata, possibly reflecting some wind deflation.

Mammals

Compared with fish and shellfish remains, mammal bones were relatively rare in the excavated samples. Roughly 49 g of mammal bone were recovered from 1/8-inch residuals in West Unit 1 and about 54 g of mammal bone in West Unit 2. None of the mammal bones from West Unit 1 were identifiable to family or below. Of the bones from West Unit 2, however, one sea otter rib weighing 7.3 g was found in Stratum 1A. The other bones were small fragments of mammal bone characterized by the presence of cancellous bone and relatively thin cortical layers. Because the Channel Islands contain relatively few terrestrial mammals and most of the identified bones from the surface were from marine mammals, the majority of these bones are probably from marine mammals.

Mammal bones were even less abundant in the East Unit, with just 10 g recovered in East Unit 1 and 14.2 g in East Unit 2. None of these small bone fragments were identifiable to family or below. These bones are also thought to represent the remains of marine mammals.

Table 4.8. Fish Remains from East Unit 2 at SMI-87.

Taxon	Wt.	% Wt.[a]	NISP	% NISP	MNI	% MNI
Teleost						
Clinidae (kelpfish)	0.1	1.7	1	1.3	1	7.1
Cottidae (sculpin)	0.1	1.7	2	2.5	2	14.3
Scorpaenichthys marmoratus (cabezon)	0.8	13.6	4	5.0	1	7.1
Embiotocidae (surfperch)	3.6	61.0	47	58.8	4	28.6
Labridae (senorita or wrasse)	0.2	3.4	15	18.8	2	14.3
Scorpaenidae						
Sebastes spp. (rockfish)	1.1	18.6	11	13.8	4	28.6
Teleost undif.	10.3	—	339	—	—	—
Elasmobranch	0.8	—	3	—	—	—
Total	17.0	—	422	—	14	—

Note: Based on 1/8-inch recovery and all weights given in grams. Volume = 0.097 m³.

[a] Percentages for fish bones are based on specimens identified to family, genus, and species.

Because mammal bones tend to be more widely distributed in site deposits than fish and shellfish remains, a systematic surface collection of mammal bones was performed at SMI-87. All diagnostic cranial, limb, and other bones were collected from the surface with the position where they were found noted. These bones were later analyzed in the laboratory. While such surface samples are inherently more problematic than excavated samples, the larger sample has some advantages in that it provides information on the types of marine mammals that were hunted or scavenged by the occupants of SMI-87.

Unlike in the excavation units, a number of identifiable bones were recovered from the site surface (Table 4.9). Most of these bones appear to have come from the upper components of the West and East Dunes, which date between roughly 3100 and 2400 cal BP. As with the surface-collected artifacts,

however, a few of these specimens may have come from earlier site components. Roughly 217 (8.2 kg) marine mammal bones from at least 16 individual animals were recovered from the surface. Of these, 199 (7.2 kg) bones from 13 individuals were recovered from the West Dune, and 18 (1 kg) bones from four individuals were obtained from the East Dune. The West Dune sample is more diverse, reflecting the larger number of bones recovered from this area. At least six marine mammal taxa were identified, including harbor seal, Guadalupe fur seal, Steller sea lion, California sea lion, sea otter, and Risso's dolphin (*Grampus griseus*), the latter identified by a few nearly complete crania. An island fox mandible and dog cranium were also recovered from the surface of the West Dune.

Due to the relatively small number of mammal bones recovered from the site, determining the relative abundance of these taxa is problematic. For

Table 4.9. Marine Mammal Remains from Surface Collections at SMI-87.

Taxon	West Dune			East Dune			Total					
	Wt.[a]	NISP	MNI	Wt.	NISP	MNI	Wt.	% Wt.[b]	NISP	% NISP	MNI	% MNI
Phocidae												
Phoca vitulina (harbor seal)	184.4	4	2	—	—	—	184.4	2.3	4	4.3	2	11.8
Otariidae	1158.4	24	—	447.6	7	—	1606.0	20.1	31	33.3	—	—
Arctocephalus townsendi (Guadalupe fur seal)	135.9	2	1	78.0	2	1	213.9	2.7	4	4.3	2	11.8
Eumetopias jubatus (Steller sea lion)	1011.0	2	1	—	—	—	1011.0	12.7	2	2.2	1	5.9
Zalophus californianus (California sea lion)	591.9	4	2	320.8	4	1	912.7	11.5	8	8.6	3	17.6
Otariidae Subtotal	2897.2	32	4	846.4	13	2	3743.6	47.0	45	48.4	6	35.3
Pinniped undif.	97.2	2	—	68.9	2	—	166.1	2.1	4	4.3	—	—
Carnivora												
Enhydra lutris (sea otter)	232.6	14	3	19.9	1	1	252.5	3.2	15	16.1	4	23.5
Cetacea												
Grampus griseus (Risso's dolphin)	3001.6	11	2	—	—	—	3001.6	37.7	11	11.8	2	11.8
Small cetacean	131.4	7	1	—	—	—	131.4	1.6	7	7.5	1	5.9
Medium cetacean	427.5	6	1	63.3	1	1	490.8	6.2	7	7.5	2	11.8
Sea mammal undif.	234.4	123	—	16.7	1	—	251.1	—	124	—	—	—
Total	7206.3	199	13	1015.2	18	4	8221.5	—	217	—	17	—

[a] All weights in grams.

[b] Percentages do not include undifferentiated sea mammal bone.

example, NISP values for each taxa are relatively small, and the MNI values only range between 1 and 4 per taxon. The bones of otariids dominate the assemblage (48 percent of NISP), followed by sea otter (roughly 16 percent of NISP), cetaceans (27 percent of NISP), and phocids (4 percent of NISP). However, the sample clearly demonstrates that the people who occupied SMI-87 obtained a variety of pinnipeds, sea otters, and small to medium cetaceans, probably using spears or harpoons and watercraft. Absent from the sample are elephant seals that are abundant in the area today and would have represented relatively large and attractive food and raw material sources.

Birds

Relatively few bird bones were recovered from SMI-87. This pattern follows the general trend in Channel Islands sites, where birds are usually supplementary resources. Birds may have been scavenged or hunted by the occupants of SMI-87, but because of the small number of bird remains it is difficult to determine how birds were obtained. Although bird bones appear to be relatively rare at SMI-87, they were important for making bone tools (e.g., gorges).

In West Unit 2, only 27 bird bones weighing just 3.4 g were recovered. Of these, only one carpometacarpus from Stratum 1E was identified as a northern fulmar (*Fulmarus glacialis*). In West Unit 1, only 7.8 g of fragmentary bird bones were recovered, and none were identifiable. Similarly, only 7 bird bone fragments weighing just 0.4 g were recovered in East Unit 2, and none were diagnostic. East Unit 1 yielded only 1.6 g of fragmentary bird bones, and none were diagnostic. Since bird bones are limited at the site, it is probable that many of the bird remains are from individuals scavenged off of beaches or other areas and were used primarily for making tools.

Dietary Reconstruction

To estimate the relative importance of various faunal classes, I also calculated the significance of each animal category using meat weight multipliers (see Chapter 3). Because of the high evidence for deflation in the upper site deposits from the West and East units, dietary reconstructions were calculated using the remains (1/8-inch) only from the lower site deposits (Strata 1D, 1E, and 1F), which presumably provide a more representative picture of the overall site economy.

Dietary reconstructions using the weight method suggest that fish (rockfish, perch, etc.) were the most important component of the diet in West Unit 1 (46 percent of overall meat yield). Shellfish (mussels, abalones, etc.) contribute roughly 40 percent of the overall meat yield, marine mammals about 12 percent, and birds only about 2 percent. When just fish and shellfish are compared, fish make up about 53 percent and shellfish about 47 percent of the total meat yield, suggesting a fairly balanced economy.

For the East Unit, shellfish dominate the overall meat yield, contributing roughly 79 percent, followed by fish (18 percent), marine mammals (4 percent), and birds (0.3 percent). When just fish and shellfish are compared, shellfish make up about 82 percent and fish about 18 percent of the total meat yield. These data also mirror the NISP and raw weights for these various classes, which demonstrate that the East Unit contains considerably fewer vertebrate remains than the West Unit. This is surprising since the East Unit is roughly 500 years younger than the West Unit, and most models of Channel Islands subsistence suggest a decrease through time in the importance of shellfish and concomitant increases in fish (Kennett 2005; Vellanoweth et al. 2002). These discrepancies could be related to sampling bias, or differences in site function through time. Collectively, the data from the East and West Units suggest that at SMI-87 people relied on a relatively balanced economy where shellfish and fish, supplemented by marine mammals and birds, composed most of the diet. These patterns differ from subsistence practices at sites dating later in time.

SYNTHESIS

SMI-87 was a large site occupied between about 4,500 and 2,500 years ago. Excavation and surface data illustrate that the most intensive human occupation occurred between about 3200 and 2500 cal BP. The presence of rock platforms, which likely represent hearths or other living features, the large size and prominent location of the site, the presence of a human burial, and the diverse artifact and faunal assemblages all suggest that this was probably the main village on Cuyler Harbor between about 3000 and 2500 cal BP. Radiocarbon dating of other sites in the Cuyler area, including a Historic period village (SMI-163, see Chapter 6), suggests that the Cuyler area was a focus of ancient human settlement on San Miguel Island.

Archaeological data from reconnaissance, excavation, and surface collection illustrate that people at SMI-87 conducted a wide range of activities, including a number of complex coastal subsistence practices, the production and maintenance of tools, basket making, and the use of shell beads. In many ways, however, this 3,000-year-old community is quite different from Late period or Historic Chumash villages (see Chapters 6). At SMI-87, beads and other ornamental artifacts are relatively rare, represented by just 19 specimens (excluding *Olivella* detritus) or roughly 24 percent of the entire artifact assemblage. Many of these artifacts were surface finds, with just 10 artifacts recovered in the excavated samples (23/m^3). In contrast, at SMI-163, over 470 beads, blanks, and beads in production (1780/m^3, excluding bead detritus) were recovered in Unit 2 alone. Collectively, these data suggest that exchange practices and bead production on San Miguel Island around 3,000 years ago were much less intensive than they were later in time.

Although ornaments and beads are rare at SMI-87, artifacts and faunal remains associated with relatively sophisticated subsistence practices are abundant in the assemblage, including chipped-stone, bone, and shell hunting/fishing implements. The hunting and fishing tools include Monterey chert points and bone barbs that may be the remains of harpoons or thrusting spears, small bone bipoints that are probably fishing gorges, bone pry bars, stone net weights, and a j-shaped single piece shell fishhook. It is also likely that composite bone fishhooks were used. The presence of cetaceans, billfish, sea otters, and abundant kelp forest fish bones suggests that people were using watercraft to hunt and fish. Collectively, these artifacts are associated with a wide range of coastal subsistence activities, and the occurrence of stone points, some of which might be made from mainland Monterey chert, also suggests that people procured this stone on the mainland and transported it to San Miguel or obtained it through trade with mainlanders. The presence of Cico chert, siliceous shale, sandstone, and metavolcanic tools suggests that people also utilized local stone resources. Stone bowls and pestles indicate that people were probably exploiting terrestrial plants. Numerous large, chipped-stone picks observed on the site surface may also have been used in manufacturing ground-stone tools such as mortars and pestles (Conlee 2000).

The faunal remains associated with these tools demonstrate a relatively balanced economy, including shellfish, fish, marine mammals, and birds. Shellfish and fish appear to have been the focus of the economy, but the presence of abundant pinniped and cetacean bone on the site surface suggests that marine mammals were also economically important. Kennett (2005) suggested that by around 3,000 years ago, the number and types of fauna being taken increased, a pattern that is reiterated at SMI-87. This diversity of animal remains supports the idea that this site was a village or residential base. While houses may have been present at one time, deflation of the upper midden deposits has obscured any surface evidence for such residential features.

Unfortunately, few sites of this age have been reported or excavated on the northern Channel Islands. Kennett and Conlee (2002:162) suggested that between about 3000 and 1300 cal BP (1050 BC and AD 650), people began focusing their settlement and subsistence strategies on the coast, with less attention devoted to the island interior than earlier in time. This may have resulted in more permanent coastal villages, but there also appears to have been some residential mobility (Kennett 2005; Kennett and Conlee 2002). The presence of a number of cemeteries on the islands (e.g., SCRI-333, SRI-5, and SRI-41; see Kennett 2005; King 1990:33) dated to around this time or earlier also suggests that sedentism and settled village life had increased. While people may have remained fairly mobile, it is likely that domestic features are present at other sites of this age and that their absence is due in large part to the dearth of research, or more recent villages obscuring older domestic features located stratigraphically below them. The large stone pavements or hearths at SMI-87 appear to be remnants of domestic features dating to around 3,000 to 2,500 years ago, but the site deposits are so badly eroded that it is difficult to determine precisely what they represent.

The data from SMI-87 paint a complicated picture of an early Late Holocene village on San

Miguel Island. The dearth of beads and other ornaments stands in contrast to many Late period or Historic Chumash villages, but the relatively complex and diverse subsistence activities and tools suggest that the occupation of the site involved a wide variety of activities and possibly a sedentary group lived at this site. Future research in sites on the Channel Islands dated to this time should provide important details on this significant but poorly understood period.

5

Late Holocene Occupation of
Otter Harbor

During the last 1,500 years, several significant environmental and cultural events occurred throughout North America. The pace of cultural change in a variety of areas appears to have intensified during this time, including several significant developments on the Channel Islands (Arnold 2001b; Kennett 2005). Environmental changes during the Medieval Climatic Anomaly (Jones et al. 1999) and new technologies such as the bow and arrow (Blitz 1988; Kennett 2005), for example, played an important role in spurring cultural developments throughout the Americas. On the Channel Islands, archaeologists have argued that bead making and exchange increased near the end of the Middle period, subsistence strategies became more complex and intensive, and sociopolitical hierarchy and rank became increasingly stratified and based on heredity (Arnold 1992a, 2001b; Arnold et al. 1997a; Kennett 2005; Raab and Larson 1997). Many of these changes, however, appear to have their foundation in cultural developments that occurred earlier in the Holocene (Erlandson and Rick 2002a). Because of the relatively limited amount of research on sites dating to the early portions of the Late Holocene, the context of many of these cultural developments is poorly understood.

In this chapter, I present the results of surface collection, mapping, and excavation at two large shell middens in the vicinity of Otter Harbor on northwestern San Miguel Island. The first of these sites is SMI-481, a stratified shell midden located on Otter Point with components spanning the Early, Middle, and Late Holocene. I focus on the analysis of materials from Unit 1, excavated in dense deposits dated to roughly 1150 cal BP (AD 800) and representing some of the most complex and diverse occupations of the site. I then present data from SMI-468, a village dated between 1150 and 490 cal BP

(AD 800 to 1500), located on the western margins of Simonton Cove and about 500 m from SMI-481. I focus on materials from two strata dated to roughly 1150 to 750 cal BP (AD 800 to 1200). Together these two sites provide important perspectives on human occupation of San Miguel Island from AD 800 to 1300 and insight into changing cultural and environmental relationships on the Channel Islands. These two sites build on the previous chapter by providing perspectives on human daily activities and ecology during another phase of the Late Holocene.

SMI-481: SITE SETTING AND CONTEXT

Located on Otter Point in a large dune complex, SMI-481 contains at least 10 discrete archaeological deposits spanning about 7,300 years. Like SMI-87, this is one of the larger archaeological sites on San Miguel, covering an area roughly 600 × 420 m (Greenwood 1978). The site extends from Otter Point to Otter Creek with numerous discontinuous and dense shell midden deposits (Figure 5.1). A series of midden deposits is located in a roughly 30-m-high dune (big dune) on the western site area, with several small, intermediate dunes capped by midden to the east, and midden deposits over 2 m deep along the eastern site margin. Two sandy coves (Amphitheater Cove and Otter Harbor) provide beaches for safely landing boats. There is also abundant kelp forest and rocky intertidal habitat adjacent to the site, and freshwater is available in Otter Creek and springs in Simonton Cove to the east and Running Springs to the west. The site lacks surface house depressions, but its enormous, stratified deposits suggest it was a large occupational site for several millennia.

The remarkable archaeological sequence at SMI-481 provides a unique case study for understanding a variety of environmental and cultural

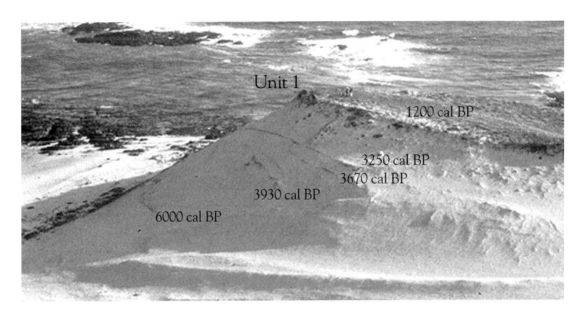

Figure 5.1. Close-up of big dune at SMI-481 showing many of the dated archaeological strata and location of Unit 1 (note two people on top of dune for scale). Photo by J. Erlandson.

issues, with most research currently focused on the nearly continuous 7,300-year sequence located in the big dune. For example, Erlandson et al. (2005b) recently used aspects of the site chronology to help understand the timing and intensity of Holocene dune building on San Miguel Island. Vellanoweth et al. (2006) targeted two roughly 6,000-year-old "red abalone" and "mussel" middens located on top of each other. Subsistence data from these two shell middens show two distinct strategies focused on a variety of invertebrate and vertebrate species. The site also played an important role in documenting the human history of sea otter hunting and associated ecological changes in San Miguel Island marine environments (Erlandson et al. 2005a).

Adjacent to the big dune is Otter Cave (SMI-605), a small rockshelter with archaeological deposits dated to roughly 6600 cal BP (Erlandson et al. 2005c). Small-scale testing of this cave showed heavy emphasis on rocky intertidal shellfish (black turban and California mussel) and small amounts of fish and other vertebrates, suggesting it was probably a temporary or seasonal camp (Erlandson et al. 2005c). The Otter Cave deposits contain relatively few formal artifacts, but one of the largest concentrations of *Dentalium pretiosum* shell artifacts found on the Channel Islands was identified at the site (Erlandson et al. 2001a).

LATE HOLOCENE OCCUPATION OF OTTER POINT

Field Research and Stratigraphy

My research at SMI-481 focused on dense shell midden deposits on the top of the roughly 30-m-high dune on the western site margin (Figure 5.2). Excavation of a 0.4 m × 0.8 m unit (Unit 1) and systematic surface collection during summer 2000 yielded large faunal samples, including the remains of marine mammals, swordfish, nearshore fishes, sea birds, and a variety of shellfish. This unit was excavated as two contiguous 0.4 × 0.4 m units (Units 1a and 1b) in a series of five natural strata. The midden deposits throughout the unit were situated in a dark gray, grayish brown, or light brownish gray sand to a brown or black loamy sand (Figure 5.3). A total of 0.157 m^3 was excavated, with roughly 0.08 m^3 from Unit 1a and 0.077 m^3 from Unit 1b.

Unit 1a was sifted through 1/16-inch mesh, and all screen residuals were retained. Unit 1b was sifted through 1/8-inch mesh, and only vertebrate faunal remains, artifacts, and whole shell valves were collected. While wind appears to have impacted portions of the SMI-481 deposits, preservation in Unit 1 was generally excellent (Rick 2002). To supplement the relatively small sample from the excavation, systematic surface collection of artifacts

Figure 5.2. Stratum 1 and location of Unit 1 at SMI-481 before excavation. Note dense faunal remains.

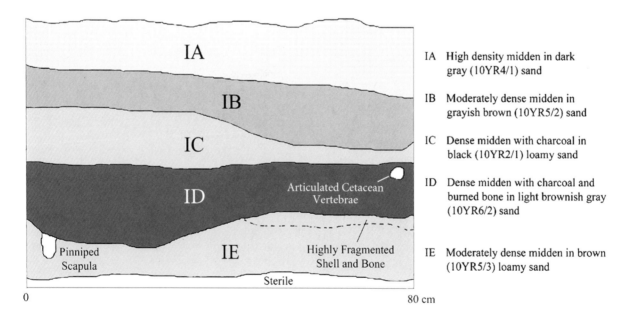

Figure 5.3. Stratigraphic profile from Unit 1 at SMI-481.

and marine mammal bones was performed on the top of the dune. All of these surface materials appear to be from Stratum 1 and are roughly contemporary with the excavation data.

Chronology

Twenty radiocarbon dates from the SMI-481 site complex suggest human occupations from about 7250 to 430 cal BP (Table 5.1). Thirteen of these

Table 5.1. Radiocarbon Dates from SMI-481.

Sample #	Provenience	Material	Uncorrected ^{14}C Age	^{13}C/^{12}C Adjusted Age	Calendar Age Range (cal BP), 1 sigma	Calendar Age Range (AD/BC), 1 sigma
OS-33353	East site margin, upper strata	California mussel	—	1000 ± 35	470 (430) 380	AD 1480 (1520) 1570
Beta-139977	Top of vertical face	Red abalone	860 ± 60	1290 ± 60	670 (640) 560	AD 1280 (1310) 1390
Beta-180925	Eastern middle dune complex	California mussel	1120 ± 80	1540 ± 80	940 (880) 760	AD 1010 (1070) 1200
Beta-145429	Unit 1; Stratum 1E, base	Black abalone	1230 ± 60	1660 ± 60	1050 (960) 920	AD 900 (990) 1040
Beta-150317	Unit 1, Stratum 1E, base	California mussel	1400 ± 60	1830 ± 60	1240 (1170) 1070	AD 710 (780) 880
OS-27182	Unit 1, Stratum 1A, top	Black abalone	—	1870 ± 35	1260 (1220) 1160	AD 690 (730) 790
Beta-139978	Vertical exposure bottom	Black abalone	1550 ± 70	1980 ± 70	1360 (1290) 1240	AD 590 (660) 710
Beta-139980	West Stratum 1 top	Black abalone	1560 ± 60	1990 ± 60	1370 (1300) 1260	AD 580 (650) 690
Beta-139979	West Stratum 1 bottom	Black abalone	1600 ± 60	2030 ± 60	1410 (1330) 1280	AD 540 (620) 670
OS-38218	Middle dune complex	Abalone fishhook	—	2150 ± 50	1530 (1480) 1400	AD 420 (470) 550
Beta-180924	Southern dune complex	California mussel	1820 ± 50	2250 ± 50	1680 (1580) 1520	AD 270 (370) 430
Beta-148498	4 m below dune crest, II	Black abalone	3180 ± 70	3610 ± 70	3340 (3250) 3160	1390 (1300) 1210 BC
Beta-148500	7–7.5 m below dune crest, IV	California mussel	3280 ± 100	3710 ± 100	3470 (3360) 3250	1520 (1410) 1300 BC
Beta-148499	5–5.5 m below dune crest, III	California mussel	3540 ± 60	3970 ± 60	3760 (3670) 3580	1810 (1720) 1630 BC
Beta-148501	8–8.5 m below dune crest, VI	Red abalone	3790 ± 40	4220 ± 40	4080 (3980) 3910	2130 (2030) 1960 BC
Beta-134836	Red abalone midden	Red abalone	5140 ± 80	5570 ± 80	5840 (5700) 5600	3890 (3750) 3650 BC
Beta-145318	Mussel lens	California mussel	5330 ± 80	5750 ± 80	5980 (5900) 5840	4030 (3950) 3890 BC
Beta-145317	Red abalone lens	Red abalone	5430 ± 70	5870 ± 70	6160 (6000) 5930	4210 (4050) 3980 BC
OS-27939	Northern tip of Otter Point	California mussel	—	6340 ± 50	6620 (6540) 6460	4680 (4590) 4510 BC
Beta-134837	Base of vertical dune	Red abalone	6520 ± 80	6950 ± 80	7330 (7250) 7180	5380 (5300) 5230 BC

Note: All dates were calibrated using Calib 4.3 (Stuiver and Reimer 1993, 2000). A ΔR of 225 ± 35 years was used for all shell samples, and ^{13}C/^{12}C ratios were determined by the radiocarbon labs, or an average of +430 years was applied (Erlandson 1988b).

^{14}C dates are from the Late Holocene, with this occupation spanning most of the last 3,500 years. Human settlement occurred on the big dune, in a series of small dunes located just east of the big dune (Middle Dune Complex), and in extremely dense deposits on the eastern site margin. Some of the most intense occupations occurred between about 1300 and 400 cal BP.

Three radiocarbon dates from Unit 1 bracket these deposits between roughly 1260 and 920 cal BP, corresponding with the end of King's (1990) Middle period and just before Arnold's (1992a) Transitional period. Additional dates obtained by Kennett from the top of the dune extend the occupation back about 150 years to roughly 1400 cal BP. While these dates are statistically similar, the most probable age of the Unit 1 occupation is from the dates obtained on samples from the actual unit (1260 and 920 cal BP). Since these three dates are also statistically similar, the most accurate age for the site deposits is probably the average of the three dates from Unit 1. Averaging these dates using Calib 4.3 provides a 1 sigma age range of roughly 1250 to 1050 cal BP (AD 700 to 900), with an average of about 1150 cal BP (AD 800). Because of this relatively narrow time span and the similar constituents in the five strata, all of the materials from Strata 1A to 1E have been lumped together for the present analysis. The surface materials collected from the top of the dune could be either from the deposits dated in this study or by Kennett. Consequently, the best estimate for their age is between about 1400 and 1000 cal BP.

ARTIFACTS

A total of 69 artifacts (excluding bead detritus or chipped-stone debitage) was recovered during surface collection and excavation of Stratum 1 (Table 5.2). This includes 20 artifacts from Unit 1a, 21 artifacts from Unit 1b, and 28 artifacts from the surface. As in most Late Holocene Channel Islands sites, shell artifacts were the dominant materials recovered, with 48 specimens (roughly 70 percent of total artifact assemblage). These were followed by chipped-stone artifacts with 12 specimens (17 percent), and nine bone artifacts (13 percent). Most of the bone and stone artifacts were found on the surface (86 percent), while

most of the shell artifacts were recovered from the excavation units (79 percent).

The shell artifacts are made from red and black abalone, California mussel, and *Olivella*. At least 40 *Olivella* shell artifacts (83 percent of shell artifacts; Figure 5.4) were identified, including four barrel beads, a spire-lopped bead, 21 wall disk beads, and 14 wall disk beads in production (BIP). The presence of abundant wall disk beads and absence of *Olivella* callus beads supports the late Middle period age of these deposits (King 1990). Roughly 520 g per m^3 of *Olivella* bead detritus were also recovered in Unit 1a, a relatively low value for bead detritus on the Channel Islands but fairly comparable with other sites of this age (Kennett and Conlee 2002). Arnold and Graesch (2001:78) also reported relatively low values for late Middle period deposits at SCRI-191, with a mean density of roughly 2,200 per m^3, a value higher than that obtained for SMI-481. The presence of beads, bead blanks, and bead detritus suggests that people were making beads at the site, but in relatively small numbers. Six abalone shell artifacts (13 percent of all shell artifacts) were recovered from Stratum 1, including a worked black abalone rim, a red abalone fishhook blank, two abalone plain shank fishhooks, and two worked pieces of abalone (Figure 5.5). Finally, a small, ground, roughly teardrop-shaped piece of California mussel may be a bead blank.

Bone artifacts are relatively rare, with just nine specimens. The bone artifacts are generally small

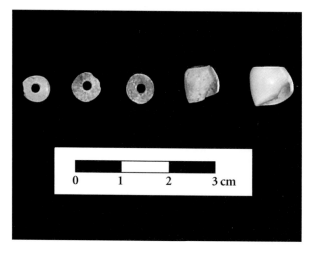

Figure 5.4. *(Left to right):* Three *Olivella* wall disks and two barrel beads; all from SMI-481, Stratum 1.

Table 5.2. Artifacts from Stratum 1 at SMI-481 (1/8-inch).

Artifact	Unit 1a	Unit 1b	Surface	Total
Shell Artifacts				
Haliotis cracherodii worked rim	1	—	—	1
H. rufescens fishhook blank	—	1	—	1
Haliotis spp. plain shank fishhook	—	1	1	2
Haliotis spp. worked	—	2	—	2
Mytilus bead blank	—	1	—	1
Olivella barrel bead	2	1	1	4
Olivella spire-lopped bead	—	—	1	1
Olivella wall disk bead	6	9	6	21
Olivella wall disk BIP	9	4	1	14
Shell undif. worked	1	—	—	1
Subtotal	19	19	10	48
Bone Artifacts				
Bird bone worked	—	—	2	2
Mammal bone club	—	—	1	1
Mammal bone pry bar	—	—	1	1
Mammal bone wedge	—	1	1	2
Mammal bone worked	1	—	—	1
Medium cetacean bone knife	—	—	2	2
Subtotal	1	1	7	9
Stone Artifacts				
Cico chert macrodrill	—	—	2	2
Cico chert microdrill retouched on all sides	—	—	1	1
Monterey chert utilized/retouched flake	—	—	1	1
Quartzite utilized/retouched flake	—	—	1	1
Sandstone donut stone in production	—	—	1	1
Volcanic utilized/retouched flake	—	—	4	4
Volcanic core/hammerstone	—	1	—	1
Volcanic hammerstone	—	—	1	1
Subtotal	—	1	11	12
Total	20	21	28	69

and fragmentary, making it difficult to determine a function. These include two pieces of worked bird bone, a fragment of worked mammal bone, two mammal bone wedges, a mammal bone pry bar, a large marine mammal bone that appears to be a club, and two medium cetacean jaw bones that may be blunt knives.

The chipped-stone assemblage is also relatively small, with just 12 artifacts. The chipped-stone artifacts include two macrodrills, an irregularly shaped microdrill that is worked on all three sides, retouched/utilized flakes, hammerstones, and a donut stone in production. The majority (83 percent) of these tools were made of volcanics or

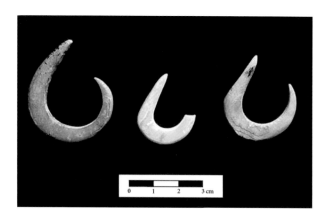

Figure 5.5. Fishhooks from SMI-481: Two abalone fishhook from Stratum 1 (*left*) and one abalone hook from Middle Dune Complex directly AMS ^{14}C dated to ca. 1480 cal BP (*right*).

Cico chert that could have been obtained on the island.

Relatively few artifacts associated with subsistence were recovered from Stratum 1. These include two shell fishhooks, retouched/utilized flakes that may be cutting tools, a bone club possibly used to club seals or other animals, a donut stone in production probably intended for a digging stick weight, and two blunt bone knives that may have been used for gouging or other purposes. In contrast, at SMI-87 and SMI-163, a wide variety of objects associated with fishing and hunting was recovered, including projectile points and bone barbs not recovered at SMI-481 (see Chapters 4 and 6). The dearth of subsistence objects in the Stratum 1 deposits is also interesting because faunal remains (see below) from the site are extremely diverse, with a variety of fishes, mammals, birds, and shellfish. SMI-481 is located on a fairly isolated part of the island, but highly visible and easily accessible to boaters, suggesting that illegal collecting may in part have reduced the number of artifacts on the surface. However, this is also the case at SMI-87, where a diverse artifact assemblage was recovered from the surface. It is likely that more subsistence related artifacts would have been discovered if a larger volume had been excavated, but the low numbers of subsistence artifacts is peculiar.

Finally, a small assemblage of artifacts from Late period (ca. 450 cal BP [AD 1500]) deposits on the eastern site margin contains grooved shank fishhooks, callus beads, a rare *Erato vitulina* shell bead, triangular microblades, and other artifacts characteristic of the Late period. Vellanoweth et al. (2006) also recovered an *Olivella* barrel bead, a bone gorge, a bone awl fragment, two sandstone anvils, a sandstone abrader, and chipped-stone debitage from the roughly 6,000-year-old deposits in the big dune. The artifacts from these two components differ from the artifacts recovered from the Stratum 1 deposits, illustrating temporal variability in the types of artifacts used at the site.

SUBSISTENCE STRATEGIES

The most common materials recovered from SMI-481 were faunal remains, including shellfish, fish, bird, and mammal remains. All of the faunal remains described below are from 1/8-inch residuals of Unit 1 or from surface collections. Because only minor differences were noted in the importance of various shell categories in the individual levels, the following discussion refers to the site deposits as a whole. Data from individual levels are available in Rick (2004a)

Shellfish and Invertebrates

Over 14 kg and a minimum of 2,466 shellfish and other invertebrate remains were recovered from Unit 1a (Table 5.3). Of the 14 kg of shell, a minimum of 27 taxa, including family, genus, species, and other categories, were identified. Shellfish remains are extremely dense throughout the unit and suggest heavy use of shellfish throughout the time represented by this sample. Except for 5.2 g of land snail (< 0.1 percent), all of the invertebrate remains are marine in origin.

The Unit 1a sample is dominated by rocky intertidal shellfish, suggesting people were primarily exploiting available local intertidal habitats. The vast majority of the shellfish sample by weight and MNI is made up of California mussel, with about 60 percent of the weight and 53 percent of the MNI. California mussel is followed by red and black abalone, with 9 percent and 7 percent of the shell weight, but only about 2.3 percent and 1.5 percent of the MNI, respectively. Sea urchin makes up about 7 percent of the shell weight, a relatively high value for this species. Platform mussel constitutes only about 1 percent of the total weight, but about 10 percent of the MNI. Owl limpets contribute

Table 5.3. Shellfish and Invertebrate Remains from Unit 1a at SMI-481.

Taxon	Wt.	% Wt.	MNI	% MNI
Acmaea mitra (white-capped limpet)	0.9	< 0.1	1	< 0.1
Barnacle undif.	228.1	1.6	—	—
Calliostoma spp. (top snails)	0.4	< 0.1	1	< 0.1
Chama pellucida (agate jewelbox)	3.6	< 0.1	2	0.1
Chiton undif.	79.5	0.6	—	—
Clam undif.	0.2	< 0.1	1	< 0.1
Collisella pelta (shield limpet)	46.2	0.3	25	1.0
Corallina spp. (coralline algae)	3.5	< 0.1	—	—
Crab undif.	159.8	1.1	—	—
Crepidula spp. (slipper shells)	5.7	< 0.1	54	2.2
Cryptochiton stelleri (gumboot chiton)	13.9	0.1	—	—
Diodora aspera (rough keyhole limpet)	5.1	< 0.1	2	0.1
Fissurella volcano (volcano limpet)	0.3	< 0.1	1	< 0.1
Gastropod undif.	4.7	< 0.1	24	1.0
Haliotis cracherodii (black abalone)	953.1	6.7	57	2.3
Haliotis rufescens (red abalone)	1283.6	9.1	37	1.5
Haliotis spp. (abalone undif.)	94.8	0.7	20	0.8
Land snail	5.2	< 0.1	25	1.0
Limpet undif.	32.7	0.2	362	14.7
Lottia gigantea (owl limpet)	390.9	2.8	109	4.4
Mytilus californianus (California mussel)	8411.9	59.5	1295	52.5
Nacre undif.	99.5	0.7	—	—
Olivella biplicata (purple olive)	41.7	0.3	—	—
Pollicipes polymerus (gooseneck barnacle)	245.4	1.7	—	—
Septifer bifurcatus (platform mussel)	161.3	1.1	250	10.1
Serpulorbis squamigerus (scaled worm snail)	6.3	< 0.1	—	—
Strongylocentrotus spp. (sea urchins)	958.1	6.8	—	—
Tegula brunnea (brown turban)	227.4	1.6	37	1.5
Tegula funebralis (black turban)	402.2	2.8	107	4.3
Tegula spp. (turban undif.)	231.9	1.6	56	2.3
Undif. shell	30.2	0.2	—	—
Total	14,128.1	—	2466	—

Note: Based on 1/8-inch recovery and all weights in grams. Volume = 0.08 m^3.

about 3 percent of the weight and 4 percent of the MNI, and brown, black, and undifferentiated turban make up about 6 percent of the total weight and 8 percent of the MNI.

A variety of small limpets are also present in the assemblage, constituting less than 1 percent of the shell weight, but 15 percent of the MNI. These small limpets are only a minor component of the sample and may have been brought to the site incidentally with other shellfish, kelp, etc. Similarly, small barnacles (Barnacle undif. and *Pollicipes polymerus*) contribute about 3 percent of the total shell weight, but were probably brought to the site as by-products when collecting other shellfish or kelp. All other shellfish taxa make up less than about 3 percent of the overall shell weight or MNI. This includes *Olivella biplicata* shells (0.3 percent of weight) that appear to have been collected largely for the production of beads and ornaments.

Fish

Roughly 760 g and 6,017 fish bones were recovered and analyzed from 1/8-inch residuals in Unit 1b (Table 5.4). A minimum of 80 fishes, representing 17 individual taxa, were identified in the Unit 1b assemblage, including rockfishes, surfperch, California sheephead, and cabezon. Sixty-one percent of the fish bone by weight and 25 percent by NISP were identified to family, genus, or species. Most of the unidentified teleost bones are spines and highly fragmentary bones. All of the fish represented in the sample could have been captured

Table 5.4. Fish Remains from Unit 1b at SMI-481.

Taxon	Wt.	% Wt.[a]	NISP	% NISP	MNI	% MNI
Teleost						
Atherinidae (silversides)	0.2	< 0.1	7	0.5	1	1.3
Bothidae (right eye flounders)						
Paralichtys californicus (California halibut)	7.5	1.6	7	0.5	1	1.3
Clupeidae (sardines)	3.8	0.8	440	29.2	14	17.5
Cottidae (sculpin)	0.3	0.1	4	0.3	2	2.5
Scorpaenichthys marmoratus (cabezon)	82.0	17.7	169	11.2	10	12.5
Embiotocidae (surfperch)	48.8	10.5	454	30.1	12	15.0
Damalichthys vacca (pile perch)	7.7	1.7	91	6.0	4	5.0
Hexagrammidae (greenling)	0.1	< 0.1	7	0.5	3	3.8
Ophiodon elongatus (lingcod)	35.1	7.6	39	2.6	6	7.5
Labridae (senorita or wrasse)	0.7	0.2	62	4.1	3	3.8
Semicossyphus pulcher (California sheephead)	22.3	4.8	12	0.8	5	6.3
Scorpaenidae						
Sebastes spp. (rockfish)	42.6	9.2	198	13.1	13	16.3
Sphyraenidae (barracudas)						
Sphyraena argentea (California barracuda)	1.1	0.2	8	0.5	2	2.5
Stichaeidae (prickleback)	0.4	0.1	1	0.1	1	1.3
Xiphiidae/Istiophoridae (swordfishes, billfishes)	208.2	44.9	3	0.2	1	1.3
Teleost undif.	295.0	—	4507	298.7	—	—
Subtotal	755.8	—	6009	—	78	—
Elasmobranch						
Elasmobranch, undif.	0.1	—	1	—	—	—
Triakidae (smoothhounds, soupfin, etc.)	3.1	0.7	6	0.4	1	1.3
Galeorhinus galeus (soupfin)	<0.1	<0.1	1	0.1	1	1.3
Subtotal	3.3	0.7	8	0.5	2	2.6
Total	759.1	—	6017	—	80	—

Note: Based on 1/8-inch recovery and all weights in grams. Volume = 0.077m^3.

[a] Percentages based on specimens identified to family, genus, and species.

and eaten by humans, although some of the smaller taxa (e.g., Atherinidae, Clupeidae) may represent the stomach contents of marine mammals, sea birds, or other large fishes. This is more likely at SMI-481 where the abundance of marine mammal bones (see below) indicates that some fishes may be natural rather than cultural in origin. However, the dearth of unequivocal digestive traces (staining, pitting, etc.) and some burning on these small fish bones suggests that the majority of the sample is cultural in origin.

The overall abundance of fishes is relatively balanced, with clupeids and surfperch accounting for about 30 to 36 percent of the NISP and 18 to 20 percent of the MNI. Cabezon account for about 11 percent of the NISP and 13 percent of the MNI. Rockfish also make up about 13 percent of the NISP and 16 percent of the MNI. The presence of a few billfish vertebrae suggests that these fishes were being captured and consumed. Other fishes, including California barracuda, sheephead, wrasse or señorita, halibut, shark, and sculpins are relatively minor contributors to the overall sample.

Most of the fish present in the SMI-481 sample suggest that, like most Channel Islanders, people were largely exploiting nearby kelp forest and rocky nearshore habitats. The presence of billfish remains suggests that offshore environments necessitating sturdy watercraft were also occasionally utilized. Two circular shell fishhooks were found in Stratum 1, indicating that people relied heavily on hook-and-line fishing. Nets may also have been used to capture smaller fish, while harpoons were probably used to capture billfish and other large taxa.

Mammals

A total of 2,773 mammal bones weighing over 15 kg was analyzed from the excavation and surface collection in Stratum 1. These are the most dense concentrations of marine mammal remains in any of the sites that I analyzed, a factor partly related to the proximity of this site to Otter Point, Point Bennett, and Castle Rock where pinnipeds are abundant today.

Of the 2,773 mammal remains analyzed, 2,408 are from the two excavation units (Table 5.5). The

Table 5.5. Mammal Remains from Unit 1a and Unit 1b at SMI-481.

	Unit 1a			Unit 1b			Total					
	Wt.	NISP	MNI	Wt.	NISP	MNI	Wt.	% Wt.[a]	NISP	% NISP	MNI	% MNI
Otariidae	715.2	105	—	1220.4	85	—	1935.6	44.3	190	63.8	—	—
Arctocephalus townsendi (Guadalupe fur seal)	319.2	10	3	99.1	3	2	418.3	9.6	13	4.4	5	35.7
Callorhinus ursinus (northern fur seal)	11.7	1	1	—	—	—	11.7	0.3	1	0.3	1	7.1
Zalophus californianus (California sea lion)	1169.5	11	3	169.3	2	1	1338.8	30.6	13	4.4	4	28.6
Subtotal	2215.6	127	7	1488.8	90	3	3704.4	84.7	217	72.8	10	71.4
Phocidae	—	—	—	20.7	1	1	20.7	0.5	1	0.3	1	7.1
Pinniped undif.	239.5	47		109.9	6		349.4	8.0	53	17.8	—	—
Subtotal	2455.1	174	7	1619.4	97	4	4074.5	93.2	271	90.9	11	78.6
Small cetacean	—	—	—	286.8	17	1	286.8	6.6	17	5.7	1	7.1
Carnivora												
Enhydra lutris (sea otter)	6.4	9	1	4.8	1	1	11.2	0.3	10	3.4	2	14.3
Mammal undif.	535.6	1297	—	947.6	813	—	1483.2	—	2110		—	—
Total	2997.1	1480	8	2858.6	928	6	5855.7	—	2408	—	14	—

Note: Based on 1/8-inch recovery and all weights in grams. Volume 1a = 0.08 m^3 and volume 1b = 0.077 m^3.

[a] Percentages do not include undifferentiated mammal bone, most of which is probably from sea mammals.

majority of the bones by count (88 percent), however, are highly fragmented and burned pieces of cancellous and cortical bone identifiable only as mammal remains. Because no large terrestrial mammals were identified in the sample, it is probable that the vast majority of these bones are from marine mammals. The samples from both Unit 1a and Unit 1b are relatively similar, so these two samples have been lumped together for the present analysis. As with the other faunal remains, I refer to the unit as a whole, because stratigraphic variation in the distribution of mammal remains was fairly limited and the number of bones identified to species or genus in individual levels is relatively low. A wide range of bones including cranial and postcranial elements was recovered, suggesting that whole skeletons were deposited on site. In some cases it appears that complete or mostly complete marine mammal carcasses were being hauled up to the top of the dune. Over 50 percent of the bones appear to be burned, suggesting that they were also being cooked and processed on site.

The majority of mammal remains identified in the excavated samples are from otariids (72.8 percent of NISP), including 190 bones from undifferentiated otariids (64 percent), 13 from Guadalupe fur seals (4 percent), one northern fur seal (0.3 percent), and 13 California sea lions (4.4 percent). The remains of phocids are relatively rare in the sample, including just one undifferentiated phocid bone (0.3 percent). Sea otters are fairly common, with 10 bones (3.4 percent). Small cetaceans (5.7 percent) are also relatively abundant, including a strand of 17 articulated vertebrae. About 53 bones (18 percent) are identified as undifferentiated pinniped.

The data from the systematic surface collections are fairly comparable to the excavated data, but a much higher percentage of these bones is identifiable to family or species levels. Three hundred and sixty-five bones (9.2 kg) from at least 25 individuals were recovered from the surface collection (Table 5.6). Similar to the excavated data, this includes cranial remains, long bones, flipper bones, vertebrae, scapulae, and other elements, supporting the idea that complete skeletons were being deposited on site. This also suggests that these animals were being directly hunted and/or scavenged by the people who occupied SMI-481 rather than obtained through exchange (see Colten 1993).

As in the excavated sample, otariids are the most abundant mammal category, with 104 undifferentiated otariid bones (36 percent of NISP), 34 Guadalupe fur seal bones (12 percent), 22 northern fur seal bones (8 percent), one Steller sea lion bone (0.3 percent), and 16 California sea lion bones (6 percent). Again the remains of phocids are quite rare, with just one elephant seal bone (0.3 percent) and four harbor seal bones (1.4 percent). Five cetacean bones were also recovered from the surface (2 percent of the assemblage), and sea otters were fairly abundant with 14 bones (5 percent). About 91 undifferentiated pinniped bones (31.2 percent) were also identified in the surface sample.

Table 5.7 presents data on all of the bones from the excavated and surface samples that were identified to species, including 129 bones from 35 individuals representing seven species (Figure 5.6). The most abundant taxon in the assemblage is Guadalupe fur seal, with 47 bones (36 percent) and 12 individuals (34 percent). This is followed by California sea lions with 29 bones (22 percent) and seven individuals (20 percent), and northern fur seals with 23 bones (18 percent) and eight individuals (23 percent). Sea otters are also fairly abundant with 24 bones (19 percent) from five individuals (14 percent). Phocids are again relatively rare, with just one elephant seal bone (1 percent) representing one individual (3 percent), and just four harbor seal bones (3 percent) from one individual (3 percent). These findings are comparable to data from SMI-602 and SMI-528 on Point Bennett (Walker et al. 2002). At both of these sites, Guadalupe fur seals make up 43 to 50 percent of the total marine mammal NISP identified to species. Sea otters contribute about 18 to 19 percent of the NISP, and northern fur seals provide about 15 to 16 percent. California sea lions supply only about 8 to 12 percent of the NISP at SMI-528 and SMI-602 compared with roughly 23 percent at SMI-481. The remains of phocids are also relatively rare at SMI-528 and SMI-602, constituting between about 2 and 15 percent of the NISP.

The age and sex of 95 of the bones from the SMI-481 collection were estimated using comparative collections and the expertise of pinniped researchers at the National Marine Mammal Laboratory in Seattle. Only bones that were identified to species were included in the age and sex analysis. The remains of mandibles, maxillae, teeth, and complete long bones of otariids were used to

Table 5.6. Marine Mammal Remains from Stratum 1 Surface Collection at SMI-481.

	Wt.	% Wt.	NISP	% NISP	MNI	% MNI
Otariidae	3458.5	41.2	104	35.6	—	—
Arctocephalus townsendi (Guadalupe fur seal)	1465.8	17.5	34	11.6	7	28.0
Callorhinus ursinus (northern fur seal)	378.3	4.5	22	7.5	7	28.0
Eumetopias jubatus (Steller sea lion)	6.1	0.1	1	0.3	1	4.0
Zalophus californianus (California sea lion)	1278.0	15.2	16	5.5	3	12.0
Phocidae						
Mirounga angustirostris (elephant seal)	110.3	1.3	1	0.3	1	4.0
Phoca vitulina (harbor seal)	90.0	1.1	4	1.4	1	4.0
Pinniped undif.	1342.0	16.0	91	31.2	—	—
Small cetacean	19.1	0.2	1	0.3	1	4.0
Medium/Large cetacean	16.1	0.2	4	1.4	1	4.0
Carnivora						
Enhydra lutris (sea otter)	224.2	2.7	14	4.8	3	12.0
Mammal undif.[a]	828.6	—	73	—	—	—
Total	9217.0	—	365	—	25	—

[a] All weights in grams. Percentages do not include undifferentiated mammal bone, most of which is probably from sea mammals.

Table 5.7. Marine Mammal Remains Identified to Species from SMI-481.

	NISP	% NISP	MNI	% MNI
Otariidae				
Arctocephalus townsendi (Guadalupe fur seal)	47	36.4	12	34.3
Callorhinus ursinus (northern fur seal)	23	17.8	8	22.9
Eumetopias jubatus (Steller sea lion)	1	0.8	1	2.9
Zalophus californinanus (California sea lion)	29	22.5	7	20.0
Phocidae				
Mirounga angustirostris (elephant seal)	1	0.8	1	2.9
Phoca vitulina (harbor seal)	4	3.1	1	2.9
Carnivora				
Enhydra lutris (sea otter)	24	18.6	5	14.3
Total	129	—	35	—

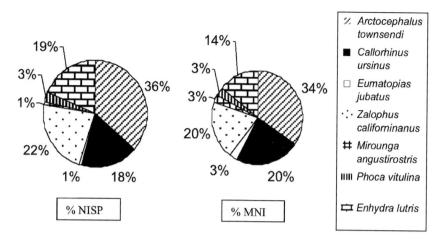

Figure 5.6. Summary of marine mammal remains identified to species from SMI-481.

determine the age and sex of remains identified to species. Because of the small sample size and general lack of sexual dimorphism, harbor seal and sea otter bones were not aged and sexed. While the sample of aged and sexed specimens is relatively small, these data provide insight on the overall age and sex composition of the sample.

A total of 22 bones from the two excavation units provided age and/or sex data for otariid remains. These 22 bones are from at least seven individuals, including three Guadalupe fur seals, three California sea lions, and one northern fur seal. Of the nine Guadalupe fur seal bones that were aged or sexed, eight are female and one mandible is from a juvenile male. Four of the bones are from adult females, one is from a one- to two-year-old female, while the other bones did not produce reliable age estimates. One northern fur seal bone appears to come from a female, probably an adult. In contrast to the fur seal remains, the majority of the California sea lion bones are from adult or subadult males. Six of the California sea lion bones are from adult males, and six are from juvenile or subadult males.

Seventy-two otariid bones that were identified to species from the surface collections were aged or sexed, including 34 Guadalupe fur seal bones (MNI = 7), 22 northern fur seal bones (MNI = 7), 15 California sea lion bones (MNI = 3), and one Steller sea lion bone (MNI-1). The age and sex of individuals represented by these bones from the surface collection are similar to those from the units. Thirty-

three of the Guadalupe fur seal bones are from females; just one is from a male. Nearly all of the remains appear to be from adult or subadult females. Twenty northern fur seal bones are from adult or subadult females and the other two bones were from one- to two-year-olds or yearlings that could not be sexed. A maxilla fragment with teeth is from a male Steller sea lion pup. Similar to the results from the excavated samples, all of the California sea lion remains are from adult or subadult males. Two additional bones classified only as otariids appear to be from individuals less than one year old, but since these bones were not identified to species, these findings are questionable. Finally, a mandible and tooth are from an adult female elephant seal.

Ultimately, the data from the excavation units and surface collection at SMI-481 are dominated by adult or subadult animals (94 percent), with just six bones (6 percent) from one- to two-year old or younger animals. The vast majority of the fur seal remains are from females (96 percent), and all of the California sea lion remains are from males. These data suggest that most of these animals were obtained from haul-outs on land or offshore rocks and not from a rookery. Had the occupants of this site exploited a rookery, considerably higher numbers of pup remains and female California sea lions probably would have been recovered (see Etnier 2002). The available data suggest that hunting may have occurred at sea, on offshore rocks such as Castle Rock, or possibly from the periphery of a rookery. California sea lions and Guadalupe and northern fur seals are currently most abundant during the late spring and summer on San Miguel Island (DeLong and Melin 2002; Stewart and Yochem 2002), raising the possibility that many of these animals may have been taken during these seasons. These animals have been seen on the island at various times of the year (Stewart and Yochem 2002), however, suggesting that more data are needed from a variety of San Miguel sites to test and refine these seasonality inferences.

Birds

All of the bird bone from Units 1a and 1b were analyzed in detail. Thirty-five bird bones weighing 9.9 g were recovered in Unit 1a, and 3.7 g and 17 bird bones were identified in Unit 1b (Table 5.8). As in many Channel Islands sites, the number of bird bones at SMI-481 is considerably lower than other faunal classes. From both units, seven individual birds from at least three different species were identified, including Cassin's auklet, Brandt's/Double-crested cormorants, and gulls. All of these birds are common residents on the island and could have been scavenged or captured. Because the amount of total bird bone is low, it is difficult to estimate the importance of the various taxa.

Dietary Reconstruction

I calculated a dietary reconstruction for the SMI-481 assemblage using the weight method, providing another rough estimate of the relative importance of various faunal classes. Dietary reconstructions based on all of the faunal remains (1/8 inch) obtained from Unit 1a suggest that marine mammals are the dominant contributor of meat to the diet, providing roughly 72 percent of the meat yield; fish make up roughly 21 percent, shellfish only 7 percent, and birds less than 1 percent. These data, along with the high density by NISP and weight of mammal remains, suggest that people at SMI-481 were focused on marine mammals for subsistence. These data differ from all of the other archaeological sites I excavated, where marine mammals are usually only a supplementary part of the diet. The high proportion of marine mammals may reflect the proximity of SMI-481 to the Point Bennett pinniped rookery, to haul-outs near Otter Point and Running Springs, and to nearby Castle Rock where

Table 5.8. Bird Remains from Unit 1a and Unit 1b at SMI-481.

Taxon	Unit 1a			Unit 1b			Total					
	Wt.	NISP	MNI	Wt.	NISP	MNI	Wt.	% Wt.[a]	NISP	% NISP	MNI	%MNI
Alcidae	0.1	2	—	—	—	—	0.1	0.7	2	3.8	—	—
Ptychoramphus aleuticus (Cassin's auklet)	0.5	2	1	0.1	1	1	0.6	4.4	3	5.8	2	28.6
Laridae												
Large gull cf. *Larus occidentalis* (western gull)	1.0	2	1	0.6	1	1	1.6	11.8	3	5.8	2	28.6
Larus californicus (California gull)	0.3	1	1	0.4	1	1	0.7	5.1	2	3.8	2	28.6
Phalacrocoracidae												
Phalacrocorax spp. (Brandt's/ Double-crested cormorant)	3.5	2	1	—	—	—	3.5	25.7	2	3.8	1	14.3
Aves undif.	4.5	26	—	2.6	14		7.1	52.2	40	76.9	—	—
Total	9.9	35	4	3.7	17	3	13.6	—	52	—	7	—

Note: Based on 1/8-inch recovery and all weights in grams. Volume 1a = 0.08 m^3 and volume 1b = 0.077m^3.

[a] Percentages based on specimens identified to family, genus, and species.

pinnipeds congregate today. The dominance of marine mammals at this site also illustrates the local variability of Chumash subsistence strategies.

When only fish and shellfish are compared, fish provide roughly 75 percent of the total meat yield, and shellfish contribute only about 25 percent. These findings are similar to data provided by Kennett and Conlee (2002) for Santa Rosa and San Miguel sites of this age, where fish clearly are dominant and shellfish appear to be supplemental.

DISCUSSION

The Otter Point area is environmentally rich, with a wide variety of fauna and fairly reliable freshwater. The faunal remains from SMI-481 suggest that people were exploiting a range of animals and habitats, including rocky intertidal and kelp forest habitats for shellfish and fish, and other environments for marine mammals. The presence of billfish in the site deposits suggests that people were using sophisticated watercraft (i.e., plank canoes) and other technology (harpoons, etc.) at this time (see Arnold 1995; Arnold and Bernard 2005; Davenport et al. 1993; Gamble 2002). The abundant marine mammal remains are distinct from the other sites and suggest people may also have been using watercraft to obtain marine mammals from Castle Rock and other offshore islets.

Compared with those at SMI-163 and other later sites (see Chapter 6), both subsistence and ornamental artifacts are relatively rare at SMI-481. The absence of stone points or other artifacts

clearly associated with pinniped hunting contrasts with the findings at SMI-87 (Chapter 4), where numerous items probably associated with pinniped hunting were found. It is possible that people relied primarily on simple technologies such as clubs and other tools to hunt these animals, that perishable technologies such as wood spears were used, or that many of the items used to hunt these animals were lost during hunting endeavors.

The diverse faunal data from Stratum 1 suggest that SMI-481 was a residential base used by Chumash peoples for a wide variety of activities. Burning on many of the marine mammal bones and some fish bones indicates that food remains were processed and consumed on site. Evidence of bead production and other activities, however, suggests that this site was more than just a hunting camp. The deposits appear to represent a relatively narrow window of time, perhaps a century or so of occupation. The dense nature of the faunal assemblage suggests that human population at the site may also have been relatively high. Unfortunately, domestic features were not identified on the surface or during excavation.

SMI-468: SITE SETTING AND CONTEXT

SMI-468 is a village and shell midden located about 0.5 km east of SMI-481. The site sits on a terrace roughly 1 m above the beach, with a steep terrace rising directly south of the site (Figure 5.7). With occupations spanning the late Middle through Late

Figure 5.7. SMI-468 site setting and landscape.

periods, the site is situated between Otter Creek and Simonton Cove and adjacent to SMI-469 to the west and SMI-467 to the east. SMI-468 has a commanding view of Otter Harbor, Simonton Cove, and Harris Point. A freshwater seep is located in the small sea cliff on the northeastern site margin. The site is covered by dense ice plant, exotic grasses, and other low-lying vegetation that heavily obscure surface visibility. The sea-cliff exposure provides a cross section of the midden, and a few rodent (rat?) tailings also supply a glimpse of some of the subsurface materials.

At least 10 C-shaped berms are present across the site and appear to be the remains of house depressions (Figure 5.8). These berms are largely composed of dense shell midden deposits and are situated in three main clusters located in a roughly east–west trending line. It is unclear if these berms were shaped by wind or were built as windbreaks or some other function. Excavation units and auger holes in these berms support the idea that these are houses or some other kind of structural feature, but complete excavation of one of these berms is needed to determine their precise layout and function. Sea-cliff erosion will likely bisect one of these in the future, providing a stratigraphic cross section

of the features. Adjacent SMI-469 also contains two smaller berms that may be related to the occupation at SMI-468.

Field Research and Stratigraphy

Fieldwork at SMI-468 was designed to obtain representative faunal and artifact samples, to help determine the function of the house berms, and to obtain details on the spatial and temporal distribution of archaeological materials. Mapping and excavation were conducted at SMI-468 in summer 2001. Because of the dense ground cover, systematic surface collections were not performed at SMI-468.

Two 0.5 × 0.5 m units were excavated at the site. Unit 1 is located in the midden berm of House 7, and Unit 2 is located in the midden berm of House 3. Both of these units contain dense concentrations of well-preserved faunal remains and artifacts. Unit 1 was excavated to a depth of roughly 1 m. Based on soil color and composition and the density of the midden deposits, four distinct strata were identified in the unit (Figure 5.9). Two radiocarbon dates from the top and bottom of Unit 1, however, suggest that these strata were deposited relatively rapidly, dating to around the time of the Transitional period (see below). Stratum I is a gen-

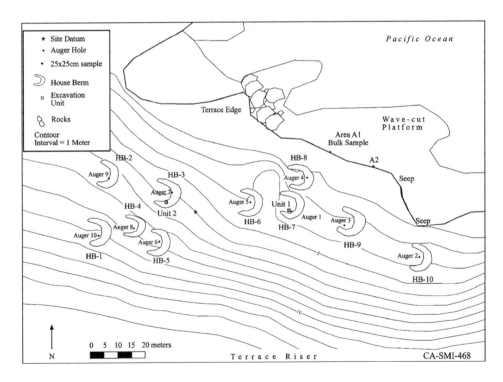

Figure 5.8. Map of SMI-468 showing location of house berms, units, and auger holes.

erally highly fragmented, low-density shell midden. Stratum II contains a dense shell midden deposit with low fragmentation and excellent preservation. Stratum III is similar to Stratum II, but has better preservation and numerous whole shell valves and a slightly darker soil. Stratum IV is a densely compacted basal layer with small bits of fragmented shell midden, some of which had probably been trampled into this level. The small bits of shell persist in this level for roughly 10 cm at which time sterile deposits are encountered. An auger hole was excavated through sterile deposits in this unit down another 50 cm. Stratum IV could represent a house floor or some other living surface associated with the midden berm adjacent to the unit. Defining house floors in California is complex (see Gamble 1995), and because of the small size of the excavation unit, it is difficult to determine more precisely if this was in fact a house floor or a post-depositional feature (see Stein 1992).

Unit 2 has three distinct strata that represent a longer period of occupation than Unit 1 (see below). The deposits in this unit are generally similar to those in Unit 1. However, Unit 2 does not contain the compact, low-density, and highly fragmented shell midden found in the upper 30 cm (Stratum I) in Unit 1. Stratum I in Unit 2 is a dense shell midden deposit with generally good preservation (Figure 5.10). Stratum II also contains a dense shell midden, but fragmentation of faunal remains

in this level is slightly lower than in Stratum I, and the soil is less consolidated than in Stratum I. Stratum III is a relatively compact, sandy loam with a low to moderately dense shell midden. Near the bottom of this level, the midden density becomes quite low and fragmented, similar to the possible floor feature in Unit 1, Stratum IV. An auger hole was excavated through sterile deposits in the bottom of this unit for another 50 cm.

To provide information on the extent and depth of the site deposits, characteristics of the midden constituents, and the nature of the human occupation, 10 auger holes were excavated across the site. Each of these auger holes was placed adjacent to one of the house berms (see Figure 5.8). In most of these berms, shell midden deposits are dense and are similar to those encountered in Units 1 and 2. However, House 10 contains a low-density shell midden deposit, suggesting that occupation of the far eastern portion of the site may have been relatively ephemeral. Radiocarbon samples were pulled *in situ* from the side walls of all of the auger holes. To provide a general chronology for these areas of the site, samples from Houses 1, 2, 4, 5, 6, 9, and 10 were dated. Two dates from the sea cliff obtained by Kennett were adjacent to the berm of House 8. Along with the dates from the units for Houses 3 and 7, all of the houses at the site have at least one radiocarbon date associated with them. While some of these houses may contain multiple occupations,

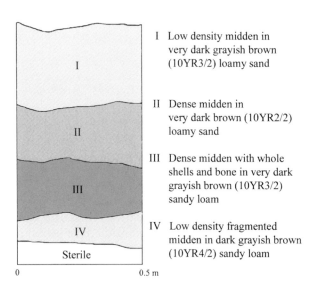

I Low density midden in very dark grayish brown (10YR3/2) loamy sand

II Dense midden in very dark brown (10YR2/2) loamy sand

III Dense midden with whole shells and bone in very dark grayish brown (10YR3/2) sandy loam

IV Low density fragmented midden in dark grayish brown (10YR4/2) sandy loam

Figure 5.9. Stratigraphic profile from SMI-468, Unit 1.

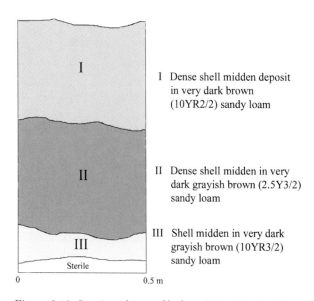

I Dense shell midden deposit in very dark brown (10YR2/2) sandy loam

II Dense shell midden in very dark grayish brown (2.5Y3/2) sandy loam

III Shell midden in very dark grayish brown (10YR3/2) sandy loam

Figure 5.10. Stratigraphic profile from SMI-468, Unit 2.

Table 5.9. Radiocarbon Dates from SMI-468 and SMI-469.

Sample #	Provenience	Material	Uncorrected ^{14}C Age	^{13}C/^{12}C Adjusted Age	Calendar Age Range (cal BP), 1 sigma	Calendar Age Range (AD/BC), 1 sigma
			SMI-468			
OS-33418	House 10, auger 2, 50–53 cm	California mussel	—	1040 ± 30	490 (460) 430	AD 1460 (1490) 1520
OS-34807	Unit 2, Stratum I	California mussel	—	1210 ± 30	620 (550) 530	AD 1330 (1400) 1420
OS-39312	House 4, auger 8, 45–47 cm	California mussel	—	1220 ± 35	630 (560) 530	AD 1320 (1390) 1420
Beta-107986	Sea cliff, 0–5 cm	Black abalone	820 ± 60	1250 ± 60	650 (620) 540	AD 1300 (1330) 1410
OS-39314	House 6, auger 5, 59–60 cm	California mussel	—	1400 ± 25	750 (710) 670	AD 1200 (1250) 1280
OS-39311	House 9, auger 3, 54–56 cm	California mussel	—	1460 ± 25	820 (760) 720	AD 1130 (1190) 1230
Beta-107985	Sea cliff, 50 cm	California mussel	1040 ± 70	1470 ± 70	890 (780) 690	AD 1060 (1170) 1260
OS-39333	Unit 2, Stratum II	California mussel	—	1490 ± 35	880 (790) 740	AD 1070 (1160) 1210
Beta-107349	SE house berm, 5–10 cm, top of unit 1	Black abalone	1070 ± 80	1500 ± 80	910 (820) 720	AD 1040 (1130) 1230
OS-39310	House 8, auger 4, 56–58 cm	Red abalone	—	1520 ± 35	910 (850) 780	AD 1050 (1100) 1180
OS-33356	Unit 1, west wall, 87–88 cm, base of unit	Black abalone	—	1530 ± 30	910 (870) 790	AD 1040 (1080) 1160
OS-39313	House 1, auger 10, 45–47 cm	California mussel	—	1620 ± 35	970 (930) 910	AD 980 (1020) 1050
OS-33357	Unit 2, Stratum III	California mussel	—	1760 ± 30	1150 (1080) 1040	AD 800 (880) 910
OS-33419	House 2, auger 9, 60–62 cm	California mussel	—	1850 ± 35	1240 (1180) 1140	AD 710 (770) 810
OS-39334	House 5, auger 6, 42 cm	California mussel	—	1860 ± 35	1250 (1200) 1150	AD 700 (750) 800
OS-33421	Unit 2, duplicate of OS-33357	California mussel	—	1900 ± 30	1270 (1240) 1180	AD 680 (710) 770
			SMI-469			
OS-33354	Berm on west side of site, 15 m from sea	California mussel	—	1810 ± 30	1190 (1150) 1080	AD 760 (800) 870

Note: All dates were calibrated using Calib 4.3 (Stuiver and Reimer, 1993, 2000). A ΔR of 225 ± 35 years was used for all shell samples, and ^{13}C/^{12}C ratios were determined by the radiocarbon labs, or an average of +430 years was applied (Erlandson 1988b).

the radiocarbon chronology for each of these house berms provides important insight on the larger occupation of the site.

In the rest of this chapter, I present the results of artifact and faunal analysis from Units 1 and 2. I focus on the Transitional period deposits in Unit 1 and the late Middle period deposits in Unit 2 (see below). During the summer of 1997, Kennett and I excavated a small bulk sample from midden deposits

exposed in the sea cliff at the site (see Figure 5.7). I also present the results of midden analysis from this bulk sample (Area A Bulk Sample). The data from these samples provide details on the occupation of SMI-468 and its relationship to nearby SMI-481.

Chronology

Sixteen radiocarbon dates were obtained from the site deposits, including samples from the excavation units, *in situ* from auger holes, and from bulk samples obtained by Kennett (Table 5.9). These radiocarbon dates suggest human occupation, spanning roughly 700 years, including the late Middle, Transitional, and Late periods. The earliest date from the site produced a calibrated intercept of roughly 1200 cal BP (AD 750) from near the base of the deposits in House Berm 5. A ^{14}C date from House 2 also produced a date of roughly 1180 cal BP (770 cal BP). The most recent date from the site, 460 cal BP (AD 1490), is from a relatively low-density deposit in House 10, located on the eastern margin of the site.

The majority of the site occupation ranges from 900 to 600 cal BP (ca. AD 1000 to 1350) or roughly the duration of the Transitional period (AD 1150 to 1300). This includes 10 dates from two excavation units, four houses, and sea-cliff exposures, suggesting a relatively dense occupation during this time period. Four ^{14}C dates from Unit 2 and Houses 2 and 5 date to the late Middle period, and three dates from Houses 4 and 10 and Unit 2 produced dates during the Late period or immediately after the transition. The Transitional period was identified by Arnold (1992a) as a time in Chumash history when formal craft specialization and other aspects of cultural complexity may have developed on the Channel Islands (see Chapter 2). There also appears to have been substantial village abandonment and reorganization during this time period as a response to prolonged drought and possibly decreased marine productivity (see Arnold 1992a, 1992b, 2001a, 2001c; Arnold et al. 1997a; Jones et al. 1999; Kennett and Kennett 2000; Yatsko 2000). Consequently, Channel Islands sites dating to this time period are relatively rare (Erlandson et al. 2001b). The presence of a continuous occupation before, during, and after the Transitional period at SMI-468 makes this assemblage highly significant.

The radiocarbon dates from the various houses and units on the site present an interesting cluster. First, the oldest dates for the site come from the house berms on the western site boundary, with both Houses 2 and 5 producing late Middle period dates. The western site area also produced dates of AD 1160 and 1390, suggesting it was in use during the Transitional period and/or Late period. A single date from a house berm at adjacent SMI-469 to the west was also late Middle period in age dating to ca. AD 800. These early dates on the western site area

correspond with the deposits from the top of the dune (Stratum 1) at SMI-481. The middle cluster of house features, including Houses 6, 7, 8, and 9, produced dates exclusively during the Transitional period, including five dates between AD 1080 and 1250. Kennett obtained two dates from the sea cliff in front of these features which also fall within the Transitional period. Finally, House 10, a small berm with low-density deposits, was dated to the Late period or roughly AD 1490. The distinct spatial and temporal patterning of the site occupation suggests a lengthy and complex occupation.

Radiocarbon dates from the top and bottom of the Unit 1 deposits suggest that they date to a relatively narrow window of time between about 910 and 720 cal BP (AD 1040 to AD 1230). Unit 2, however, contains three different occupations. The Stratum III deposits appear to date to roughly 1150 cal BP (AD 800), representing some of the earliest occupation of the site. Two dates from the same shell for this basal deposit produced intercepts of 1240 to 1070 cal BP (AD 710 and 880), a difference possibly the result of dating different growth rings on the same shell (see Culleton et al. 2006). Here I present the average of these two dates, ca. 1150 cal BP. A date of ca. 790 cal BP (AD 1160) was obtained for Stratum II, roughly corresponding with the occupation in Unit 1. A single California mussel shell from near the top of Stratum I was dated to roughly 550 cal BP (AD 1400). Finally, the Area A Bulk Sample excavated by Kennett dates to roughly 780 cal BP (AD 1170).

ARTIFACTS

From Units 1 and 2, 233 artifacts, including 96 shell, seven bone, 80 stone, and 50 asphaltum artifacts were recovered (Table 5.10). As in many sites of this age, the artifact assemblage is dominated by *Olivella* beads, bead blanks, and BIP (31 percent of all artifacts), as well as microdrills and microblades (33 percent of all artifacts).

In Unit 1, 226 artifacts were recovered (958 per m[3]). Most of these are *Olivella* shell artifacts, including 13 wall disk bead blanks, 22 wall BIP, and 15 wall beads (Figure 5.11). A smaller proportion of the *Olivella* shell assemblage (23 percent) is made up of nine callus blanks and six callus BIP. Three *Olivella* barrel beads were also identified. The presence of wall beads, bead detritus, and callus bead-making artifacts in these deposits is similar to other assemblages dated to the Transitional period (see Arnold and Graesch 2001:81). The density of *Olivella* bead detritus in the assemblage is 3,386 g per m^3, a value that is comparable to some Santa Cruz Island sites of this time period, where values generally range between 3,000 and 6,200 g per m^3 (Arnold and Munns 1994). Other shell artifacts in the assemblage include two pieces of worked black abalone, six red abalone epidermis BIP, three red abalone disk beads, and four *Mytilus* fishhook fragments.

Bone artifacts are relatively rare in the sample, with just one piece of a ground/polished fragment of marine mammal bone, a worked mammal rib that is similar to Gifford's (1940) E and F series (knife, scraper, or strigil), four bone barbs, and a bone awl fragment (Figure 5.12). Stone artifacts were common in Unit 1, with at least 80 specimens, not including debitage. Microblades and microdrills were the most abundant stone artifacts, with 38 trapezoidal microblades or microdrills, 20 triangular unprepared microdrills or microblades, 15 triangular prepared microblades or microdrills, and four undiagnostic microdrills. The dominance of trapezoidal and unprepared microliths (75 percent of all microliths) in Unit 1 is similar to most Transitional period assemblages that are dominated by unprepared microliths with fewer prepared specimens (Arnold et al. 2001; Preziosi 2001:158). Because no cores were present in the sample, it appears that people were likely obtaining finished microblades and/or drills through trade or making them in other areas of the site. The other stone artifacts identified in the assemblage include a heat-treated or burned chert biface, and two retouched chert flakes. Two tarring pebbles and 40 fragments of asphaltum with basketry impressions were also recovered.

In the late Middle period sample from Unit 2, only nine shell artifacts were recovered (see Table 5.10). Again most of these (67 percent) are *Olivella* shell artifacts, including five wall disk BIP and one blank. *Olivella* bead detritus densities are relatively low (856 g per m^3), but are comparable with other late Middle period sites on the Channel Islands (Arnold and Graesch 2001; Arnold and Munns 1994; Kennett and Conlee 2002). A red abalone shell fishhook midsection and worked fragment of abalone were also recovered. Finally, one *Dentalium neo-hexagonum* bead was identified in the assemblage. *Dentalium* beads are relatively rare on the Channel Islands, but the presence of *Dentalium neohexagonum* in the assemblage is consistent with the findings from most late Channel Islands sites which generally contain this species, versus early sites which generally contain *Dentalium pretiosum* (Arnold and Graesch 2001; Erlandson et al. 2001a; King 1990). Finally, one *Olivella* wall disk bead, two wall disk BIP, one red abalone BIP, one trapezoidal microdrill, and one trapezoidal microblade were recovered from the Area A Bulk Sample.

SUBSISTENCE STRATEGIES

The most common materials recovered from SMI-468 are faunal remains, including shellfish, fish, bird, and mammal remains. All of the faunal remains described below are from 1/8-inch residuals from units 1 and 2. Additional details on data from individual levels are available in Rick (2004a).

Shellfish and Invertebrates

UNIT 1

A variety of shellfish and invertebrate remains was found in Unit 1. In the analyzed sample, 15.3 kg of shell from at least 2,738 individuals and a minimum of 29 different taxa were identified (Table 5.11). The sample is dominated by rocky intertidal taxa. The differences in the species composition between the analyzed levels is relatively minor, suggesting continuity in shellfish-collecting strategies throughout the relatively brief time of occupation represented by this unit.

California mussel is the dominant taxa by both weight (68 percent) and MNI (62 percent). Black abalone is the second most abundant taxon with 6 percent of the weight and 2 percent of the MNI. Red abalone provides 4 percent of the weight but only 1 percent of the MNI. Black turban contribute 4 percent of the weight and 6 percent of the MNI. As in previous samples, platform mussels provide only 1 percent of the weight but 11 percent of the MNI. A variety of small limpets are also present in the sample, representing less than 1 percent of the shell weight, but over 8 percent of the MNI. These small limpets were probably brought to the site incidentally with other shellfish, kelp, etc. Similarly, small barnacles (Barnacle undif. and *Pollicipes polymerus*) make up about 3 percent of the total shell weight, but most were probably incidental by-products.

Table 5.10. Artifacts from Unit 1 (All Levels) and Unit 2, Stratum III at SMI-468 (1/8-inch).

Artifact	Unit 1	Unit 2
Shell Artifacts		
Dentalium neohexagonum bead	—	1
Haliotis cracherodii worked	2	—
Haliotis rufescens BIP[a]	6	—
Haliotis rufescens disk bead	3	—
Haliotis rufescens fishhook fragment	—	1
Haliotis rufescens worked	1	—
Haliotis spp. worked	—	1
Mytilus grooved-shank fishhook fragment	3	—
Mytilus fishhook fragment	1	—
Mytilus disk BIP	2	—
Mytilus disk bead	3	—
Olivella barrel bead	3	—
Olivella callus blank	9	—
Olivella callus BIP	6	—
Olivella wall disk BIP	22	5
Olivella wall blank	13	1
Olivella wall disk bead	15	—
Subtotal	89	9
Bone Artifacts		
Mammal bone medium barb	3	—
Mammal bone large barb	1	—
Mammal bone awl	1	—
Mammal rib knife or scraper	1	—
Worked mammal bone	1	—
Subtotal	7	—
Stone Artifacts		
Biface chert	1	—
Retouched/Utilized chert flake	2	—
Trapezoidal microblade	16	—
Trapezoidal microdrill	22	—
Triangular unprepared microblade	11	—
Triangular unprepared microdrill	9	—
Triangular prepared microblade	5	—
Triangular prepared microdrill	10	—
Undiagnostic microdrill	4	—
Subtotal	80	—
Other Artifacts		
Asphaltum w/ impressions	40	—
Tarring pebble	10	—
Subtotal	50	—
Total	226	9

[a] BIP= bead in production.

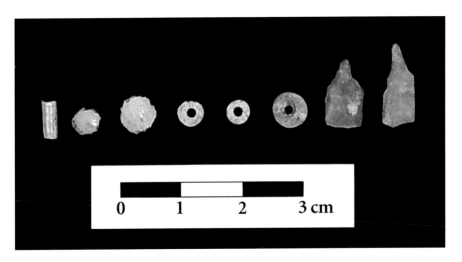

Figure 5.11. Shell beads, bead blanks, and microdrills from SMI-468. *From left to right:* *Dentalium neohexagonum* bead, *Olivella* wall disk bead blanks (2), *Olivella* wall disk beads (2), red abalone disk beads, trapezoidal microdrill, triangular prepared microdrill.

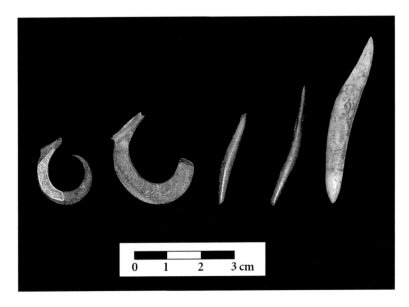

Figure 5.12. *(Left)* Two California mussel shell fishhooks; *(right)* three mammal bone barbs; all from SMI-468. Note that the two smaller bone barbs are burned.

UNIT 2

As in Unit 1, the shellfish and invertebrate remains from Unit 2, Stratum III were relatively dense. Roughly 2.9 kg of shell from at least 390 individuals and 22 different taxa were identified (Table 5.12). The sample is also dominated by rocky intertidal taxa.

California mussel is the dominant taxon by both weight (39 percent) and MNI (33 percent). Red abalone is considerably more abundant in this unit, pro-viding 12.5 percent of the weight but only 1.5 percent of the MNI. Black abalone provides 11.5 percent of the weight and 3.6 percent of the MNI. Black turbans contribute 4.8 percent of the weight and 7.9 percent of the MNI, similar to that in Unit 1. Sea urchins are fairly abundant with 5 percent of the shell weight, compared with 2.5 percent in Unit 1. Small limpets, slippers, and barnacles are also present, but were probably brought to the site as inci-dental by-products. All other shellfish taxa are minor

Table 5.11. Shellfish and Invertebrate Remains from Unit 1 at SMI-468.

Taxon	Wt.	% Wt.	MNI	%MNI
Astraea undosa (wavy turban)	0.5	< 0.1	4	0.1
Barnacle undif.	311.2	2.0	—	—
Calliostoma spp. (top snails)	0.8	< 0.1	12	0.4
Chiton undif.	190.3	1.2	—	—
Corallina spp. (coralline algae)	4.5	< 0.1	—	—
Crab undif.	54.4	0.4	—	—
Crepidula spp. (slipper shells)	4.4	< 0.1	52	1.9
Cryptochiton stelleri (gumboot chiton)	71.9	0.5	—	—
Dendraster excentricus (sand dollar)	1.0	< 0.1	—	—
Diodora aspera (rough keyhole limpet)	12.6	0.1	9	0.3
Fissurella volcano (volcano limpet)	2.4	< 0.1	8	0.3
Gastropod undif.	5.8	< 0.1	26	0.9
Haliotis cracherodii (black abalone)	851.8	5.6	53	1.9
Haliotis rufescens (red abalone)	603.0	3.9	25	0.9
Haliotis spp. (abalone undif.)	45.6	0.3	1	<0.1
Hinnites multirugosus (giant rock scallop)	15.2	0.1	1	<0.1
Land snail	9.3	0.1	20	0.7
Limpet undif.	101.5.	0.7	233	8.5
Lottia gigantea (owl limpet)	204.8	1.3	57	2.1
Margarites succinctus (tucked margarite)	3.5	< 0.1	7	0.3
Megathura crenulata (keyhole limpet)	3.5	< 0.1	1	< 0.1
Mytilus californianus (California mussel)	10,330.0	67.6	1707	62.3
Nacre undif.	493.2	3.2	—	—
Nucella spp. (dogwinkles)	0.2	< 0.1	1	< 0.1
Olivella biplicata (purple olive)	260.7	1.7	—	—
Pelecypod	1.1	< 0.1	2	0.1
Pollicipes polymerus (gooseneck barnacle)	164.7	1.1	—	—
Septifer bifurcatus (platform mussel)	199.1	1.3	312	11.4
Serpulorbis squamigerus (scaled worm snail)	1.3	< 0.1	—	—
Strongylocentrotus spp. (sea urchins)	404.2	2.6	—	—
Tegula brunnea (brown turban)	74.1	0.5	13	0.5
Tegula funebralis (black turban)	675.6	4.4	167.0	6.1
Tegula spp. (turban undif.)	134.4	0.9	27	1.0
Undif. Shell	41.7	0.3	—	—
Total	15,278.3	—	2738	—

Note: Shellfish and invertebrate remains from levels 30–40 cm, 50–60 cm, and 70–80 cm. Based on 1/8-inch recovery and all weights in grams. Volume = 0.077 m³.

contributors to the shell weight or MNI, including *Olivella biplicata* (1.2 percent of weight) and platform mussels (1.5 percent of weight).

AREA A BULK SAMPLE

A small sample of shellfish and invertebrate remains was also analyzed from the lower portion of the Area A Bulk Sample obtained from the sea cliff by Kennett. This bulk sample is small, with a volume of just 0.005 m^3. However, over 460 g of shellfish from 57 individuals and 50 g of fish, mammal, and bird bone was recovered (Table 5.13). The vertebrate remains have not been identified beyond general categories, but the shellfish remains from the lower level of this sample have been analyzed. At least 16 different taxa were identified and, as in the other two units, the sample is dominated by rocky intertidal taxa.

California mussel is the dominant taxon, with 73 percent of the weight and MNI. The second most abundant taxon by weight is sea urchin, with 5.1 percent, a relatively high percentage for this taxon. Black abalone provides 4.9 percent of the weight, and red abalone contributes about 2.0 percent. Black turbans contribute about 3.4 percent of the weight and 8.8 percent of the MNI. Small limpets and barnacles are relatively limited in the sample with just 0.2 percent and 3.2 percent of the weight, respectively. All other taxa are relatively limited in the assemblage, including *Olivella*, with just 1 percent of the total shell weight.

Fish

UNIT 1

Fish remains from the analyzed sample in Unit 1 are abundant. About 567 g and 5,915 individual fish bones were recovered and identified to the most specific taxonomic category possible (Table 5.14). Of these, roughly 1,114 (19 percent) bones were identified to family, genus, or species, including at least 19 different taxa.

Rockfish are abundant, constituting roughly 46 percent of the weight, 28 percent of the NISP, and 23 percent of the MNI. Labrids are also common in the sample, with the highest percentage of the NISP (43 percent), but only about 5 percent of the weight and 14 percent of the MNI. Undifferentiated surfperch and pile perch are also abundant, contributing roughly 15 percent of the weight and NISP and about 12 percent of the MNI. Sheep-head, lingcod, and cabezon are also present, and, because the bones of these fishes are relatively heavy, they combine for about 30 percent of the total weight, but only about 5 percent of the NISP and 8 percent of the MNI.

Smaller fishes, such as greenling, atherinids, and small sculpins, were also identified in the sample and make up about 5 percent of the MNI. Small clupeids, however, make up about 4.4 percent of the NISP, but 24 percent of the MNI. Some of the clupeid remains may have been introduced to the site as stomach contents of marine mammals or other animals, but the good preservation and abundance of these remains suggest that many of them are cultural in origin. Barracuda and an ocean sunfish ossicle were also identified in the sample. These two species combine for less than 1 percent of the NISP and only about 5 percent of the MNI, suggesting they were not a dominant part of the SMI-468 fishery. These larger taxa are generally found in deep waters, necessitating watercraft and sophisticated fishing tackle, but they can also be found inshore, making it difficult to discern precisely where these fishes were caught. Three different elasmobranchs were also identified in the sample, including bat ray, triakids, and a probable salmon shark. Elasmobranchs, however, make up only about 1 percent of the total fish NISP.

Only minor differences were noted in the abundance of the various taxa between the analyzed levels. The most significant difference involves labrids, which make up about 49 percent of the NISP in the lower level and only about 5 percent in the upper deposit (Rick 2004a). This discrepancy may represent a one-time significant catch of labrids in the lower deposits, rather than a wholesale change in fishing tactics through time. Most of the fishes in the sample are relatively common in nearshore kelp forest and rocky reef habitats surrounding the islands, suggesting that people fished primarily in the waters near SMI-468. It is possible that people occasionally ventured into offshore waters to obtain barracuda, ocean sunfish, and other fishes. A variety of techniques could have been used to catch the fishes represented in the sample, including hook and line, spearing, and netting. Single-piece shell fishhooks were recovered from the site, supporting the use of hook and line. The small labrids, clupeids, and other taxa were probably obtained with nets.

Table 5.12. Shellfish and Invertebrate Remains from Unit 2, Stratum III at SMI-468.

Taxon	Wt.	% Wt.	MNI	% MNI
Barnacle undif.	57.4	2.0	—	—
Calliostoma spp. (top snails)	0.8	< 0.1	5	1.3
Chiton undif.	69.9	2.4	—	—
Corallina spp. (coralline algae)	4.0	0.1	—	—
Crab undif.	28.0	1.0	—	—
Crepidula spp. (slipper shells)	0.5	< 0.1	6	1.5
Cryptochiton stelleri (gumboot chiton)	6.0	0.2	—	—
Gastropod undif.	4.2	0.1	17	4.4
Haliotis cracherodii (black abalone)	335.5	11.5	14	3.6
Haliotis rufescens (red abalone)	363.5	12.5	6	1.5
Haliotis spp. (abalone undif.)	0.6	< 0.1	1	0.3
Land snail	0.6	< 0.1	9	2.3
Limpet undif.	56.0	1.9	104	26.7
Lottia gigantea (owl limpet)	133.5	4.6	25	6.4
Megathura crenulata (giant keyhole limpet)	1.6	0.1	1	0.3
Mytilus californianus (California mussel)	1120.8	38.5	129	33.1
Nacre undif.	247.0	8.5	—	—
Olivella biplicata (purple olive)	35.1	1.2	—	—
Pollicipes polymerus (gooseneck barnacle)	24.2	0.8	—	—
Septifer bifurcatus (platform mussel)	42.7	1.5	14	3.6
Serpulorbis squamigerus (scaled worm snail)	0.5	< 0.1	—	—
Strongylocentrotus spp. (sea urchins)	145.4	5.0	—	—
Tegula brunnea (brown turban)	42.9	1.5	12	3.1
Tegula funebralis (black turban)	140.6	4.8	31	7.9
Tegula spp. (turban undif.)	41.0	1.4	16	4.1
Undif. Shell	9.4	0.3	—	—
Total	2911.7	—	390	—

Note: Based on 1/8-inch recovery and all weights in grams. Volume = 0.041 m³.

UNIT 2

Fish bones are considerably less abundant in the analyzed sample from Unit 2, with just 115 g and 1,807 fish bones (Table 5.15). However, the sample contains at least 11 different taxa, including 10 teleosts and one elasmobranch. Of the 1,807 fish bones analyzed, 14 percent by NISP were identified to family, genus, or species, a slightly lower value than that for Unit 1.

Similar to Unit 1, rockfish are the most abundant taxon, with about 48 percent of the weight, 36 percent of the NISP, and 22 percent of the MNI. The remains of labrids are again fairly common, with 29 percent of the NISP and 13 percent of the MNI. Surfperches are also relatively abundant, with 16 percent of the NISP and 17 percent of the MNI. Small fishes, including atherinids and clupeids, combined for about 7 percent of the NISP and 13 percent of the MNI. The remains of cabezon and sheephead account for 32 percent of the weight, but only 9 percent of the NISP and 17 percent of the MNI. Undifferentiated mackerel were

Table 5.13. Faunal Remains from Area A Bulk Sample at SMI-468.

| Taxon | Lower Stratum | | | |
	Wt.	% Wt.[a]	MNI	% MNI
Barnacle undif.	6.9	1.5	—	—
Chiton undif.	0.8	0.2	—	—
Coronula diadema (whale barnacle)	0.5	0.1	1	1.8
Crab undif.	5.7	1.2	—	—
Crepidula spp. (slipper shells)	1.9	0.4	2	3.5
Gastropod undif.	0.1	< 0.1	1	1.8
Haliotis cracherodii (black abalone)	22.5	4.9	1	1.8
Haliotis rufescens (red abalone)	9.2	2.0	1	1.8
Limpet undif.	1.0	0.2	—	—
Lottia gigantea (owl limpet)	12.4	2.7	2	3.5
Mytilus californianus (California mussel)	334.6	72.7	41	71.9
Nacre undif.	4.7	1.0	—	—
Olivella biplicata (purple olive)	4.5	1.0	—	—
Pollicipes polymerus (gooseneck barnacle)	8.0	1.7	—	—
Strongylocentrotus spp. (sea urchins)	23.6	5.1	—	—
Tegula brunnea (brown turban)	1.7	0.4	1	1.8
Tegula funebralis (black turban)	15.8	3.4	5	8.8
Tegula spp. (turban undif.)	4.0	0.9	2	3.5
Undif. shell	2.3	0.5	—	—
Shellfish Subtotal	460.2	—	57	—
Bird bone	0.5	1.0	—	—
Fish bone	33.2	66.4	—	—
Mammal bone	16.3	32.6	—	—
Vertebrate Subtotal	50.0	—	—	—
Total	510.2	—	—	—

Note: Based on 1/8-inch recovery and all weights in grams. Volume = 0.005 m^3.

[a] Percentages for shellfish and invertebrates and vertebrate remains are separate.

also identified in the sample, making up about 2 percent of the NISP. What appears to be a tooth from a blue shark was the only elasmobranch identified in the sample.

All of the fish identified in the Unit 2 sample could have been taken from nearshore kelp forests or rocky reefs, using hook and line, nets, and spears. For the most part, the types of fishes and abundance of each taxon identified in Unit 2 and Unit 1 are similar. Both are dominated by rockfish, labrids, and surfperch, with smaller amounts of clupeids, atherinids, cabezon, sheephead, and other fishes. The only difference between the two is the absence of barracuda and ocean sunfish in Unit 2. However, these are both relatively rare in Unit 1, probably representing incidental catches rather than distinct differences in the overall fishery. These data suggest relative continuity in the fishery at SMI-468 across the late Middle and Transitional periods, with an increase in the number of taxa in the Transitional period assemblage.

Mammals

Mammal remains from the analyzed samples of Units 1 and 2 were relatively limited. Four hundred

Table 5.14. Fish Remains from Unit 1 at SMI-468.

Taxon	Wt.	% Wt.[a]	NISP	% NISP	MNI	% MNI
Teleost						
Atherinidae (silversides)	0.1	0.1	1	0.1	1	1.4
Clinidae (kelpfish)	0.3	0.2	2	0.2	1	1.4
Clupeidae (sardines)	0.7	0.5	49	4.4	18	24.3
Cottidae (sculpin)	< 0.1	0.1	1	0.1	1	1.4
Scorpaenichthys marmoratus (cabezon)	14.8	10.1	28	2.5	2	2.7
Embiotocidae (surfperch)	16.4	11.2	139	12.5	7	9.5
Damalichthys vacca (pile perch)	4.8	3.3	29	2.6	2	2.7
Hexagrammidae (greenling)	0.1	0.1	3	0.3	2	2.7
Ophiodon elongatus (lingcod)	17.9	12.3	15	1.4	2	2.7
Labridae (senorita or wrasse)	7.1	4.9	481	43.3	10	13.5
Semicossyphus pulcher (California sheephead)	10.3	7.1	14	1.3	2	2.7
Mackerel undif.	1.0	0.7	15	1.4	2	2.7
Molidae (molas)						
Mola mola (ocean sunfish)	0.5	0.3	1	0.1	1	1.4
Scorpaenidae						
Sebastes spp. (rockfish)	66.9	45.9	316	28.4	17	23.0
Sphyraenidae (barracudas)						
Sphyraena argentea (California barracuda)	1.0	0.7	2	0.2	2	2.7
Stichaeidae (prickleback)	2.2	1.5	7	0.6	1	1.4
Small teleost undif.	0.1	—	3	—	—	—
Teleost undif.	420.6	—	4800	—	—	—
Subtotal	564.9	—	5906	—	71	—
Elasmobranch						
Elasmobranch undif.	0.2	—	1	—	—	—
Lamnidae (mackerel sharks)						
Lamna ditropis (salmon shark)?	0.1	0.1	2	0.2	1	1.4
Myliobatidae						
Myliobatis californica (California bat ray)	0.3	0.2	2	0.2	1	1.4
Triakidae (smoothhounds, soupfin, etc.)	1.2	0.8	4	0.4	1	1.4
Subtotal	1.8	—	9	—	3	—
Total	566.7	—	5915	—	74	—

Note: Based on 1/8-inch recovery and all weights in grams. Fish remains are from the 30–40 cm and 70–80 cm levels. Volume = 0.051 m³. All specimens noted with a ? mark are tentative identifications.

[a] Percentages based on specimens identified to family, genus, and species.

Table 5.15. Fish Remains from Unit 2, Stratum III at SMI-468.

Taxon	Wt.	% Wt. [a]	NISP	% NISP	MNI	% MNI
Teleost						
Atherinidae (silversides)	0.1	0.3	3	1.2	1	4.3
Clinidae (kelpfish)	0.1	0.3	1	0.4	1	4.3
Clupeidae (sardines)	0.2	0.6	15	5.8	2	8.7
Cottidae (sculpins)						
Scorpaenichthys marmoratus (cabezon)	4.8	13.5	13	5.1	2	8.7
Embiotocidae (surfperches)	3.9	11.0	40	15.6	4	17.4
Hexagrammidae (greenlings)						
Ophiodon elongatus (lingcod)	0.6	1.7	2	0.8	1	4.3
Labridae (senorita or wrasse)	1.8	5.1	75	29.2	3	13.0
Semicossyphus pulcher (California sheephead)	6.7	18.8	9	3.5	2	8.7
Mackerel undif.	0.4	1.1	5	1.9	1	4.3
Scorpaenidae						
Sebastes spp. (rockfish)	16.9	47.5	93	36.2	5	21.7
Teleost undif.	79.7	—	1550	—	—	—
Subtotal	115.2	—	1806	—	22	—
Elasmobranch						
Carcharhinidae						
Prionace glauca (blue shark)?	<0.1	0.3	1	0.4	1	4.3
Total	115.3	—	1807	—	23	—

Note: Based on 1/8-inch recovery and all weights in grams. Volume = 0.041 m^3. All specimens noted with ? marks are tentative identifications.

[a] Percentages based on specimens identified to family, genus, and species.

and twenty-five mammal bones weighing 330.1 g were recovered and analyzed from Unit 1 (Table 5.16). Of these bones, roughly 97 percent by NISP (20 percent of the weight) are small, highly fragmentary mammal bones or undifferentiated bone fragments. The majority of these are small fragments of cancellous or cortical bones that are probably from marine mammals. Over 90 percent of the NISP identified to more specific categories is from marine mammals, including one element each from northern fur seal and California sea lion (15.4 percent combined), four otariid bones (30.8 percent), four undifferentiated pinniped bones (30.8 percent), one phocid bone (7.7 percent), and one elephant seal bone. A reptile or amphibian vertebra was also identified.

In Unit 2, 119.6 g and 485 mammal and other bones were recovered and analyzed. Again roughly 97 percent by NISP of these bones are small and fragmentary bits of cancellous or cortical bone that are probably from marine mammals. The only diagnostic bones in the sample are 12 bones from an undifferentiated otariid and one bone from a rodent (probably deer mouse). The data from both the units illustrate that marine mammal remains dominate the mammalian sample.

Birds

Bird bones are relatively rare in the samples. The sample from Unit 1 produced the most bird bone and yielded the only bones identifiable to genus. Forty-two bones weighing 10.5 g from at least two

Table 5.16. Mammal and Reptile/Amphibian Remains from Units 1 and 2 at SMI-468.

Taxon	Unit 1						Unit 2, Stratum II					
	Wt.	% Wt.[a]	NISP	% NISP	MNI	% MNI	Wt.	% Wt.	NISP	% NISP	MNI	% MNI
Pinniped	38.2	30.1	4	30.8	—	—	—	—	—	—	—	—
Otariidae	14.3	11.3	4	30.8	—	—	24.2	99.6	12	92.3	1	50.0
Callorhinus ursinus (northern fur seal)	20.6	16.2	1	7.7	1	25.0	—	—	—	—	—	—
Zalophus californianus (California sea lion)	12.9	10.2	1	7.7	1	25.0	—	—	—	—	—	—
Phocidae	24.0	18.9	1	7.7	—	—	—	—	—	—	—	—
Mirounga angustirostris (elephant seal)	16.8	13.2	1	7.7	1	25.0	—	—	—	—	—	—
Sea Mammal Subtotal	126.8	99.9	12	92.3	3	75.0	24.2	99.6	12	92.3	1	50.0
Reptile/Amphibian	0.1	0.1	1	7.7	1	25.0	—		—	—	—	—
Rodent	—	—	—	—	—	—	0.1	0.4	1	0.7	1	50.0
Mammal undif.	202.8	—	407	—	—	—	95.1	—	464	—	—	—
Undif. bone	0.4	—	5	—	—	—	0.2	—	8	—	—	—
Subtotal	203.3	—	413	—	1	—	95.4	—	473	—	1	—
Total	330.1	—	425	—	4	—	119.6	—	485	—	2	—

Note: Based on 1/8-inch recovery and all weights in grams. The Unit 1 mammal remains are from the 30–40 cm and 70–80 cm levels. Volume = 0.051 m³.

[a] Percentages do not include undifferentiated mammal bone or undifferentiated bone. Most undifferentiated mammal bone is probably from sea mammals.

Table 5.17. Bird Remains from Unit 1 at SMI-468.

Taxon	Wt.	% Wt.[a]	NISP	% NISP	MNI	% MNI
Pelecanidae						
Pelecanus spp. (pelican)	0.5	22.7	1	50.0	1	50.0
Phalacrocoracidae						
Phalacrocorax spp. (Brandt's/Double-crested cormorant)	1.7	77.3	1	50.0	1	50.0
Aves undif.	8.3	—	40	—	—	—
Total	10.5	—	42	—	2	—

Note: Based on 1/8-inch recovery and all weights in grams. Bird remains are from the 30–40 cm and 70–80 cm levels. Volume = 0.051 m³.

[a] Percentages based on specimens identified to family, genus, and species.

individuals were recovered in Unit 1 (Table 5.17). Of these bones, 95 percent (NISP) are undiagnostic and fragmentary bird bones. A pelican radius and Brandt's/Double-crested cormorant mandible, however, were identified in the sample. These two birds are relatively common on the island today and could have been scavenged or captured. In Unit 2, only 1.6 g and 23 undiagnostic and fragmentary bird bones were identified in the sample. Similarly, in the Area A Bulk Sample, only 0.5 g (100 g per m³) of undifferentiated bird bone was recovered.

Dietary Reconstruction

To provide another measure of the significance of various faunal categories, I calculated a dietary reconstruction for Units 1 and 2 and the Area A Bulk Sample (1/8-inch) using the weight method. Dietary reconstructions for Unit 2 provide an indication of the relative importance of various animal categories during the late Middle period. These data indicate that fish and marine mammals contributed roughly 41 percent and 37 percent of the meat yield, respectively, shellfish about 23 percent, and birds less than 1 percent. When just fish and shellfish are compared, fish provide roughly 64 percent and shellfish about 36 percent. Collectively, these data suggest a fairly balanced economy between fish and marine mammals, supplemented by shellfish and birds.

Dietary reconstructions for Unit 1 suggest that fish contributed most of the meat represented (57 percent), followed by marine mammals (29 percent), shellfish (13 percent), and birds (<1 percent). When just fish and shellfish are compared, fish provide roughly 81 percent of the meat, and shellfish about 19 percent. These data are similar to those provided by Kennett and Conlee (2002) for Santa Rosa and San Miguel sites of this age, where fish clearly are dominant and shellfish appear to be primarily a supplemental part of the economy. Marine mammals appear to still be fairly significant, probably indicative of the site's proximity to Castle Rock, Point Bennett, and other areas where pinnipeds abound.

Finally, dietary reconstructions for the Area A Bulk Sample suggest that fish were the most abundant contributor, with roughly 61 percent of the meat yield. Marine mammals follow, with roughly 26 percent, shellfish contribute about 12 percent, and birds provide less than 1 percent of the overall meat yield. When just fish and shellfish are com-

pared, fish provide 84 percent and shellfish only 16 percent. Collectively, the data from Unit 1 and the bulk sample suggest that during the Transitional period, people at the site focused largely on fish, with smaller amounts of marine mammals, shellfish, and birds. The Unit 2 sample suggests a more balanced economy, with fish and marine mammals dominating.

DISCUSSION

SMI-468 has dense shell midden deposits and a series of 10 well-defined house berms or other domestic features. Occupation of the site spans roughly 700 years (ca. 1150 to 450 cal BP [AD 800 to 1500]) of the late Middle, Transitional, and Late periods. On San Miguel Island, a cave site on Harris Point (SMI-264), a shell midden located near Green Mountain on the island's interior (SMI-464), a shell midden on Simonton Cove (SMI-396), and a sample from Unit G3 at Daisy Cave have produced Transitional period dates. Currently, the only other sites with documented Transitional period occupation include four sites (SRI-2, SRI-15, SRI-85, and SRI-97) on Santa Rosa Island and four sites (SCRI-191, SCRI-236, SCRI-240, and SCRI-474) on Santa Cruz Island (Arnold 2001c; Kennett and Conlee 2002; Munns and Arnold 2002). This fairly small number of sites makes SMI-468 important for understanding broad cultural changes on the Channel Islands.

The available data from SMI-468 suggest that people were conducting a wide range of activities at the site, including fishing, marine mammal hunting, shellfish collecting, bead making, and other activities. The artifact assemblage from the site is dominated by wall beads, blanks, BIP, and trapezoidal microliths, with smaller amounts of *Olivella* callus bead materials and triangular prepared microliths that support the site chronology. The site appears to be a classic late Middle period and Transitional period Chumash community with domestic features and a diverse array of activities.

Arnold (1992a, 2001b; Arnold et al. 1997a) suggested that Channel Islanders were faced with fluctuating marine water temperatures and resources during the Transitional period, which, along with a period of drought, spurred a reorganization of Island Chumash society, including ascribed leadership and increased craft specialization and exchange.

The role of drought in prompting cultural changes during this time has also recently been emphasized by a variety of researchers (e.g., Jones et al. 1999; Kennett and Kennett 2000; Raab and Larson 1997; Yatsko 2000). The data from SMI-468 suggest that marine environmental conditions on San Miguel Island during the Transitional period were relatively productive (see also Erlandson 1993; Kennett 2005; Kennett and Kennett 2000; Raab and Larson 1997). The diversity and abundance of resources increases substantially from the late Middle period to Transitional period samples. For example, at least 19 fish taxa and 29 shellfish taxa were identified in the Transitional period sample, compared with just 11 fish taxa and 22 shellfish taxa in the late Middle period sample. The density of fish and shellfish remains is also higher in the Transitional period sample, with 198 kg per m^3 of shellfish and 11 kg per m^3 of fish bone, compared with 71 kg per m^3 of shellfish and 2.8 kg per m^3 of fish bone in the late Middle period sample. The density of mammal bones is also higher in the Transitional period samples, with 6.5 kg per m^3 compared with 2.9 kg per m^3 in the late Middle period sample. These data may partly reflect the larger sample size for the Transitional period component, but the faunal data from SMI-468 demonstrate intensified marine subsistence during the Transitional period. In a recent analysis of faunal remains from Santa Cruz Island, Colten (2001) and Pletka (2001a) also noted the variability and diversity of human subsistence strategies during the Transitional period, a pattern generally consistent with the data from SMI-468.

SMI-468 and other Channel Islands sites also raise questions about the effects of drought during the Transitional period. SMI-468 is one of five sites on San Miguel Island that have components dated to the Transitional period. Other sites (e.g., SMI-150 and SMI-536) produced dates that are near the end of the Transitional period and beginning of the Late period. Compared with the situation on Santa Cruz and Santa Rosa islands, freshwater is considerably more limited on San Miguel Island. Springs are present across the island and small creeks also flow, but a sustained drought would presumably have had a pronounced effect on people living on San Miguel. A spring is located in front of SMI-468 today, a feature that probably helped draw people to this spot. However, this is a relatively small spring,

and nearby Otter Creek is also fairly poorly watered compared with other island drainages. In short, SMI-468 does not appear to be an ideal spot for people to coalesce to combat drought. This suggests that either the population at SMI-468 was low, that the period of drought during the Transitional period was more variable than previously recognized, or that the hydrology of the area has changed significantly. Determining population size is difficult from the archaeological record, but the large size of the site and at least five houses dated to the Transitional period suggest that this was a fairly sizable community. While island watersheds are currently regenerating, the hydrology in this area has probably not radically changed from what it was during the Transitional period.

Although a number of important cultural changes happened during the Transitional period, the data from SMI-468 suggest that these varied locally depending on a number of cultural and environmental factors (see also Gamble 2005). The recent identification of two Transitional period sites on Santa Barbara Island, well known for its lack of freshwater, also suggests that human responses to climatic changes during the Transitional period were more variable than previously presumed (Rick and Erlandson 2001). It is this local variability that should be the focus of future research on environmental and cultural changes during the Transitional period (see also Arnold 2001b; Pletka 2001a). With continued radiocarbon dating efforts across the Channel Islands, it is likely that more Transitional period components will be identified and provide further insight on cultural developments during this period.

The SMI-468 ^{14}C chronology suggests that people lived at the site until around AD 1400 or the early portions of the Late period. It appears that the settlement on this portion of the island then shifted toward the area of Otter Creek where Protohistoric and Historic period occupations have been identified at SMI-470 (see Chapter 6).

SYNTHESIS

The Otter Harbor area of San Miguel Island has been a center of human occupation for millennia. Shell middens in the area date more or less continuously from around 7,300 years ago through the Historic period. The rich and productive kelp forests, rocky reefs, pinniped haul-outs, and shellfish beds were clearly attractive to people who settled in the area. Freshwater from a small creek and a series of seeps is limited but fairly reliable. Between about AD 800 and 1400, SMI-481 and SMI-468 were two of the main settlements on San Miguel Island. Berm features at SMI-468 also suggest the presence of a series of houses at this site.

Human daily activities at these sites were diverse. Subsistence pursuits included fishing, marine mammal hunting, shellfish collecting, and scavenging or hunting for birds. Boats were probably being employed for fishing and possibly to obtain marine mammals from offshore rocks and islets. The faunal remains from these sites provide insight into the marine ecology of the re-gion, suggesting a relatively similar composition of marine animals and habitats as in the present day, except for the once locally extinct and now-seldom-reported Guadalupe fur seal and sea otter. Dietary reconstructions suggest a shift through time from marine mammals to fishes, a pattern that has also been reported for San Miguel Island by Walker et al. (2002).

The people who occupied these sites also made beads, fishhooks, chipped-stone tools, and bone artifacts. Undoubtedly, some of these arti-facts and possibly faunal remains were incorpo-rated into the broader Santa Barbara Channel regional exchange system and interaction sphere. I will return to the data from these two sites again in Chapter 7 for a broad comparative analysis.

6

Historic Period San Miguel Island

The Historic era was a time of dramatic change and cultural devastation for Native peoples throughout the Americas. At various points during the Historic period, introduced diseases such as smallpox, influenza, measles, and syphilis dramatically reduced Native populations, disrupted interaction and trade systems, and forever altered traditional ways of life (Boyd 1999b; Erlandson and Bartoy 1995; J. Johnson 1999b; Lightfoot 2005; Ramenofsky 1987; Stannard 1992; Thomas 1989, 1990, 1991; Walker and Johnson 1992; Walker et al. 1989). Exotic plants and animals also severely impacted Native subsistence strategies and had a profound effect on natural and cultural landscapes. Along the Pacific Coast of North America, interaction with European explorers began in the sixteenth century as they began to investigate the coast for trade routes and new lands to conquer (see Erlandson and Bartoy 1995; Lightfoot 2005:50–51; Lightfoot and Simmons 1998; Preston 1996, 2002). Following these sporadic early explorations, contact between Native Americans and Europeans intensified during the late eighteenth and early nineteenth centuries.

While a large body of research has been assembled on pre and post-contact lifeways on the southern California coast and Channel Islands (e.g., Arnold 1990; Arnold, ed. 2001; Arnold and Graesch 2004; Erlandson and Bartoy 1995; Erlandson et al. 2001b; Graesch 2001, 2004; J. Johnson 1982, 1988, 1989, 1999a, 2001; Kennett 2005; Kennett et al. 2000; Walker et al. 1989), we still know relatively little about the lifeways of Chumash peoples on contact period San Miguel Island. For example, what were the responses of peoples on this outer island to European colonialism? How did the effects of contact and colonialism on San Miguel Island compare with those on Santa Cruz and Santa Rosa islands and the adjacent mainland? What were the effects of European contact and the introduction of new plants, animals, and agrarian systems on traditional subsistence practices on the islands? Finally, how can ethnohistoric and ecological data from the Channel Islands be integrated with archaeological data to produce a more complete picture of Historic period and prehistoric Chumash lifeways?

In this chapter, I present the results of surface collection and excavation at SMI-163, located on the north-central coast of San Miguel Island. This village appears to have been occupied primarily from about 450 to 150 cal BP (AD 1500 to 1800) with an ephemeral component dated to around 1200 cal BP (AD 750). Ethnohistoric and archaeological data suggest that this is the probable location of *Tuqan*, the largest of two named historic villages on San Miguel Island and the possible location where Juan Rodriguez Cabrillo wintered on his journey from New Spain (Mexico) in 1542–1543 (see Erlandson and Bartoy 1995; see Kelsey 1986 for a different interpretation of Cabrillo's winter harbor). These factors, along with the good preservation of archaeological materials at SMI-163, make it an excellent case study for examining Chumash daily activities and lifeways during the Historic period. Several other San Miguel Island sites (SMI-470, SMI-516, SMI-536, and SMI-602) have also recently been radiocarbon dated to the Protohistoric and/or Historic periods, including SMI-470, the probable location of the Chumash village of *Niwoyomi* (J. Johnson 1999a; Kennett 2005). San Miguel was once thought to have been an isolated island with comparatively low population densities. These new sites, however, raise questions about the nature of San Miguel Island occupations during the late prehistoric, Protohistoric, and Historic periods. To augment the data from SMI-163, I also summarize current knowledge about other Protohistoric and Historic sites, including a map and sample of faunal and artifact data from SMI-470.

I begin this chapter by presenting a brief overview of the contact history and Mission period in the Santa Barbara Channel region and Channel Islands. I then summarize the results of field and laboratory research at SMI-163 and briefly describe the nature and context of the other Protohistoric and Historic archaeological sites on San Miguel Island. I conclude the chapter by offering new perspectives on the Chumash occupation of San Miguel Island.

EUROPEAN EXPLORERS, MISSIONIZATION, AND THE ISLAND CHUMASH

The postcontact period is divided into four general phases: Protohistoric (AD 1542 to 1769), Mission (AD 1769 to 1834), Mexican/Rancho (AD 1834 to 1849), and American (AD 1850 to present). These periods provide a framework for examining the scale and pace of cultural changes in the wake of European contact (Figure 6.1; Costello and Hornbeck 1989). Contact during the Protohistoric period was generally sporadic, occurring mostly with early European explorers, but some contacts were more sustained and some early voyages could be undocumented (Erlandson and Bartoy 1995; Lightfoot and Simmons 1998). The first Europeans to contact the Island Chumash were probably crew members of an expedition led by Juan Rodriguez Cabrillo, who may have wintered on San Miguel Island in 1542–1543 (see Costello and Hornbeck 1989; Erlandson and Bartoy 1995; Wagner 1929). Limited contacts may have also occurred among members of later maritime expeditions, including undocumented voyages associated with the Manila Galleon trade. Contact during the Mission period and the subsequent Rancho period was intense, marking the end of a hunting-and gathering-life-style, which had flourished along the coast for over 10,000 years. Conversion of the Chumash was complete by AD 1822 (J. Johnson 1982, 1999b; McLendon 1999:13), with many islanders coming to the missions between AD 1815 and 1816 during a period of environmental instability (Larson et al. 1994). Because of their relative isolation, people on the Channel Islands had a different experience than many people on the mainland during the contact period.

The effects of introduced diseases and new technologies on traditional Chumash culture and on Native peoples throughout the Americas during the Protohistoric period is a hotly contested subject. Some researchers suggest that early voyages by European explorers had limited, localized, or no impacts on traditional lifeways (e.g., Arnold et al. 2004:7–8; Kelsey 1985; Landberg 1965:19; Lightfoot and Simmons 1998:161–164), while others argue that disease epidemics from these early voyages may have caused declines in population and social upheaval (Erlandson and Bartoy 1995; Erlandson et al. 2001b; Preston 1996, 2000). The debate continues because little is known about the extent and scale of the early maritime voyages throughout California, as these trips were often shrouded in secrecy or people kept relatively poor records. Protohistoric versus Mission period chronologies are also difficult to define because of inherent errors of radiocarbon dating samples from recent times (Erlandson et al. 2001b). While Historic period artifacts (glass beads, metal, etc.) can be used to determine site age, these are relatively rare in some island sites and frequently yield fairly gross chronologies. Recently, some archaeologists have suggested that possible declines in Native populations from early undocumented epidemics may have also led to a rebound in local resources, suggesting a link between disease epidemics and ecology in California and elsewhere (Broughton 1999; Butler 2000; Erlandson et al. 2004a; Preston 1998).

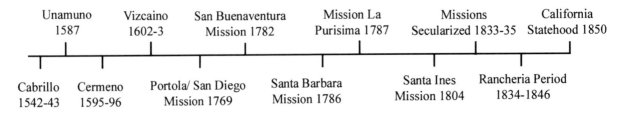

Figure 6.1. Dates of major historic expeditions and founding of the missions in the Santa Barbara Channel region (dates obtained from Costello and Hornbeck [1989]).

Virtually all scholars agree that early in the Mission period, dramatic changes in Chumash society had occurred. The Spanish campaign to bring the Chumash to the missions for conversion and labor was relatively quick and dramatic. There are examples of resistance, however, including a rebellion in AD 1824 at the missions (Blackburn 1975), as well as less hostile and somewhat poorly understood forms, including continued use of traditional artifacts and ideology (Bamforth 1993; Castillo 1989). Epidemic diseases were rampant both in the close quarters of the missions and among people still living outside the missions, resulting in dramatic declines in populations (Walker and Johnson 1992). Not only did populations decline, but people were taught to denounce their traditional values and worldviews as part of the conversion process (Castillo 1989). They were also subjected to hard labor on the missions, and new diets may have caused other health problems (Walker et al. 1989). The introduction of cattle grazing and agriculture in the area also proved to be devastating for traditional hunting-and gathering-rounds.

Because the Spanish never established a mission on the islands, most Island Chumash became affiliated with the missions later than mainlanders (J. Johnson 1982, 2001:53). Cross-channel voyages were made to bring the Chumash ashore for conversion and life in the mission system. This proved increasingly difficult for the Spaniards, as boats and lives were apparently lost during some voyages (Hudson et al. 1978:148–150; J. Johnson 1999a: 66). The last few elderly islanders were brought to the mainland in 1822, although a small group returned briefly during the Chumash Revolt in 1824 (J. Johnson 2001:59). Prior to this time, the Island Chumash followed a different trajectory than mainlanders and had considerably more cultural continuity. For example, most islanders were baptized between AD 1814 and 1817 (J. Johnson 1999b: 104), roughly 30 years after the missions were established at San Buenaventura and Santa Bárbara. Despite the dramatic changes to Chumash society during the colonial era, people continued to make beads and other trade items and to practice traditional subsistence pursuits on the islands during much of the Mission period, suggesting continuity in traditional lifeways after European contact (Arnold et al. 2004; Arnold and Graesch 2001; Graesch 2004; Rick 2004c).

Following the collapse of the Mission system around AD 1834, the Mexican government formally claimed California. Comparatively little is known about the Chumash during the Rancho or Mexican period. Many Chumash dissolved into the labor force of the new Mexican homesteads, but a few rancherías persisted in the area that were composed of Island Chumash and other peoples following the secularization of the missions (Johnson and McLendon 1999b, 2000). Despite the roughly 500 years of cultural change and population loss during the contact era, the Chumash survived and are undergoing a major cultural revival and florescence, including people who can trace their lineages back to specific villages on the Channel Islands or adjacent mainland (see McLendon and Johnson 1999).

Many questions remain about the details of Island Chumash lifeways during the contact period. Introduced disease epidemics during the Mission period and possibly earlier affected Channel Islanders, but what about subsistence practices and changes in material culture and exchange? Since agriculture was not instituted on the islands until much later than it was on the mainland, did Island Chumash subsistence remain largely unchanged after contact? How did the introduction of glass beads, needles, and other artifact forms change the traditional economic systems of people on San Miguel Island? Arnold (1990, 2001b), Arnold and Graesch (2001, 2004), Graesch (2001, 2004), and Kennett et al. (2000) have examined these issues on Santa Cruz Island, and Kennett (2005) and J. Johnson (1982, 1993, 1999a, 2001) provided an overview of the northern Channel Islands in general. However, systematic excavation of Historic period sites on San Miguel Island has been considerably more limited. In the remainder of this chapter, I use archaeological data to explore the dynamics of Chumash lifeways on contact era San Miguel Island.

HISTORIC PERIOD
SAN MIGUEL ISLAND

Ethnohistoric sources suggest that there were two named Chumash villages on San Miguel Island, *Tuqan* and *Niwoyomi* (J. Johnson 1982, 1999a). Based on baptismal counts from mission records, both of these villages are thought to have been relatively small. *Tuqan*, also the Chumash name for San Miguel Island, is the larger of the two and is thought to be in the Cuyler Harbor area (J. Johnson 1999a:66). The village of *Tuqan* was the home of the island chief Cristóbal Mascál, who, according to J. Johnson (1999a:66), was married four times at Mission La Purísima. Baptismal counts for this village are relatively small, with just 34 baptisms, 29 at La Purísima, and five at Santa Bárbara (J. Johnson 1999a:53). J. Johnson (1999a: 66) suggested that poorly documented canoe accidents and losses at sea may have underestimated the actual population of this village.

Early twentieth-century excavations at a cemetery by Glidden were performed at a possible historic site on San Miguel Island (Erlandson and Bartoy 1995:166–167; Heye 1921). This site may have been located on a terrace above Cuyler Harbor, but the precise location is unknown, and recent attempts to locate a historic village above Cuyler Harbor have not yet been successful. Erlandson and Bartoy (1995) suggested that a Late period/Protohistoric radiocarbon date obtained by Hubbs may be from SMI-536 located just above Cuyler Harbor, but other dates from this site are Late period in age (see below). The village at SMI-163 and an adjacent cemetery (SMI-162) and large shell midden (SMI-159) with probable Historic/Protohistoric period artifacts or radiocarbon dates suggest this complex of sites is probably the location of *Tuqan*.

Niwoyomi, the other of the two named villages, has one of the lowest baptismal counts for any of the island villages, with just three baptisms at Mission La Purísima (J. Johnson 1999a:53). This led J. Johnson (1999a:66) and Kennett (2005:104) to conclude that *Niwoyomi* was a small "ranchería" or satellite community, possibly with only a single household. Archaeological data suggest that the village of *Niwoyomi* may be located at SMI-470, a site located near Otter Harbor, which has produced Historic and Protohistoric radiocarbon dates and a few probable contact period artifacts.

SMI-163: SITE SETTING AND CONTEXT

SMI-163 is located on a prominent point near Cuyler Harbor and Prince Island (Figure 6.2). The site is flanked primarily by rocky intertidal environments, with a small sandy cove located on its eastern edge, which is ideal for landing a boat. A slope

rises steeply to the south of the site, providing a relatively circumscribed area surrounding the village complex. Freshwater is available from a series of springs around Cuyler Harbor.

SMI-163 contains archaeological deposits well over 1 m deep with abundant evidence of bead making, marine fishing, and other activities. At least six visible house depressions of varying size are visible on the surface (Figure 6.3). Surface exposures, auger holes, and excavation of three test units demonstrate variability in the site constituents. Recently deposited dune sand and dense ice plant and *Coreopsis* cover much of the site area, somewhat obscuring the surface. Auger tests, however, revealed midden underneath portions of this sand and vegetation cover, suggesting that the village is probably larger than indicated by surface features and midden exposures alone. A cemetery located at adjacent SMI-162 appears to be related to the village at SMI-163.

A dry rock wall probably postdating the Chumash occupation of the site is located just above the beach on the northeast site margin. On the rocks above the beach adjacent to the northwestern site margin, a large concentration of asphaltum that is a few meters in diameter has washed ashore. Such asphaltum masses probably come ashore from seeps just offshore of San Miguel Island (see Braje et al. 2005b: 209; Heye 1921:20; Roberts 1991:14). If present during the time of occupation, this would have been a ready source of asphaltum for the site occupants.

Field Research and Stratigraphy

During 1999 and 2001, I excavated three units at SMI-163: Unit 1 in House 1; Unit 2 on the rim of House 5; and Unit 3 on the rim of House 1. I also conducted laser transit mapping, obtained artifact samples from 10 surface units from disturbed/eroded deposits across portions of the site, and excavated auger holes to determine the extent and depth of the deposits and obtain *in situ* radiocarbon samples from various portions of the site.

Unit 1 is a 0.5 × 1 m unit excavated on the inside edge of House 1, the largest house on the site based on surface exposures. This unit was excavated in 5-cm arbitrary levels through moderately dense shell midden deposits, and all residuals were screened over 1/16-inch mesh. Cultural deposits in this unit were relatively shallow, extending to a

Figure 6.2. SMI-163 location and setting.

depth of roughly 40 cm, with a volume of 0.186 m^3. The deposits were in a dark brown (10YR3/3) loamy sand throughout the upper 25 to 30 cm. At a depth of roughly 30 cm, the soil lightened in color and became increasingly compact. Small fragments of shell and bone were compacted into this lens, and around 5 cm below this, bedrock was encountered. This relatively thin compacted lens is probably the floor of House 1.

Unit 2 is a 0.5 × 0.5 m unit excavated to a depth of roughly 120 cm in the midden berm of House 5. An auger hole placed in the bottom of this unit indicates the deposit extends at least another 80 cm. Stratigraphic variation in the deposits is minimal, so this unit was excavated in arbitrary 10-cm levels, and all residuals were screened over 1/16-inch

mesh. The shell midden deposits are extremely dense and in a dark grayish brown (10YR4/2) sandy loam. The volume of Unit 2 is 0.269 m^3. Preservation in this unit is excellent, with hundreds of whole, articulated shell valves, fish bones, and other materials encountered *in situ*. Radiocarbon dating and the limited stratigraphic variation in this unit suggest that it was deposited relatively rapidly, perhaps during a century or less.

Unit 3 was excavated on the rim of House 1, near a small "bomb crater" feature probably created during the use of the island by the U.S. Navy. All sediments were screened over 1/16-inch mesh. This unit contains at least two components. The first is a small deposit located near the base of the unit at a depth of roughly 50 cm, in a very dark brown

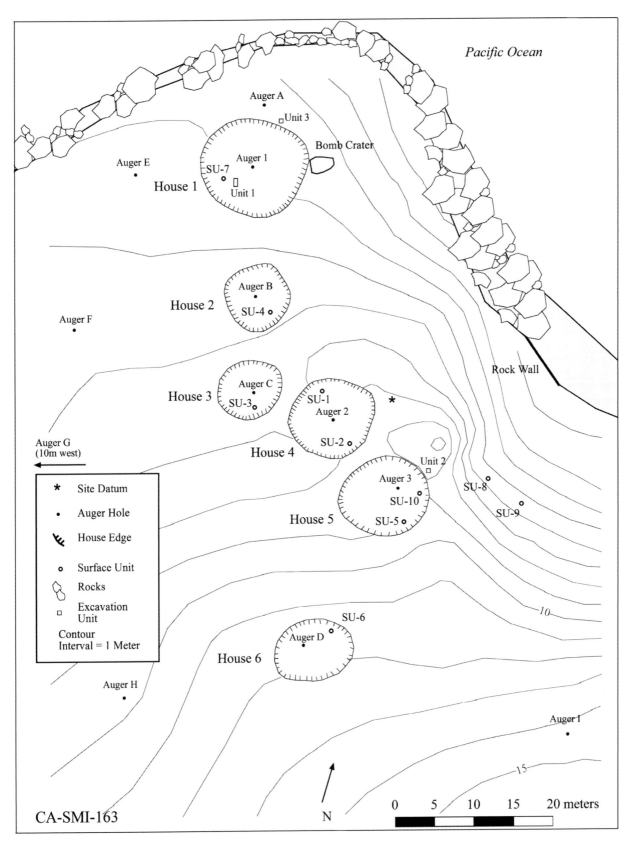

Figure 6.3. Map of SMI-163 showing location of house depressions, units, and auger holes.

(10YR2/2) sand. Most of the deposits were found in the upper 40 cm of the unit, in a dark brown (10YR3/3) sand. These appear to be some of the earliest deposits from the site (see below).

To supplement the data from Units 1, 2, and 3, I also excavated 10 surface units. These units were excavated in discrete areas (about 0.5 × 0.5 cm) of midden exposures disturbed by small rodent burrows or other erosional processes. Because these areas were disturbed, the depth of the materials is unknown but does not appear to be more than about 10 cm. Volume for the surface units was obtained using measured buckets, and all deposits were screened over 1/16-inch mesh. While the stratigraphic controls on these surface units were not as good as on the test units, they provide quantitative and volume-controlled data on the types of artifacts found in various houses and other areas of the site that were not deeply excavated. Twelve auger holes were also excavated around the site perimeter and in each of the six house depressions. Radiocarbon samples were pulled from each of these auger holes and dated, providing a chronology of the site occupation and dates for each of the houses. Here I focus on the data from Units 1 and 2 and all the surface units. These data provide evidence of human daily activities at the site during the Protohistoric and Historic periods.

Chronology

Fourteen ^{14}C dates from the excavation units and auger holes provide information on the antiquity and duration of the Chumash occupation of SMI-163 (Table 6.1). The earliest dates from the site were from a component at the base of Unit 3 dated to roughly 1200 cal BP (AD 750). Two separate AMS dates from a single California mussel shell yielded calibrated intercepts of 1260 and 1130 cal BP (AD 690 and 820), with an average of ca. 1200 cal BP. The vast majority of the site occupation, however, occurred between roughly 450 and 150 cal BP (AD 1500 and 1800), with 12 ^{14}C dates falling in this interval.

A ^{14}C date obtained from a *Mytilus* shell at the base of the House 1 deposits yielded a calibrated intercept of roughly 150 cal BP (AD 1800), suggesting that this house was occupied during the Historic period. The presence of needle-drilled *Olivella* wall beads in this unit supports the radiocarbon date. ^{14}C dates from the top and bottom of

Unit 2 in House 5, obtained on single black abalone and California mussel shells, produced intercepts of roughly 290 cal BP (AD 1660) for the base of the deposit and about 150 cal BP (AD 1800) for the top, suggesting occupation during the Protohistoric and Historic periods. No needle-drilled beads were found in this sample and the two surface units in House 5 (see below), and another date obtained from about 67 cm deep inside House 5 produced a calibrated intercept of 380 cal BP (AD 1570), suggesting that much of the occupation represented in this house is probably Protohistoric in age. The best estimate for the age of the materials for Unit 2 is probably the average of the two dates obtained for this unit, ca. 220 cal BP (AD 1730).

Two ^{14}C dates were also obtained from red abalone beads in production from Unit 2. Because most of the red abalone in the site deposits appears to be for making beads or fishhooks, these beads were dated to determine if people were collecting shells that were "fresh" or if they were obtaining shells that had washed up on the beach or from other nearby older archaeological sites. These beads yielded intercepts of 650 and 440 cal BP (AD 1300 and 1510), or roughly 150 to 500 years older than the dates obtained on subsistence remains from the same deposits. These data suggest that people sometimes used "old shells" to make beads.

Five ^{14}C dates were obtained from *in situ* samples removed from auger holes in unexcavated houses and peripheral site areas. A ^{14}C date from a shell obtained at a depth of 43 cm in a deposit that was at least 70 cm deep in House 3 produced a calibrated midpoint of 270 cal BP (AD 1680). Another ^{14}C date from a shell obtained at a depth of 64 cm and buried in a 20-cm-thick deposit in House 6 produced a calibrated intercept of 290 cal BP (AD 1660). A ^{14}C date on charcoal from a small probe in House 4 excavated by Kennett yielded an intercept of 380 cal BP (AD 1570). A final date from a shell obtained at 29 cm below the surface in a 40- to 50-cm-thick deposit in an auger hole in House 2 produced an intercept of 290 cal BP (AD 1660). Collectively, the dates from these auger holes, probes, and excavation units provide dates for all of the houses visible on the site surface. These data suggest that each of these houses was occupied primarily during the Protohistoric period, with Historic period dates obtained from Houses 1 and 5.

Table 6.1. Radiocarbon Dates from SMI-163.

Sample #	Provenience	Material	Uncorrected ^{14}C Age	^{13}C/^{12}C Adjusted Age	Calibrated Age Range (cal BP), 1 sigma	Calibrated Age Range (BC/AD), 1 sigma
OS-27183	Top of Unit 2, House 5	Black abalone	—	655 ± 60	270 (150) 0	AD 1690 (1800) 1950
Beta-145428	House 1, 25 cm	California mussel	330 ± 60	760 ± 60	270 (150) 0	AD 1690 (1800) 1950
OS-33376	House 3, auger C, 43 cm	California mussel	—	830 ± 25	290 (270) 240	AD 1660 (1680) 1710
OS-33375	House 6, auger D, 64 cm	California mussel	—	880 ± 35	320 (290) 270	AD 1630 (1660) 1680
OS-33417	Unit 2, ca. 110 cm, bottom of excavation	California mussel	—	880 ± 30	320 (290) 270	AD 1630 (1660) 1680
OS-33377	House 2, auger B, 29 cm	California mussel	—	885 ± 35	330 (290) 270	AD 1630 (1660) 1680
Beta-138430	House 5, auger 3, 67cm	Black abalone	510 ± 70	950 ± 70	450 (380) 290	AD 1500 (1570) 1670
OS-37142	Auger 2, ca. 40 cm	California mussel	—	955 ± 50	440 (390) 300	AD 1510 (1560) 1650
CAMS-14365	House 4, probe, 10 cm	Charcoal	310 ± 60	310 ± 60	470 (380) 300*	AD 1490 (1570) 1650
OS-34803	Unit 2 RAB 2, 70–80 cm	Red abalone BIP[a]	—	1010 ± 40	480 (440) 390	AD 1470 (1510) 1560
OS-34805	Unit 3, middle section, 27–28 cm	California mussel	—	1060 ± 35	500 (470) 440	AD 1450 (1480) 1510
OS-34802	Unit 2 RAB 1, 10-20 cm	Red abalone BIP[a]	—	1320 ± 30	680 (650) 630	AD 1270 (1300) 1320
OS-33374	Unit 3, 52-54 cm	California mussel	—	1790 ± 25	1170 (1130) 1060	AD 780 (820) 890
OS-33420	Duplicate of OS-33374	California mussel	—	1930 ± 30	1290 (1260) 1230	AD 660 (690) 720

Note: All dates were calibrated using Calib 4.3 (Stuiver and Reimer 1993, 2000), and applying a ΔR of 225 ± 35 years for all shell samples (see Kennett et al. 1997). ^{13}C/^{12}C ratios were determined by the radiocarbon labs, or an average of +430 years was applied (Erlandson 1988b).

[a] BIP = bead in production.

Additional ^{14}C dates were obtained on some of the sites in the surrounding area. These include dates ranging from ca. 5860 to 1350 cal BP (3910 BC and AD 600) from the SMI-161 site complex located to the south. SMI-159, a heavily vegetated shell midden deposit located adjacent to SMI-163, yielded a date of 925 ± 50 (OS-37140), with a calibrated intercept of 320 cal BP (AD 1630), and 1 sigma range of 420 to 280 cal BP (AD 1530–1670). This date corresponds with the occupation of SMI-163, suggesting that the village is probably larger than previously thought. Although no radiocarbon dates have been obtained from the midden or cem-

etery at adjacent SMI-162, the presence of *Olivella* thin-lipped, cup, and wall beads, and red abalone disk beads suggests that the site (or at least the cemetery) is roughly contemporaneous with SMI-163 and SMI-159.

ARTIFACTS

Unit 1

A relatively small sample of artifacts was recovered from 1/8-inch residuals in Unit 1 (Table 6.2). This is similar to the low density of faunal and other materials in this unit, suggesting that it most likely represents a relatively brief occupation during the

Table 6.2 Artifacts from Unit 1 at SMI-163 (1/8-inch).

Level (cm)	0–10	10–15	15–20	20–25	25–30	Total
Shell Artifacts						
Haliotis rufescens bead blank	—	—	1	—	—	1
H. rufescens bead	—	—	—	1	—	1
Olivella callus bead blank	—	—	—	1	—	1
Olivella callus cup bead	2	—	—	1	—	3
Olivella wall bead blank	—	—	1	6	1	8
Olivella wall BIP	—	—	—	1	—	1
Olivella wall bead	1	3	4	2	1	11
Olivella whole shell punched/drilled	—	—	—	1	1	2
Shell Subtotal	3	3	6	13	3	28
Bone Artifacts						
Mammal bone awl/gouge	—	—	1	—	—	1
Total	3	3	7	13	3	29

Historic period. Portions of these deposits may be material that slumped in from the house rim adjacent to the unit. Twenty-nine artifacts (156 per m³) were recovered, of which 28 (97 percent) were made from *Olivella* or red abalone shells, with only one bone artifact (3 percent). As in the samples from the other excavation units, *Olivella* artifacts dominate the assemblage, with 26 specimens (90 percent), including one callus bead blank, three callus beads, one wall bead in production, 11 wall beads, and two punched whole shells. Like other Historic period assemblages, wall beads, BIP, and blanks are more abundant than callus materials, making up 77 percent of the *Olivella* assemblage (see Arnold and Graesch 2001:82). *Olivella* detritus densities are also low for this assemblage with just 270 g per m³. One red abalone bead and one red abalone bead blank were also recovered, but these occur in considerably lower densities than in Unit 2 (see below). Of the total *Olivella* assemblage, four of the wall beads (36 percent) appear to have been drilled with a needle. Finally, a mammal bone awl or gouge that may have been used for a variety of functions (basketry, flaking, punching, etc.) was also recovered from the unit.

Unit 2

A much larger sample of artifacts was recovered from Unit 2 (Tables 6.3, 6.4). The abundant artifacts occur with an abundance of faunal remains, including some of the highest densities for all of the sites I excavated. A total of 651 artifacts (2420 per m³) was recovered from the unit, including 516 shell artifacts (1918 per m³), 100 chipped-stone artifacts (372 per m³), six bone artifacts (22 per m³), and 29 asphaltum impressions, tarring pebbles, or other artifacts (108 per m³). The 516 shell artifacts include 339 abalone artifacts, six California mussel artifacts, 165 *Olivella* artifacts, and 12 additional shell artifacts (Figure 6.4). These values do not include *Olivella* and red abalone bead-making detritus.

At SMI-163, artifacts made from red abalone dominate the assemblage. The majority of the abalone assemblage is made up of red abalone epidermis disk beads (n = 9), bead blanks (n = 132), and BIP (n = 164). Similar to a pattern noted by Arnold and Graesch (2001), virtually all of the red abalone shell from Unit 2 is broken, and most of it appears to be related to making artifacts. Numerous other artifacts appear to be preblanks, chipped/modified fragments, broken shell, and detritus also associated with bead making (Rick 2004a, 2004c). Analysis of 1/16-inch residuals from Unit 2 also suggests that many BIP are present in the smaller fraction. The low number of complete beads compared with BIP at SMI-163 appears to be related to two factors. First, there is a high incidence of breakage in red abalone beads, particularly during the drilling

Table 6.3. Shell Artifacts from Unit 2 at SMI-163 (1/8-inch).

Level (cm)	0–10	10–20	20–30	30–40	40–50	50–60	60–70	70–80	75–80	80–90	90–100	Total
Dentalium neohexagonum bead	—	—	—	—	—	—	—	—	—	1	—	1
Haliotis cracherodii bead blank	—	—	—	—	—	—	1	—	—	—	—	1
H. cracherodii ornament	—	—	—	1	—	—	—	—	—	—	—	1
H. cracherodii worked	1	—	22	1	—	—	—	—	—	—	—	24
H. rufescens bead blank	3	5	25	17	20	7	14	9	9	10	13	132
H. rufescens BIP[a]	20	1	27	23	3	11	55	16	4	1	3	164
H. rufescens bead	—	1	—	2	1	1	3	1	—	—	—	9
H. rufescens grooved-shank fishhook	—	—	—	—	—	1	—	—	—	—	—	1
H. spp. worked	—	—	1	1	5	—	—	—	—	—	—	7
Haliotis subtotal	24	7	75	45	29	20	73	26	13	11	16	339
Megathura crenulata worked	—	—	—	1	—	—	—	—	—	—	—	1
Mytilus disk bead blank	—	—	—	—	—	—	—	—	—	—	1	1
Mytilus disk bead	—	—	—	1	—	—	—	—	—	—	—	1
Mytilus disk BIP[a]	—	—	—	1	1	1	—	1	—	—	—	4
Olivella callus bead blank	1	—	3	4	3	2	3	1	—	4	—	21
Olivella callus BIP[a]	2	—	2	2	1	1	1	4	—	2	1	16
Olivella callus cup bead	1	—	3	2	2	8	3	1	2	1	3	26
Olivella full-lipped bead	—	—	—	—	—	1	—	—	—	—	—	1
Olivella thin-lipped bead	—	—	—	1	—	—	1	1	—	—	—	3
Olivella wall bead blank		1	9	15	4	4	4	5	—	—	3	45
Olivella wall BIP[a]	3	1	16	4	1	1	1	—	2	—	—	29
Olivella wall bead	3	2	7	5	—	—	1	—	—	—	—	18
Olivella spire-lopped bead	—	—	—	2	1	—	—	1	—	—	—	4
Olivella split punched bead	—	—	—	1	—	—	—	—	—	—	—	1
Olivella whole shell punched	—	—	—	—	—	1	—	—	—	—	—	1
Olivella subtotal	10	4	40	35	13	17	15	13	4	7	7	165
Shell undif. BIP[a]	—	—	—	1	1	1	—	—	—	—	—	3
Trivia californiana bead	—	—	1	—	—	—	—	—	—	—	—	1
Total	34	11	116	84	44	39	88	40	17	19	24	516

[a] BIP = bead in production.

phase (Arnold and Graesch 2001:91). Second, people residing at SMI-163 were probably making red abalone beads for exchange, with most of the complete beads traded to other locations. The abundance of red abalone beads, blanks, and BIP is not surprising at SMI-163, given the high proportion of "red abalone" middens (Glassow 1993a; Vellanoweth et al. 2006) on the island and the occurrence of this shell type in the generally cooler

waters surrounding San Miguel. As stated earlier, direct ^{14}C dating of two red abalone BIP indicates they are roughly 150 to 500 years older than the subsistence remains from the site, suggesting that in some cases people were probably collecting older shells from the beach, or perhaps from archaeological sites, to make red abalone beads.

In addition to red abalone bead-making artifacts, a red abalone grooved shank fishhook and

Table 6.4. Chipped-Stone, Bone, and Other Artifacts from Unit 2 at SMI-163 (1/8-inch).

Level	0–10	10–20	20–30	30–40	40–50	50–60	60–70	70–80	75–80	80–90	90–100	Total
Chipped- and Ground-Stone Artifacts												
Chert macrodrill	—	—	—	—	—	—	—	—	—	1	—	1
Chert biface frag.	—	—	—	—	—	—	—	—	—	—	1	1
Microblade core/ retouched	—	—	—	—	—	—	—	—	—	1	—	1
Trapezoidal microblade	—	—	—	—	—	—	1	—	—	1	2	4
Trapezoidal microdrill	—	—	—	—	—	—	1	1	—	—	—	2
Triangular prepared microblade	—	—	1	1	2	8	2	2	2	4	2	24
Triangular prepared microdrill	1	4	3	5	5	4	12	7	2	5	4	52
Triangular unprepared microblade	—	—	—	2	1	2	1	—	—	—	2	8
Triangular unprepared microdrill	—	—	—	—	—	2	2	2	—	—	—	6
Utilized/retouched flake	—	1	—	—	—	—	—	—	—	—	—	1
Subtotal	1	5	4	8	8	16	19	12	4	12	11	100
Bone Artifacts												
Bird bone awl/pin	1	—	—	—	—	—	1	—	—	—	—	2
Mammal bone awl	—	—	—	—	—	—	—	—	—	—	1	1
Worked mammal bone	—	—	—	—	—	1	—	—	—	—	—	1
Mammal bone barb or gorge fragment	—	—	—	—	—	—	—	—	—	1	—	1
Shark centrum bead	—	—	—	—	1	—	—	—	—	—	—	1
Subtotal	1	—	—	—	1	1	1	—	—	1	1	6
Other Artifacts												
Asphaltum w/ impressions	—	—	9	—	2	1	—	—	—	—	—	12
Asphaltum skirt weight or plug	1	—	—	—	—	—	—	—	—	—	1	2
Donut-stone fragment	—	—	—	—	—	—	—	—	1	—	—	1
Soapstone chunk	1	—	—	1	—	—	—	—	1	—	—	3
Tarring pebble	—	—	3	6	2	—	—	—	—	—	—	11
Subtotal	2	—	12	7	4	1	—	—	2	—	1	29
Total	4	5	16	15	13	18	20	12	6	13	13	135

seven pieces of worked abalone nacre were recovered in Unit 2. Twenty-four fragments of ground or chipped black abalone, one black abalone bead blank, and a black abalone drilled ornament were also recovered from the unit.

Olivella artifacts are the second most abundant type in the assemblage, with roughly 165 beads, BIP, and bead blanks. About 67 artifacts (41 percent of all *Olivella* artifacts) are from the callus portion of the shell, including 21 callus bead blanks, 16 callus

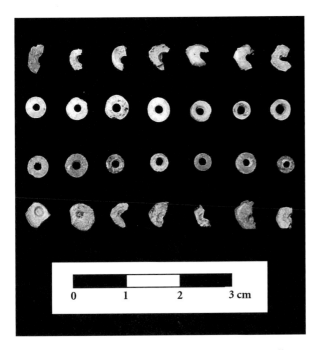

Figure 6.4. Shell beads from SMI-163. *(Top row)* Olivella wall beads (four, at left) and callus beads in production. *(Second row)* Olivella wall beads (four, at left) and callus-cup beads. *(Third row)* Red abalone disk beads. *(Bottom row)* Red abalone beads in production.

BIP, 26 callus cup beads, one full-lipped bead, and three thin-lipped beads. At least 92 artifacts (56 percent) made from the wall portion of the shell were recovered, including 45 wall bead blanks, 29 wall BIP, and 18 wall beads. The dominance of wall beads and bead-making artifacts over callus again illustrates the importance of wall beads in some postcontact sites. Four *Olivella* spire-lopped beads, one split punched bead, and a punched whole shell were also identified in the unit.

Olivella detritus was also found in Unit 2, including 1482.2 g (5510 g per m³). While this is a large amount of *Olivella* detritus, it is considerably smaller than similar aged deposits from Santa Cruz, Santa Rosa, or San Miguel islands, where densities are 10,000 g per m³ or higher (Arnold and Graesch 2001; Arnold and Muns 1994; Kennett and Conlee 2002). The production of *Olivella* artifacts appears to have been important for people living at SMI-163, but the moderate density of *Olivella* and high density of red abalone artifacts suggest that people were focused on making both red abalone and *Olivella* beads at the site. Interestingly, none of the *Olivella* wall beads or red abalone beads in Unit 2 have hole diameters that indicate they were needle-

drilled. This suggests that most of these deposits are probably Protohistoric in age. It is also possible that people on San Miguel Island may have had less access to needles because of their relative isolation. However, roughly 36 percent of the beads in Unit 1 were drilled with needles.

Other than abalone and *Olivella*, most other shell artifacts were recovered in relatively small numbers. Six California mussel shell artifacts were identified, including four disk BIP, one disk bead, and one disk blank. Mussel shell from the site was sorted quickly for bead-making artifacts, and a more detailed sort may provide slightly more mussel artifacts, but the small number of mussel beads and bead-making materials is consistent with findings from Santa Cruz Island that suggest California mussel beads were a relatively minor portion of the overall shell artifact assemblage (Arnold and Graesch 2001:104).

One *Dentalium neohexagonum* bead was also recovered from the unit. This is a relatively rare bead type in southern California, but the presence of *D. neohexagonum* rather than *D. pretiosum* in this Late site fits with C. King's (1990) chronology for this artifact type (see also Chapter 5; Erlandson et al. 2001a). Finally, three badly burned, undifferentiated shell BIP, one *Trivia californiana* punched-shell bead, and one fragment of worked *Megathura crenulata* shell were also recovered from the site.

Chipped-stone artifacts were the second most common material type found in Unit 2, including 100 artifacts (excluding debitage). Of the stone assemblage, 97 (97 percent of all chipped-stone artifacts) are microblades, microdrills, or microblade cores (Figure 6.5). Only one small microblade core was recovered, suggesting that the microblades were primarily being made elsewhere and then brought to the site or traded by other islanders. Most of the microblade assemblage is from triangular prepared microdrills (n = 52) and microblades (n = 24), making up about 78 percent of all microblades or microdrills. Only 20 microblades or microdrills were trapezoidal or unprepared blades. The presence of mostly prepared microblades is similar to patterns noted for Late period sites on Santa Cruz Island (Arnold 1987; Arnold et al. 2001:117; Preziosi 2001:159). One of the prepared microdrills is bipointed (see Figure 6.5). Other than microblades, chipped-stone artifacts are relatively rare, including one

Figure 6.5. Chert microblades (three, at left); and microdrills (three, at right) from SMI-163. All specimens are triangular prepared. Drill on far left is bipointed.

chert macrodrill, a chert biface fragment, and a utilized flake. All microblades appear to be made from Santa Cruz Island or Cico chert, but because of the small size of the specimens and macroscopic similarities between the material types (see Erlandson et al. 1997), the specific type of chert was not determined for microblades.

Bone artifacts are relatively rare in the Unit 2 deposits, with just six artifacts, including two bird bone awl/pins, a mammal bone awl, a mammal bone barb or gorge fragment, one fragment of worked mammal bone, and a shark centrum bead. Most of these artifacts probably had multiple functions, and some were for both utilitarian and ornamental purposes. Twenty-nine other artifacts were also recovered, including asphaltum artifacts and soapstone chunks. Twelve fragments of asphaltum with basketry impressions, 11 tarring pebbles, and an asphaltum skirt weight or plug were recovered, suggesting asphaltum was being used for waterproofing and other purposes. The only groundstone artifact recovered was a small donut-stone fragment. Finally, three exotic soapstone chunks were identified in the unit and were acquired through trade.

Surface Units

To provide data on the amount and type of artifacts present in the other houses, ten surface units were excavated in areas disturbed by erosion or rodent tailings (see Figure 6.3). To excavate these units, disturbed materials were scraped into a bucket using a trowel. The depth of these materials is unknown, but probably was no more than about 10 cm. Each of these surface units was about 0.5 × 0.5 m in area, with all sediments screened over 1/16-inch mesh. Only formal artifacts were collected from these surface units, and volume was obtained using measured buckets, with all of the surface units producing volumes of 6 liters (.006 m^3), except for Units 3 and 4, which were 4 liters (.004 m^3). Although these surface units were relatively small, 132 shell, chipped-stone, bone, and asphaltum artifacts (2,357 per m^3) were recovered (Table 6.5). All of the surface units produced formal artifacts, except for SU-6 located in House 6, which contained *Olivella* detritus but no formal artifacts.

SU-1 and -2 were located in House 4 and yielded 49 artifacts, including red abalone bead blanks and BIP, *Olivella* beads, blanks, and BIP, and other artifacts. One of the wall beads from SU-1 and two of the wall beads in SU-2 appear to have been drilled using a needle, the only needle-drilled beads from the surface units. SU-3 was located in House 3 and produced only four artifacts, and SU-4, located in House 2, provided just seven artifacts. SU-5 and SU-10 were located in House 5 near Unit 2 and produced 48 artifacts, including red abalone and *Olivella* bead making artifacts, a California mussel bead and fishhook, and other artifacts. SU-7, located in House 1 near Unit 1, produced only one *Olivella* cup bead and

Table 6.5. Artifacts from Surface Units at SMI-163 (1/16-inch).

Surface Unit	1	2	3	4	5	7	8	9	10	Total
Shell Artifacts										
H. rufescens bead blank	1	1	—	1	2	—	—	—	3	8
H. rufescens BIP	2	11	—	—	9	—	1	—	6	29
H. rufescens bead	—	—	—	1	1	—	—	—	—	2
H. spp. ornament	—	—	—	—	—	—	—	—	1	1
Haliotis subtotal	3	12	—	2	12	—	1	—	10	40
Mytilus disk bead	—	—	—	—	2	—	—	1	—	3
Mytilus disk BIP	—	—	—	—	—	—	—	1	2	3
Mytilus fishhook	—	—	—	—	1	—	—	—	1	2
Mytilus fishhook in production	—	—	—	1	—	—	—	—	—	1
Mytilus subtotal	—	—	—	1	3	—	—	2	3	9
Olivella callus bead blank	3	1	—	—	3	—	6	—	2	15
Olivella callus BIP	—	—	—	—	—	—	1	—	—	1
Olivella callus cup bead	—	—	—	1	—	1	1	—-	1	4
Olivella thin-lipped bead	—	—	—	—	—	—	—	—	2	2
Olivella wall bead blank	7	11	—	—	3	—	4	—	3	28
Olivella wall BIP	1	4	—	2	—	—	1	2	—	10
Olivella wall bead	3	3	2	1	—	—	1	—	3	13
Olivella spire-lopped bead	—	—	1	—	—	—	—	—	—	1
Olivella split punched bead	—	—	—	—	1	—	—	—	—	1
Olivella subtotal	14	19	3	4	7	1	14	2	11	75
Subtotal	17	31	3	7	22	1	15	4	24	124
Chipped-Stone Artifacts										
Triangular prepared microblade	—	—	—	—	—	—	—	1	1	2
Triangular prepared microdrill	—	—	—	—	1	—	—	1	—	2
Triangular unprepared microblade	—	—	1	—	—	—	—	—	—	1
Subtotal	—	—	1	—	1	—	—	2	1	5
Bone Artifacts										
Mammal bone medium barb	—	—	—	—	—	—	1	—	—	1
Other Artifacts										
Asphaltum w/impressions	—	1	—	—	—	—	—	1	—	2
Total	17	32	4	7	23	1	16	7	25	132

no other artifacts. Both SU-8 and SU-9 were located in dense deposits along the hillside in the northeastern site area and yielded 23 artifacts, including a mammal bone barb and numerous shell bead making artifacts.

Collectively, the surface units yielded an artifact assemblage similar to the two excavation units.

These data suggest that the Protohistoric and Historic period occupants of SMI-163 were engaged in the production of *Olivella* and red abalone beads, with all of the units (including SU-6 which produced detritus) containing *Olivella* beads, BIP, bead blanks, or detritus. Six of the surface units (SU-1, -2, -4, -5, -8, and -10) contain evidence of red abalone bead making, suggesting that people in Houses 2, 4, 5, and the east slope were involved in making red abalone beads. The presence of a red abalone bead and blank in Unit 1 suggests that people in House 1 were also at least partially engaged in this industry. Finally, subsistence tools in the surface units are relatively rare, with just two mussel fishhooks, a mussel shell fishhook in production, and a bone barb. This is consistent with findings in Units 1 and 2; only one mammal bone barb or gorge and a red abalone fishhook were recovered in Unit 2, and no definitive subsistence artifacts were identified in Unit 1. Surface collections from elsewhere on the site were limited because of generally dense vegetation cover. A red abalone grooved shank fishhook, California mussel fishhook blank, and a bone barb were the only other definitive subsistence artifacts recovered, suggesting these are fairly widely distributed in the deposits (Figure 6.6).

SUBSISTENCE STRATEGIES

Faunal remains, including shellfish, fish, bird, and mammal remains, were the most abundant materials recovered in the excavation units. All of the faunal remains are from 1/8-inch residuals of the excavated units. Following the previous chapters, I discuss shellfish and invertebrate remains for both units, followed by fish, mammal, and bird remains. Like many of the previous units, there is little difference in the abundance of various taxa through time. Consequently, I focus on describing the faunal samples for each unit as a whole (see Rick 2004a for a breakdown of individual levels).

Shellfish and Invertebrates

UNIT 1

Only about 1.7 kg of shellfish and other invertebrate remains were recovered from Unit 1 (Table 6.6). Except for 13.4 g of land snail (< 1 percent), all of the remains are marine in origin. Preservation of the assemblage was generally good, but relatively few whole shell valves were recovered. At least 23 different shellfish taxa from a minimum of 324 individuals were identified in the sample. Most of these are from rocky intertidal taxa. Relatively little change in the abundance of the shellfish taxa was noted in the various levels.

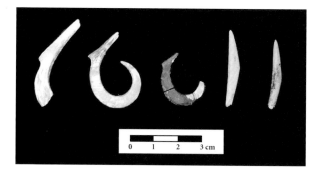

Figure 6.6. Abalone (two, at left) and mussel shell fishhooks and bone barbs from SMI-163.

California mussel is the dominant shellfish taxon represented in the sample, making up about 76 percent of the total weight and 54 percent of the MNI. Black abalone contribute about 4 percent of the weight and 2 percent of the MNI, and red abalone about 2 percent of the weight and MNI. Platform mussels provide only about 0.6 percent of the weight, but around 9 percent of the MNI. Turban shells make up about 2 percent of the total shell weight, but over 7 percent of the MNI. Small limpets contribute only about 0.3 percent of the weight, but over 13 percent of the MNI. These small limpets, along with barnacles (Barnacle undif. and *Pollicipes polymerus*), were probably brought to the site as incidental riders rather than as food sources. *Olivella*, which was probably brought to the site exclusively or primarily for bead making, makes up 3 percent of the total shell weight. All other taxa appear to have been relatively minor constituents, generally making up less than about 2 percent of the total sample.

UNIT 2

Unit 2 produced roughly 88 kg of shell, the largest and most diverse shellfish sample from all of the sites that I excavated (Table 6.7). At least 40 taxa from a minimum of 19,530 individuals were recovered. Of the 40 taxa, 99.9 percent were from marine species. Preservation of the Unit 2 sample was exceptional, with numerous whole and well-preserved mussel shells, including many specimens that still had the mussel periostracum present.

The sample is dominated by California mussel, with about 80 percent of the shell weight and 70 percent of the MNI. Most other shellfish represented in the assemblage appear to be of relatively minor

Table 6.6. Shellfish and Invertebrate Remains from Unit 1 at SMI-163 (0–40 cm).

Taxon	Wt.	% Wt.	MNI	% MNI
Barnacle undif.	48.1	2.9	—	—
Calliostoma spp. (top snails)	0.3	< 0.1	1	0.3
Chiton undif.	1.1	0.1	—	—
Corallina spp. (coralline algae)	0.1	< 0.1	—	—
Crab undif.	7.6	0.5	—	—
Crepidula spp. (slipper shells)	0.3	< 0.1	3	0.9
Cryptochiton stelleri (gumboot chiton)	8.0	0.5	—	—
Fissurella volcano (volcano limpet)	1.3	0.1	2	0.6
Gastropod undif.	1.2	0.1	6	1.9
Haliotis cracherodii (black abalone)	62.3	3.8	7	2.2
Haliotis rufescens (red abalone)	31.2	1.9	5	1.5
Haliotis spp. (abalone undif.)	15.5	0.9	4	1.2
Land snail	13.4	0.8	25	7.7
Limpet undif.	4.7	0.3	42	13.0
Lottia gigantea (owl limpet)	0.7	< 0.1	1	0.3
Megathura crenulata (giant keyhole limpet)	0.3	< 0.1	1	0.3
Mytilus californianus (California mussel)	1251.3	75.7	176	54.3
Nacre undif.	71.2	4.3	—	—
Olivella biplicata (purple olive)	50.3	3.0	—	—
Pollicipes polymerus (gooseneck barnacle)	3.1	0.2	—	—
Protothaca staminea (Pacific littleneck)	3.9	0.2	—	—
Septifer bifurcatus (platform mussel)	10.4	0.6	28	8.6
Serpulorbis squamigerus (scaled worm snail)	4.3	0.3	—	—
Strongylocentrotus spp. (sea urchins)	5.5	0.3	—	—
Tegula funebralis (black turban)	20.3	1.2	12	3.7
Tegula spp. (turban undif.)	11.4	0.7	11	3.4
Undif. shell	24.5	1.5	—	—
Total	1652.3	—	324	—

Note: Based on 1/8-inch recovery and all weights in grams. Volume = 0.186 m^3.

significance. Black abalone makes up 3 percent of the weight, but less than 1 percent of the MNI. Platform mussels contribute just 1 percent of the weight, but 9 percent of the MNI. Black turban is also relatively limited, constituting about 4 percent of the weight and MNI. Red abalone supplies about 1 percent of the weight and less than 1 percent of the MNI. Moreover, most of the red abalone shell fragments in the sample are highly fragmented or broken pieces that were probably used for making beads or other artifacts. *Olivella*, which was also used primarily for making beads, contributed about 2 per-

cent of the shell weight. Small barnacles (Barnacle undif. and *Pollicipes polymerus*) make up about 5 percent of the total shell weight, but were probably collected as by-products. Small limpets also make up less than 1 percent of the shell weight, but about 12 percent of the MNI. Many of these, too, were probably collected incidentally and were not a targeted resource. Less than 1 percent of the entire assemblage is made up of *Tivela stultorum* (Pismo clam) and *Saxidomus nuttallii* (Washington clam) that were probably obtained from sandy beach habitats in Cuyler Harbor or washed up on the beach.

Table 6.7. Shellfish and Invertebrate Remains from Unit 2 at SMI-163.

Taxon	Wt.	% Wt.	MNI	% MNI
Barnacle undif.	3432.9	3.9	—	—
Calliostoma spp. (top snails)	1.9	< 0.1	10	0.1
Chiton undif.	218.6	0.2	—	—
Clam undif.	6.4	< 0.1	4	<0.1
Collisella spp. (limpets)	14.3	< 0.1	9	<0.1
Conus californicus (California cone)	0.2	< 0.1	1	<0.1
Corallina spp. (coralline algae)	4.7	< 0.1	—	—
Coronula diadema (whale barnacle)	0.2	< 0.1	1	<0.1
Crab undif.	354.8	0.4	—	—
Crepidula spp. (slipper shells)	18.1	< 0.1	134	0.7
Cryptochiton stelleri (gumboot chiton)	328.2	0.4	—	—
Dendraster excentricus (sand dollar)	3.6	< 0.1	—	—
Diodora aspera (rough keyhole limpet)	1.0	< 0.1	1	< 0.1
Fissurella volcano (volcano limpet)	6.1	< 0.1	24	0.1
Gastropod undif.	16.7	< 0.1	217	1.1
Glans subquadrata (eccentric ribbed clam)	0.4	< 0.1	8	< 0.1
Haliotis cracherodii (black abalone)	2510.5	2.9	151	0.8
Haliotis rufescens (red abalone)	929.4	1.1	21	0.1
Haliotis spp. (abalone undif.)	311.6	0.4	5	< 0.1
Hiatella arctica (Arctic rock borer)	1.0	< 0.1	11	0.1
Hinnites multirugosus (giant rock scallop)	3.3	< 0.1	2	<0.1
Land snail	23.3	< 0.1	167	0.9
Limpet undif.	149.6	0.2	2402	12.3
Lottia gigantea (owl limpet)	317.0	0.4	83	0.4
Megathura crenulata (giant keyhole limpet)	0.8	< 0.1	11	0.1
Mytilus californianus (California mussel)	70,452.8	80.1	13,578	69.5
Nacre undif.	1040.7	1.2	—	—
Norrisia norrisii (Norris top)	1.1	< 0.1	1	< 0.1
Nucella spp. (dogwinkles)	23.1	< 0.1	57	0.3
Olivella biplicata (purple olive)	1482.2	1.7	—	—
Pectinidae (scallops)	1.9	< 0.1	5	<0.1
Pelecypod	2.1	< 0.1	9	<0.1
Pododesmus cepio (pearly monia)	0.7	< 0.1	—	—
Pollicipes polymerus (gooseneck barnacle)	747.9	0.9	—	—
Protothaca staminea (Pacific littleneck)	8.2	< 0.1	36	0.2
Saxidomus nuttalli (Washington clam)	60.4	0.1	2	< 0.1
Septifer bifurcatus (platform mussel)	758.8	0.9	1687	8.6
Serpulorbis squamigerus (scaled worm snail)	16.7	< 0.1	—	—
Strongylocentrotus spp. (sea urchins)	467.1	0.5	—	—
Tegula brunnea (brown turban)	64.9	0.1	31	0.2
Tegula funebralis (black turban)	3904.0	4.4	811	4.2
Tegula spp. (turban undif.)	132.3	0.2	42	0.2
Tivela stultorum (Pismo clam)	1.4	< 0.1	1	< 0.1
Trivia californiana (coffee bean)	1.4	< 0.1	8	< 0.1
Undif. shell	106.9	0.1	—	—
Total	87,929.2	—	19,530	—

Note: Based on 1/8-inch recovery from 0–100 cm and all weights in grams. Volume = 0.269 m^3.

Fish

UNIT 1

Only about 15.5 g and 175 specimens of fish bone were recovered from Unit 1 (Table 6.8), reflecting the relatively low density of bone from this unit. At least five teleost taxa and one undifferentiated elasmobranch were identified. Of the identified fish remains, nine rockfish bones (MNI = 1), 13 surfperch bones (MNI = 1), two California sheephead bones, three clupeid bones (MNI = 1), and one sculpin bone (MNI = 1) were identified. These fishes are similar to those recovered from the other sites and in Unit 2. Most of the fish are probably cultural in origin, but it is possible that some of the clupeid and sculpin bones may have been deposited by sea birds or other animals. Most of these fishes could have been captured using hook and line, spears, or nets.

UNIT 2

In Unit 2, 4.3 kg of fish bone were recovered. Because of the large size of the fish bone sample, 811.6 g and 9391 fish bones were analyzed from 1/8-inch residuals in the 10 to 20 cm, 50 to 60 cm, and 90 to 100 cm levels, providing an analyzed subsample from near the top, middle, and bottom of this unit (Table 6.9). All of the other levels were rough sorted for elements not encountered in the analyzed levels, but no major differences in the assemblage were noted. Because the relative importance of the various fish taxa in these levels is fairly similar, these subsamples provide a reliable estimate of the types and abundance of the various fishes present in the entire unit. Like the shellfish sample, the preservation of fish bone was outstanding, with numerous whole bones and fish scales. Thirteen percent of the analyzed sample by NISP (n = 1204), but 32 percent of the weight was identifiable to family, genus, or species.

Rockfish are the most abundant taxon in the sample, with 72 to 75 percent of the weight and NISP, and about 50 percent of the MNI. Surfperch, including pile perch, are the next most abundant category, providing about 14 percent of the NISP and 11 percent of the MNI. The relatively heavy bones of cabezon and sheephead contribute about 11 percent of the fish weight and MNI, but less than 4 percent of the NISP. Lingcod are also present in the sample, making up 5 to 6 percent of the MNI and weight and 2 percent of the NISP. A few barracuda and mackerel remains were also recovered, but generally contribute less than 1 percent of the NISP. What are probably small, burned fragments of a billfish beak were identified in several of the levels, including four fragments in the analyzed sample (0.3 percent of NISP). Most other fish appear to be of relatively minor significance.

The fish bones present in Unit 2 suggest that people were primarily exploiting nearby kelp forest and rocky nearshore habitats. The presence of billfish, and possibly barracuda and mackerel, suggests that offshore environments requiring sturdy

Table 6.8. Fish Remains from Unit 1 at SMI-163.

Taxon	Wt.	% Wt.[a]	NISP	% NISP	MNI	% MNI
Clupeidae (sardines)	0.2	3.8	3	10.7	1	16.7
Cottidae (sculpin)	0.3	5.8	1	3.6	1	16.7
Embiotocidae (surfperch)	0.9	17.3	13	46.4	1	16.7
Labridae						
Semmicossyphus pulcher (California sheephead)	0.9	17.3	2	7.1	1	16.7
Scorpaenidae						
Sebastes spp.	2.9	55.8	9	32.1	1	16.7
Teleost undif.	8.5	—	146	—		
Elasmobranch undif.	1.8	—	1	—	1	16.7
Total	15.5	—	175	—	6	—

Note: Based on 1/8-inch recovery from (0–40 cm) and all weights in grams. Volume = 0.186 m[3].

[a] Percentages based on specimens identified to family, genus, and species.

Table 6.9. Fish Remains from Unit 2 at SMI-163.

Taxon	Wt.	% Wt. [a]	NISP	% NISP	MNI	% MNI
Teleost						
Clinidae (kelpfish)	< 0.1	< 0.1	2	0.2	1	1.6
Clupeidae (sardines)	0.1	< 0.1	10	0.8	2	3.2
Cottidae (sculpin)	< 0.1	< 0.1	2	0.2	1	1.6
Scorpaenichthys marmoratus (cabezon)	22.1	8.5	35	2.9	4	6.3
Embiotocidae (surfperches)	14.8	5.7	146	12.1	6	9.5
Damalichthys vacca (pile perch)	2.7	1.0	27	2.2	1	1.6
Hexagrammidae (greenlings)	< 0.1	< 0.1	1	0.1	1	1.6
Ophiodon elongatus (lingcod)	14.7	5.7	27	2.2	3	4.8
Labridae (senorita or wrasse)	0.4	0.2	18	1.5	2	3.2
Semicossyphus pulcher (California sheephead)	6.9	2.7	7	0.6	3	4.8
Mackerel undif.	0.3	0.1	5	0.4	2	3.2
Pomacentridae						
Chromis punctipinnis (blacksmith)?	0.1	< 0.1	1	0.1	1	1.6
Scorpaenidae						
Sebastes spp. (rockfish)	188.1	72.3	897	74.5	31	49.2
Sphyraenidae (barracudas)						
Sphyraena argentea (California barracuda)	1.7	0.7	3	0.2	2	3.2
Stichaeidae (prickleback)	0.9	0.3	19	1.6	2	3.2
Xiphiidae/Istiophoridae (swordfishes, billfishes)?	6.9	2.7	4	0.3	1	1.6
Teleost undif.	550.5	—	8182	—	—	—
Subtotal	810.5	—	9386	—	—	—
Elasmobranch						
Elasmobranch undif.	1.1	—	5	—	—	—
Total	811.6	—	9391	—	63	—

Note: Based on 1/8-inch recovery and all weights in grams. Categories noted with a ? mark are tentative identifications. Volume = 0.085 m^3.

[a] Percentages based on specimens identified to family, genus, and species.

watercraft were also occasionally used. Some of the surfperches and other taxa may also have been obtained from sandy beaches. The presence of circular shell fishhooks suggests that people relied heavily on hook and line to capture fish. Nets may also have been used to catch smaller fish, while harpoons were probably used to capture billfish and other large taxa.

Mammals

UNIT 1

Mammal bones are relatively rare in the Unit 1 deposits, consisting primarily of small undiagnostic fragments. Twenty-eight bones weighing 7.1 g appear to be small fragments of marine mammal bones. Four bones weighing about 1 g are from small rodents, probably deer mice. An artiodactyl tooth, probably from a sheep that grazed historically on the island, was also found in the top of the unit. About 2.2 g of undifferentiated bone is probably mammal bone, but all of these bones are very small and fragmentary, precluding more precise identification.

UNIT 2
Six hundred and fifty mammal bones weighing 452.2 g were recovered from Unit 2 (Table 6.10). Preservation of the sample is excellent. Marine mammals, including sea otter, Guadalupe fur seal, northern fur seal, and harbor seal were identified, along with a few rodent remains and probable splinters of large land mammal bones (e.g., deer). As in samples from other Channel Islands sites, the vast majority of the mammal bones are small, fragmentary pieces of cancellous or cortical bone that are probably from marine mammals. Consequently, less than 10 percent of the assemblage by NISP was identified to specific categories, but roughly 56 percent by weight was identifiable.

Of the 29 marine mammal remains identified, over 40 percent are from otariids, including Guadalupe fur seal (6.5 percent), northern fur seal (2.2 percent), and undifferentiated otariid (32.6 percent). One sea otter bone was identified (2.2 percent), and one harbor seal bone was also present (2.2 percent). Eight bones were identified as pinniped (17.4 percent). Twelve rodent bones (26.1 percent) and five fragments of what are probably large land mammal (e.g., deer) bones were also identified. Large land mammal bone may have been acquired through trade with the mainland. People living at SMI-163 may have hunted or scavenged marine mammals or acquired them from other people living on San Miguel Island.

Birds
Bird bones are relatively rare in Unit 1, consisting of about 16 g and 19 bird bones. Most of these are fragmentary or undiagnostic specimens. Five specimens were identified to specific taxa, including 1 California gull bone, 1 Brandt's/Double-crested cormorant bone, and 3 pelagic cormorant bones.

In Unit 2, 422 bird bones were recovered, the most from any of the sites that I excavated (Table 6.11). Nineteen percent of the Unit 2 NISP were identified to species. The assemblage is dominated by alcids and cormorant remains, with both taxa accounting for between about 50 percent each of the total identified NISP. At least 11 individuals are present in the sample, including three Brandt's/Double-crested cormorants, two pelagic cormorants, three Cassin's auklets, a pigeon guillemot, a Xantus' murrelet, and a rhinoceros auklet. The abundance of bird bones from the site suggests that people may have been obtaining some birds from Prince Island, where numerous birds, including alcids and cormorants, currently breed (Guthrie 1980; Schoenherr et al. 1999:272). The presence of one bone that may be from an immature or flightless Cassin's auklet supports this contention. Birds were probably hunted and scavenged for subsistence, for making bone tools, or for their feathers or skins.

Dietary Reconstruction
For Unit 1 (1/8-inch), dietary reconstructions demonstrate that shellfish contributed about 40 percent of the meat yield, fish 30 percent, marine mammals 12 percent, and birds 17 percent. When just fish and shellfish are compared, fish contribute 43 percent of the meat and shellfish about 57 percent. The high proportion of shellfish in the Unit 1 deposits contrasts with most Late or Historic period island sites, where fish usually supply over 80 percent of the total meat yield (see Kennett and Conlee 2002). The importance of shellfish in this assemblage may reflect the small excavated sample and low density of faunal remains inside of the house depression, with many of the faunal remains slumped in from the adjacent house rim.

Dietary reconstructions for Unit 2 (1/8-inch) show a heavier reliance on marine fishes. Fishes make up about 74 percent of the total meat yield, followed by shellfish (18 percent) and marine mammals (7 percent), with birds providing only trace amounts (1.2 percent). When just fish and shellfish are compared, fish make up about 81 percent and shellfish about 19 percent. The values from Unit 2 are generally comparable to other sites of this age (Colten and Arnold 1998; Kennett and Conlee 2002; Noah 2005; Rick 2004a).

DISCUSSION
The faunal remains, artifacts, and chronological data from SMI-163 provide substantial evidence of a large Chumash community at the site during the

Table 6.10. Mammal Remains from Unit 2 at SMI-163.

	Wt.	% Wt.[a]	NISP	% NISP	MNI	% MNI
Carnivora						
Enhydra lutris (sea otter)	14.0	5.5	1	2.2	1	12.5
Pinniped	66.2	25.8	8	17.4	—	—
Otariidae	86.4	33.7	15	32.6	1	12.5
Arctocephalus townsendi (Guadalupe fur seal)	49.3	19.2	3	6.5	1	12.5
Callorhinus ursinus (northern fur seal)	16.3	6.4	1	2.2	1	12.5
Phocidae						
Phoca vitulina (harbor seal)	15.9	6.2	1	2.2	1	12.5
Subtotal	248.1	96.8	29	63.0	5	62.5
Rodent	0.2	0.1	12	26.1	2	25.0
Large land mammal?	7.9	3.1	5	10.9	1	12.5
Mammal undif.[b]	195.2	—	595	—	—	—
Undif. bone	0.8	—	9	—	—	—
Subtotal	204.1	—	621	—	3	37.5
Total	452.2	—	650	—	8	—

Note: Based on 1/8-inch recovery from 0–100 cm and all weights in grams. Categories noted with a ? mark are tentative identifications. Volume = 0.269 m^3.

[a] Percentages based on specimens identified to family, genus, and species.

[b] Mammal undif. assumed to be largely sea mammal bone.

Table 6.11. Bird Remains from Unit 2 at SMI-163.

Taxon	Wt.	% Wt.[a]	NISP	% NISP	MNI	% MNI
Alcidae (auklets)	0.1	0.1	1	1.2	—	—
Cepphus columba (pigeon guillemot)	1.7	2.4	3	3.7	1	9.1
Cerorhinca monocerata (rhinoceros auklet)	1.0	1.4	3	3.7	1	9.1
Ptychoramphus aleuticus (Cassin's auklet)	4.9	6.9	29	35.8	3	27.3
Synthliboramphus hypoleucus (Xantus' murrelet)	0.9	1.3	6	7.4	1	9.1
Phalacrocoracidae						
Phalacrocorax spp. (Brandt's/Double-crested cormorant)	57.9	81.2	33	40.7	3	27.3
Phalacrocorax pelagicus (pelagic cormorant)	4.8	6.7	6	7.4	2	18.2
Aves undif.	66.5	—	341	—	—	—
Total	137.8	—	422	—	11	—

Note: Based on 1/8-inch recovery from 0–100 cm and all weights in grams. Volume = 0.269 m^3.

[a] Percentages based on specimens identified to family, genus, and species.

Late, Protohistoric, and Historic periods, and limited evidence for occupation during the late Middle period. The site also appears to be closely related to adjacent SMI-159 and SMI-162, and probably to other sites (e.g., SMI-160) in the area, suggesting that this village may have been considerably larger than previously believed. Although early researchers who visited and excavated a cemetery in the area found glass beads, the location of this cemetery is unclear (Heye 1921:159). The available data from SMI-163 strongly support the earlier assertions of Kennett (2005) that the SMI-163 site complex is the village of *Tuqan*. Radiocarbon dates from the site support this proposition, indicating that each of the six visible house depressions contains a Protohistoric or Historic occupation.

The Chumash of *Tuqan* were clearly involved in a number of important activities, including the production of *Olivella* and red abalone beads and a variety of marine subsistence activities. Since relatively few complete red abalone beads, but high proportions of BIP, bead blanks, and detritus were present, it is likely that people were making these beads primarily for exchange with other islanders or people on the mainland (Rick 2004c). The dearth of glass beads and other historic artifacts at SMI-163 differs from Historic period deposits on Santa Cruz Island where a wide variety of historic artifacts (glass beads, metal fishhooks, bronze crucifixes, etc.) were recovered (Graesch 2001). It is possible that the more remote location of San Miguel Island may have limited the traffic of these exotic goods. It is also possible that because much of SMI-163 dates between the sixteenth and mid-eighteenth centuries, with only a few dates extending into the Mission period, much of the site was abandoned prior to the mass movement of historic goods.

The subsistence data from the site are similar to those from other Late or Historic period villages, where nearshore kelp forest and rocky shore fishes dominate the assemblage, and shellfish, birds, and marine mammals are less abundant (Colten 1993, 2001; Kennett 2005; Noah 2005; Pletka 2001a). In general, however, the types of resources found at the site are similar to those found at SMI-468 and SMI-481, although both of these sites produced more marine mammal remains. These similarities, however, suggest continuity in subsistence practices between the late Middle, Transitional, Late, and Historic periods for the Island Chumash.

Only 34 baptisms are recorded for people who resided at *Tuqan* (J. Johnson 1999a:53). The presence of at least six houses, and probably additional houses buried under midden, dune sand, and vegetation on the eastern site margin, and at SMI-159 and other adjacent sites, suggests that this village may have been considerably larger than indicated by ethnohistoric data. Introduced diseases probably took a heavy toll on people living at SMI-163 during Mission times. Given that this may have been where Cabrillo wintered in 1542–1543, such diseases might have been introduced earlier (Erlandson and Bartoy 1995). Plank canoes that may have been shipwrecked while transporting Chumash to the missions probably also led to underestimating the population of *Tuqan* (see Hudson et al. 1978; J. Johnson 1999a). The radiocarbon chronology for the site suggests that the village was occupied primarily in the latter portions of the Protohistoric period, and needle-drilled beads and other historic artifacts are relatively rare. These data suggest that the occupation of this village may have been in decline prior to the onset of the Historic period.

SMI-470: SITE SETTING, CONTEXT

Located adjacent to SMI-481, SMI-470 is part of the complex of sites located in the Otter Harbor area that includes SMI-468 (Figure 6.7). The site covers an area about 100 × 75 m and, according to Kritzman (1966, unpublished site record), included what appeared to be two house depressions or excavated areas. I have mapped four to five house depressions at the site (Figure 6.8), much of which is well vegetated, making surface visibility relatively poor. However, shell midden exposures are visible in the sea cliff and along the creek edge where the deposits are about 1 to 2 m deep and include an earlier roughly 4,000-year-old deposit. Freshwater is available in an adjacent creek and from a variety of springs in the area.

As stated previously, archaeological and ethnohistoric data suggest that SMI-470 is the probable location of *Niwoyomi*, one of the two named villages for San Miguel Island. Only a single household is represented in the mission registers for *Niwoyomi*, suggesting this may have been a relatively small community (J. Johnson 1999a). Until now, however, little was known about the occupation of SMI-470 or *Niwoyomi*.

Figure 6.7. SMI-470 site setting.

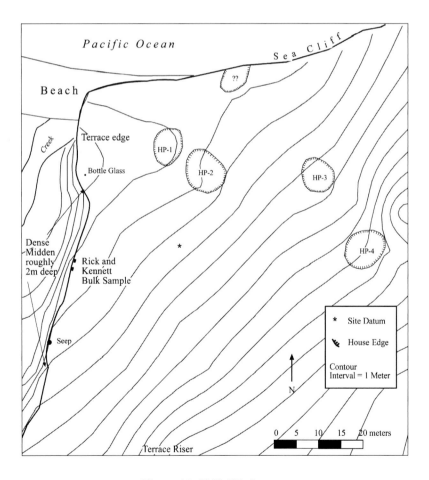

Figure 6.8. SMI-470 site map.

Field Research, Stratigraphy, and Chronology

During the summer of 2000, I collected ^{14}C samples and a bulk sample of midden constituents for general comparison with other San Miguel sites. I also visited the site in 2001 to make a laser transit map and assess the status of the midden deposits in the creek exposures. A 32-liter (.032 m^3) bulk sample was excavated in a roughly 40-cm-deep exposure in the creek bank. Because no stratigraphic distinctions were noted, this bulk sample was divided into two levels: upper (0 to 20 cm) and lower (20 to 40 cm) and screened over 1/16-inch mesh. Two ^{14}C samples were removed *in situ* from the top of the exposure and from a depth of 40 cm. The midden constituents are relatively dense and homogeneous with no evidence of any soil change, except for a break between the Late and Middle Holocene components. The excavated Late Holocene deposits are situated in a dark gray (10YR4/1) sandy loam throughout the excavated area.

Five radiocarbon dates suggest that SMI-470 has three components (Table 6.12). The oldest site occupation is represented by a low-density and highly fragmented shell midden that is situated about 2 m deep in the creek exposure. Kennett (1998) radiocarbon dated this deposit to 4220 cal BP (2270 BC). Located above this deposit and separated by sterile soils is a dense midden deposit, containing abundant *Olivella*, fish bone, and marine shellfish. Kennett (1998) obtained a date from this deposit and another from the sea cliff that produced calibrated intercepts of ca. 130 cal BP (AD 1820), suggesting that at least portions of the site were historic in age. I obtained two samples *in situ* from the bulk sample exposure. A date from the top of this exposure yielded an intercept of 420 cal BP (AD 1530), and one from the bottom produced an intercept of about 300 cal BP (AD 1660). These dates overlap at 1 sigma, and the best age estimate for the bulk sample may be the average of the two dates, or ca. 350 cal BP (AD 1600). These two dates and those obtained by Kennett suggest that this area of the site has occupations spanning the Late, Protohistoric, and Historic periods.

The Protohistoric and Historic period ^{14}C dates, presence of house depressions, and dense midden exposures support the possibility that this site is *Niwoyomi*, although other candidates (SMI-602) remain (see below). An additional component located across the creek on the far eastern edge of SMI-481 was also recently dated to ca. 470 to 380 cal BP (AD 1480–1570) (Chapter 5) and may be closely related to the occupation of SMI-470. However, only limited data are currently available from this component.

ARTIFACTS

Thirty artifacts were recovered from the upper and lower levels of the SMI-470 Bulk Sample, and five additional artifacts were recovered from the surface in slumped deposits adjacent to it (Table 6.13). The majority (77 percent) of the artifacts are made from shell. Seventeen of these are made of *Olivella*, including two callus BIP, five callus bead blanks, four lipped beads, four wall BIP, one wall bead, and a spire-lopped bead (Figure 6.9). Eleven of the beads or bead-making materials are from the callus portion of the shell, and five are from the wall region, a pattern consistent with the Late/Protohistoric or Historic period chronology of the site. *Olivella* bead detritus densities from the bulk sample are roughly 7044 g per m^3, a relatively high value for *Olivella* densities on San Miguel Island, but still in the lower range of Late period bead densities on the islands more generally (Arnold and Graesch 2001; Kennett and Conlee 2002). In addition to *Olivella* artifacts, five abalone artifacts were recovered, including three fragments of worked black abalone (chipped or ground), five pieces of worked abalone nacre, and a red abalone fishhook tip. No evidence of red abalone bead making similar to that found at SMI-163 was identified in this bulk sample. A California mussel disk BIP was also recovered.

The other artifacts from the site include three triangular prepared microblades, three triangular prepared microdrills, an asphaltum skirt weight or plug, and a medium bone barb made from mammal bone. This barb has asphaltum near its base and a well-defined S curve, and may have functioned as a composite fishhook or harpoon barb.

SUBSISTENCE STRATEGIES

Like other Channel Islands middens, the SMI-470 deposits are dominated by faunal remains, including shellfish, and fish, bird, and mammal bones.

Table 6.12. Late Holocene Radiocarbon Dates from SMI-470, -516, -536, and -602.

Sample #	Provenience	Material	Uncorrected ^{14}C Age	^{13}C/^{12}C Adjusted Age	Calibrated Age Range (cal BP), 1 sigma	Calibrated Age Range (BC/AD), 1 sigma
		SMI-470				
Beta-107344	OPC 1-A2 20cm	Black abalone	310 ± 60	740 ± 60	260 (130) 0	AD 1690 (1820) 1950
Beta-107983	OPC 1-A1 Sea Cliff 40 cm	Abalone	310 ± 70	740 ± 70	260 (130) 0	AD 1690 (1820) 1950
Beta-145305	Unit bottom, 30 cm	Black abalone	460 ± 70	890 ± 70	410 (300) 260	AD 1540 (1660) 1690
OS-27184	Unit top, 1 cm	Black abalone	—	980 ± 40	460 (420) 320	AD 1490 (1530) 1630
		SMI-516				
Beta-145312	Cave mouth, 35–40 cm above bedrock	Black abalone	430 ± 60	860 ± 60	320 (280) 250	AD 1630 (1670) 1710
Beta-145313	Cave mouth, 70 cm above bedrock	Black abalone	520 ± 90	950 ± 90	470 (380) 280	AD 1490 (1570) 1670
		SMI-536				
LJ-0955	Sandy Cliff, Cuyler Harbor	California mussel	575 ± 125	1005 ± 125	510 (430) 290	AD 1440 (1520) 1660
OS-42694	Surface of dune slope	Olivella bead	—	1260 ± 30	650 (620) 560	AD 1300 (1330) 1390
		SMI-602				
Beta-114533	Unit 2, Stratum A	California mussel	310 ± 50	730 ± 60	250 (130) 0	AD 1700 (1820) 1950
Beta-098743	Unit 2, 39 cm	California mussel	460 ± 60	900 ± 60	410 (300) 270	AD 1540 (1650) 1680
Beta-098744	Unit 5, 48 cm	California mussel	650 ± 60	1100 ± 60	530 (500) 460	AD 1420 (1450) 1500
Beta-098742	Unit 5, 10 cm	California mussel	650 ± 70	1100 ± 70	540 (500) 450)	AD 1410 (1450) 1500

Note: All dates were calibrated using Calib 4.3 (Stuiver and Reimer 1993, 2000), and applying a ΔR of 225 ± 35 years for all shell samples (see Kennett et al. 1997). ^{13}C/^{12}C ratios were determined by the radiocarbon labs, or an average of +430 years was applied (Erlandson 1988b).

The faunal remains were screened over 1/8-inch mesh and are from the upper (0 to 20 cm) and lower (20 to 40 cm) levels of the bulk sample. Due to the similarity of the deposits, all faunal remains have been lumped together.

Shellfish and Invertebrates

Roughly 8.8 kg of shell from 1913 individual shellfish and invertebrates were recovered in the upper and lower levels of the bulk sample (Table 6.14). At least 27 different taxa were identified, of which over 99 percent are from marine organisms. Preservation of the assemblage is excellent, with numerous whole mussel valves and black and red abalones.

California mussel dominates the assemblage, making up roughly 60 percent of the MNI and weight of the entire sample. Black turban is the second most important taxon, contributing about 10

Table 6.13. Artifacts from Bulk Sample and Surface at SMI-470 (1/8-inch).

Shell Artifacts	Upper	Lower	Surface	Total
Haliotis cracherodii worked	—	2	1	3
Haliotis rufescens fishhook tip	—	—	1	1
Haliotis spp. worked	—	5	—	5
Mytilus disk BIP [a]	—	1	—	1
Olivella callus BIP	—	2	—	2
Olivella callus bead blank	1	4	—	5
Olivella lipped bead	1	2	1	4
Olivella wall BIP	3	1	—	4
Olivella wall bead	—	1	—	1
Olivella spire-lopped bead	1	—	—	1
Subtotal	6	18	3	27
Other Artifacts				
Medium bone barb	—	—	1	1
Triangular prepared microblade	1	1	1	3
Triangular prepared microdrill	—	3	—	3
Asphaltum skirt weight or plug	1	—	—	1
Subtotal	2	4	2	8
Total	8	22	5	35

[a] BIP = bead in production.

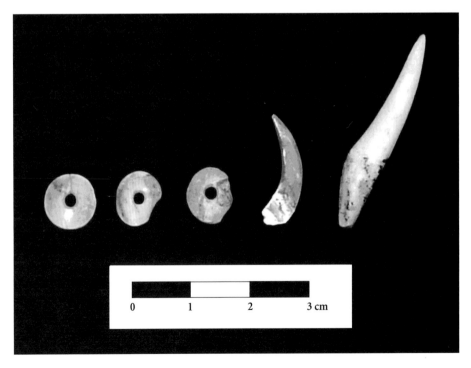

Figure 6.9. Artifacts from SMI-470. *(Left to right)*: *Olivella* wall disk bead, *Olivella callus*/lipped beads (two), abalone shell fishhook tip, bone barb.

Table 6.14. Shellfish and Invertebrate Remains from Bulk Sample at SMI-470 (Upper and Lower Deposits).

Taxon	Wt. (g)	% Wt.	MNI	% MNI
Barnacle undif.	79	0.9	—	—
Calliostoma spp. (top snails)	0.1	< 0.1	2	0.1
Chiton undif.	75.9	0.9	—	—
Corallina spp. (coralline algae)	0.7	< 0.1	—	—
Crepidula spp. (slipper shells)	5.8	0.1	41	2.1
Crab undif.	62.9	0.7	—	—
Cryptochiton stelleri (gumboot chiton)	40	0.5	—	—
Fissurella volcano (volcano limpet)	0.5	< 0.1	2	0.1
Gastropod undif.	4.4	0.1	31	1.6
Glans subquadrata (eccentric ribbed clam)	0.1	< 0.1	1	0.1
Haliotis cracherodii (black abalone)	1166.8	13.3	46	2.4
Haliotis rufescens (ribbed abalone)	263.5	3.0	9	0.5
Haliotis spp. (abalone undif.)	45.4	0.5	—	—
Land snail	3.1	<0.1	6	0.3
Limpet undif.	99.1	1.1	287	15.0
Lottia gigantea (owl limpet)	191.5	2.2	50	2.6
Margarites succinctus (tucked margarite)	2.5	< 0.1	1	0.1
Mytilus californianus (California mussel)	5191.9	59.1	1188	62.1
Nacre undif.	96.1	1.1	—	—
Nucella spp. (dogwinkles)	2.1	< 0.1	5	0.3
Olivella biplicata (purple olive)	225.4	2.6	—	—
Pollicipes polymerus (gooseneck barnacle)	89.9	1.0	—	—
Protothaca staminea (Pacific littleneck)	0.1	< 0.1	1	0.1
Septifer bifurcatus (platform mussel)	24.8	0.3	66	3.5
Serpulorbis squamigerus (scaled worm snail)	0.3	< 0.1	1	0.1
Strongylocentrotus spp. (sea urchins)	237.3	2.7	—	—
Tegula brunnea (brown turban)	19.3	0.2	5	0.3
Tegula funebralis (black turban)	833.5	9.5	164	8.6
Tegula spp. (turban undif.)	10.7	0.1	6	0.3
Tivela stultorum (Pismo clam)	0.1	<0.1	1	0.1
Undif. shell	6.5	0.1		—
Total	8779.3	—	1913	—

percent of the weight and 9 percent of the MNI. Platform mussel constitutes about 4 percent of the MNI, and sea urchin about 3 percent of the weight. Black abalone is also relatively abundant, making up about 13 percent of the shell weight, but only about 2 percent of the MNI. Owl limpets provide about 2 to 3 percent of the weight and MNI. *Olivella*, which was collected primarily for making beads, supplies about 3 percent of the total shell weight. As in the other sites, small limpets contribute about 15 percent of the MNI, but only 1 percent of the weight, suggesting these were brought to the site as by-products when collecting other shell species or supplemental resources. All other shell species appear to be only minor contributors to the sample.

Fish

Fish remains are relatively dense in the bulk sample, with 568.4 g of fish bone recovered in the bulk sample, including roughly 353.1 g of fish bone from the upper level and about 215.3 g in the lower level. All of the fish remains from the lower sample were sorted and identified to the most specific taxon possible. The bones from the upper level were rough-sorted to determine if any unusual elements or taxa not identified in the lower sample were present, but none were encountered. Since nearly 2,500 bones from at least seven different taxa were identified, this sample is probably a good estimate of the fishes present in the entire bulk sample (Table 6.15).

Preservation of the assemblage is generally good, but fragmentation of bones is relatively high, and consequently only 13 percent of the NISP (n = 333) but 32 percent of the weight was identifiable to family, genus, or species. Rockfish dominate the assemblage by all measures, making up 67 percent of

the weight, 69 percent of the NISP, and 56 percent of the MNI. Surfperch and pile perch are the second most abundant fishes, making up about 17 percent of the NISP and 13 percent of the MNI. Cabezon is fairly abundant, with 5 percent of the NISP, but 13 percent of the MNI. Prickleback remains were relatively common, making up 7 percent of the NISP. Lingcod and clupeid remains were also identified in the sample, but account for only about 1.5 and 0.3 percent of the NISP, respectively.

Most of the fishes identified are from nearshore marine habitats that could have been caught using hook and line, nets, or other tackle in kelp beds or rocky reefs. The presence of a single-piece abalone shell fishhook on the surface near the bulk sample attests to the use of this technology. During excavation of the bulk sample, a billfish fin ray spine was also noted in an eroding exposure near the area where the bulk sample was obtained.

Mammals and Birds

No diagnostic mammal bones were recovered in the sample, but most of the bones, including rib and vertebral fragments, appear to come from marine mammals. In the upper deposits, nine mammal bones weighing 13.3 g were recovered, and in the lower sample, 82 mammal bones weighing

Table 6.15. Fish Remains from Bulk Sample (Lower Deposit) at SMI-470.

Taxon	Wt.	% Wt. [a]	NISP	% NISP	MNI	% MNI
Teleost						
Clupeidae (sardines)	0.1	0.1	1	0.3	1	6.3
Cottidae (sculpin)						
Scorpaenichthys marmoratus (cabezon)	5.9	8.5	17	5.1	2	12.5
Embiotocidae (surfperch)	6.7	9.7	54	16.2	1	6.3
Damalichthys vacca (pile perch)	0.2	0.3	3	0.9	1	6.3
Hexagrammidae (greenling)						
Ophiodon elongatus (lingcod)	2.9	4.2	5	1.5	1	6.3
Scorpaenidae						
Sebastes spp. (rockfish)	46.2	66.6	229	68.8	9	56.3
Stichaeidae (prickleback)	7.4	10.7	24	7.2	1	6.3
Teleost undif.	145.9	—	2162	—	—	—
Total	215.3	—	2495	—	16	—

Note: Based on 1/8-inch recovery and all weights in grams. Volume = 0.016 m^3.

[a] Percentages based on specimens identified to family, genus, and species.

about 60.2 g were recovered. One small reptile or amphibian bone (< 0.1 g) was also found in the bulk sample.

Roughly 32 bird bones (30 g) were recovered in the upper and lower levels of the bulk sample, a relatively high number considering this is from a small 32-liter sample (Table 6.16). Thirty-four percent of the bird bone NISP was identifiable to species. Four taxa were identified, including Cassin's auklet (n = 3), pelican (n = 1), pelagic cormorant (n = 3), and Brandt's/Double-crested cormorant (n = 4). All of these birds are relatively common inhabitants of the Channel Islands and may have been scavenged or hunted on the island or offshore on Castle Rock, located near the site.

Dietary Reconstruction

A dietary reconstruction for the bulk sample (1/8-inch) provides additional insight into the relative importance of the various faunal categories at the site. The dietary reconstruction suggests that fish represented roughly 72 percent of the total meat represented in the sample, followed by shellfish at 18 percent, mammals at 8 percent, and birds about 2 percent. When just fish and shellfish are compared, fish contribute about 80 percent and shellfish

about 20 percent. These values are similar to those from Unit 2 at SMI-163 and other sites of this age where fish typically dominate the diet.

OTHER PROTOHISTORIC AND HISTORIC SITES

In recent years, a few additional sites, including a village (SMI-602), shell midden (SMI-536), and rockshelter (SMI-516), have produced ^{14}C dates that are Protohistoric or Historic in age. To provide a more detailed context of Chumash settlement of the island during this time period, I briefly synthesize these sites below. A number of sites dating to the Late period (e.g., SMI-9, SMI-150, SMI-481, and SMI-485) have also been investigated, but only sites with components dating after 400 cal BP (AD 1550) are included here.

SMI-602

SMI-602 is a large shell midden with a series of house depressions and an associated cemetery located in the middle of the Point Bennett pinniped rookery on the far west coast of the island. The site is badly eroding and has been impacted by pinnipeds hauling out on the site and by wind erosion.

Table 6.16. Bird Remains from Bulk Sample at SMI-470.

Taxon	Upper Wt.	Upper NISP	Lower Wt.	Lower NISP	Total Wt.	Total % Wt.[a]	Total NISP	Total % NISP	Total MNI	Total % MNI
Alcidae										
Ptychoramphus aleuticus (Cassin's auklet)	—	—	0.7	3	0.7	2.9	3	27.3	1	25.0
Pelecanidae										
Pelecanus spp. (pelicans)	6.6	1	—	—	6.6	27.4	1	9.1	1	25.0
Phalacrocoracidae										
Phalacrocorax spp. (Brandt's/Double crested cormorants)	—	—	12.8	4	12.8	53.1	4	36.4	1	25.0
Phalacrocorax pelagicus (pelagic cormorant)	2.3	2	1.8	1	4.1	17.0	3	27.3	1	25.0
Aves undif.	0.2	5	5.7	16	5.9	—	21	—	—	—
Total	9.1	8	20.9	24	30.0	—	32	—	4	—

Note: Based on 1/8-inch recovery and all weights in grams. Volume = 0.032 m^3.

[a] Percentages based on specimens identified to family, genus, and species.

The site covers an area roughly 90 × 80 m, with intact deposits that are about 75 cm deep, at least 10 burials, and a house floor surrounded by a stone circle (Kennett 1997, unpublished site record). The Point Bennett area is very dynamic, and from year to year, sand cover either obscures portions of the site or the wind exposes features (e.g., hearths), house depressions, and midden constituents. Subsequent visits to the site by Erlandson, Rick, and others have noted that the site contains at least seven house depressions.

The site was excavated by Doug Kennett, Phil Walker, Bob DeLong, and Terry Jones as part of a larger project investigating the long-term history of human impacts on the pinniped breeding colony currently located on Point Bennett (see Walker et al. 2002). Analysis is currently ongoing, but faunal identifications have been reported and provide important insight on this large site complex.

Four radiocarbon dates from the site indicate the presence of three components, one dated to ca. 500 cal BP (AD 1450), another to 300 cal BP (AD 1650), and a final component during the Historic period, with a calibrated intercept of 130 cal BP (AD 1820; Walker et al. 2002; see Table 6.12). Collectively, these dates suggest that the site was occupied during the Late, Protohistoric, and Historic periods. Walker et al. (2002:629) suggested that the site was occupied until around AD 1660 because no glass beads, metal, or other contact period artifacts were recovered. However, the Historic date suggests that at least a portion of the site may have been occupied during the late eighteenth or even early nineteenth century.

Preliminary analysis of faunal remains from SMI-602 suggests a heavy reliance on marine fishes. Dietary reconstructions for Unit 5 suggest that fish provide about 74 percent of the meat yield, marine mammals about 23 percent, shellfish about 2 percent, and birds less than 1 percent (Walker et al. 2000). These data contrast with reconstructions from nearby SMI-528 dated to the late Middle period, where fish make up only about 16.4 percent and marine mammals dominate with 73.1 percent, shellfish about 10.3 percent, and birds less than 1 percent (Walker et al. 2002). Walker et al. (2002) suggested that the decline of marine mammals and associated increase of fishes at SMI-602 is the result of humans over-hunting marine mammals (see also

Chapter 7). Except for preliminary data on the types of marine mammals present at SMI-602, no detailed taxonomic identification of other fauna is currently available. At least seven species are represented, including fur seals, sea lions, harbor seal, elephant seal, and sea otter (Walker et al. 2002; see Chapter 5).

Although no detailed artifact data from SMI-602 have been reported, Kennett and Conlee (2002) present bead detritus densities for all three of the dated deposits. The deposits dated to ca. AD 1450 have values ranging from about 3,576 to 3,741 g per m³, while the values for the deposit dated to AD 1650 and 1820 are considerably higher, with about 10,425g per m³ and 11,875 g per m³, respectively (Kennett and Conlee 2002:160). These data suggest an overall increase in bead-making at the site during the Protohistoric and Historic periods. Kennett and Conlee (2002:156) also indicate that triangular microblades, *Olivella* callus cup and lipped beads, circular fishhooks, and concave-base arrow points were present at the site.

While interpretations of SMI-602 will undoubtedly change and improve when the final site report is available, the current data suggest that this was likely an important site for Chumash peoples during the Late, Protohistoric, and possibly the Historic period. In many ways, analyses of this site raise more questions than they answer. For example, were there actually three Historic villages on San Miguel Island (SMI-163, SMI-470, SMI-602), or are these sites all interrelated components of two villages? Is it possible that people designated from *Tuqan* at the missions are from the island as a whole rather than from a particular village? Were some of these villages occupied seasonally or periodically? While these questions are difficult to answer, especially given the small amount of data from the excavated sites, it appears that historic and late prehistoric occupation of San Miguel Island was considerably more variable and diverse than previously recognized. This will need to be tested as more data become available.

SMI-536

Located on the western margins of Cuyler Harbor, SMI-536 was described by Kritzman (1966, unpublished site record) as a permanent campsite located near a huge landslide covering an area about 120 ×

150 m. This site is currently badly eroding down the steeply sloping hillside on which it is located. Shell midden and lithic artifacts are visible cascading about 150 m down the slope all the way to the base of Cuyler Harbor. A few patches of midden remain intact, and it is possible that other parts of the site remain buried under sand and vegetation. During site assessment work in 2003, we noted that the site contained dense concentrations of California mussels and moderate amounts of red and black abalone, along with fish and marine mammal bones. *Olivella* bead-making detritus was abundant on the surface, and *Olivella* wall detritus, two chipped-wall disk beads, and an *Olivella* callus BIP were also noted. Three rim fragments of a stone bowl were also identified.

Unfortunately, the precise location of a cemetery excavated by Glidden in 1919 is unknown (Heye 1921). As stated previously, my research and that of Kennett (2005) suggest that the complex of sites that includes SMI-163, SMI-162, and others may contain this cemetery. However, the presence of Late period artifacts at SMI-536 and its location on Cuyler Harbor raises the possibility that the site may have been associated with the excavated cemetery.

To examine this idea, Erlandson recently obtained two dates from the site, one on a mussel shell from the midden deposits, and another on an *Olivella* bead. The California mussel yielded a calibrated intercept of 3610 cal BP (1660 BC; OS-42693), while the *Olivella* bead yielded a calibrated intercept of 620 cal BP (AD 1330), suggesting that there were at least two components at the site (see Table 6.12). While the bead is probably Late period in age, this date is also similar to a date obtained by Hubbs from a shell midden on a sandy cliff in Cuyler Harbor that may be from SMI-536 (Erlandson and Bartoy 1995:167). This date produced a calibrated intercept of 430 cal BP (AD 1520), with a 1 sigma age range of 510 to 290 cal BP (AD 1440 to 1660) which extends into the Protohistoric period and is roughly contemporaneous with some of the dates from SMI-163.

Similar to SMI-602, this site also currently raises more questions than it answers. How is this site related to SMI-163? Is it a satellite of SMI-163, a site occupied just before the village was moved to the location at SMI-163, or were there two Chumash villages in the Cuyler area during the Protohistoric period? Considerably more data are needed from SMI-536 before these questions can be evaluated. The site is badly eroding, and only a remnant of what appears to have been a much more substantial site currently exists, making it a complicated but important area for future research.

SMI-516

SMI-516 is a rockshelter located on the southwest coast of the island. The site sits near the top of the southern escarpment at about 145 m above sea level and is roughly 15 × 8 m in area (Kritzman 1966, unpublished site record). According to Kritzman, the shelter consists of two irregularly shaped rooms that overlook the ocean and a steeply sloping canyon. California mussel, black abalone, owl limpet, turbans, sea urchin, and marine mammal bones were observed at the site in 1966, and some fire blackening was apparently also present in one of the rooms of the rockshelter. Erlandson recently obtained two radiocarbon samples from midden exposures at the site. The first of these dates was on a single black abalone shell from about 70 cm above bedrock which produced a calibrated intercept of 380 cal BP (AD 1570) and a 1 sigma age range of 470 to 280 cal BP (AD 1490 to 1670). The second date was also from a single black abalone shell located about 35 to 40 cm above bedrock and produced a calibrated intercept of 280 cal BP (AD 1670) and 1 sigma range of 1630 to 1710 cal BP (AD 1630 to 1710). Given the density and depth of the deposits, it appears that this site was used throughout the Protohistoric period, perhaps as a temporary or seasonal camp.

RETHINKING CHUMASH OCCUPATIONS OF SAN MIGUEL ISLAND

Collectively, the data from SMI-163, -470, and -602 illustrate relatively extensive occupation of San Miguel Island during the Protohistoric and Historic periods. Occupation of the rockshelter at SMI-516, and Late period or possibly Protohistoric occupation of SMI-536 also suggest that Protohistoric and Historic occupation of the island involved the use of a variety of site types and environments.

These data raise questions that will need to be tested with further ^{14}C dating and excavation. However, they suggest that the magnitude and scope of Chumash occupation of San Miguel Island need to be reevaluated.

Limited baptismal counts for San Miguel Island, along with its small size and relatively isolated location, have led researchers to suggest that the island may have been fairly peripheral in the larger scheme of Chumash society. Much of the problem stems from perceptions of San Miguel Island environments. San Miguel Island was ravaged for over a century by overgrazing by introduced sheep and other livestock that reduced parts of the island to a mass of drifting sand and created a huge sandspit at Cardwell Point on the east end of the island (D. Johnson 1980). As Rogers (1929:265–266) noted:

> The winds sweep unhindered across the naked mesa, undercutting the unprotected soil, and sweeping the lighter materials in dust clouds out to sea. The heavier sand particles are carried along the surface, in a blast that flays the face and hands of the pedestrian who braves these wastes. Under the lee cliffs of the island, one may, at any dry period of the year, find torrents of sand pouring into the sea. There can be but one end to this ceaseless erosion. In the course of time, San Miguel will cease to appear on our maps as an island, and will be charted as "dangerous shoals."

The Reverend Stephen Bowers, in his visit to the island in 1877, also noted:

> The sand has drifted fearfully in some places. Mr. Mills informs me that two miles of fence, an orchard of fruit trees, and a house are entirely covered and lost to view by the drifting sand. (Benson 1997:101)

This devastating historical erosion and vegetation stripping also had a profound effect on island archaeology, causing deflation, erosion, and near total loss of some sites (Rick 2002). These trends were noted by Rogers (1929:268) who, despite the presence of massive archaeological sites across San Miguel Island, felt that research efforts were more promising on Santa Rosa and Santa Cruz because of less erosion. The limited amount of freshwater has also been cited as a major hindrance to sustained human habitation on the island (Vellanoweth and Grenda 2002:72–73).

During surveys by Kritzman and Rozaire in the 1960s, Greenwood in the 1970s, and other more recent surveys, vegetation stripping and wind erosion were still occurring. However, nearly 700 archaeological sites on virtually all parts of the island have been documented. Recent research also suggests that numerous previously unrecorded sites exist on the south coast of San Miguel Island (Braje and Erlandson 2005; Braje et al. 2005a). Under the management of Channel Islands National Park, the island's vegetation and watersheds have been dramatically recovering. Freshwater sources also appear to be expanding, as we have documented new springs and the expansion of some existing creeks during just the last five to ten years. The island was probably never as well watered as Santa Rosa or Santa Cruz, but clearly freshwater was not as limited as some scholars have noted.

These changing perspectives on San Miguel Island's vegetation communities, freshwater, and rich marine fauna, as well as the presence of at least three villages that date to the Protohistoric and Historic periods, suggest that the role of San Miguel Island in the larger Chumash interaction sphere needs to be revisited. Indeed, the island's comparative dearth of water and terrestrial vegetation may have been a hindrance, but this could have been surmounted through water storage as it was on the other islands. Data from SMI-163, -470, -602, and other sites illustrate that Chumash peoples on San Miguel Island were actively engaged in producing *Olivella* and red abalone beads and other items (e.g., stone bowls) for exchange. Densities of *Olivella* bead detritus are often lower than at some Santa Rosa or Santa Cruz Island sites, but people still actively participated in this system.

The Historic period also marks the final respite for Chumash people on San Miguel Island before they were removed to the missions along with the other islanders by about AD 1822. Radiocarbon dates and artifact data from SMI-163 suggest that this village was largely in a state of decline by the onset of the Historic period. Populations may have been in decline from earlier disease epidemics, people may have relocated the village to an unknown location, or people may have moved to other islands or the mainland. The available data suggest, however, that Late prehistoric and Protohistoric period occupation of the island was more substantial than previously presumed. Future research at SMI-536, forthcoming data from SMI-602, and further dating of island sites should provide important insight into changing human use of San Miguel Island during the last 500 years.

While the effects of introduced diseases on Chumash populations and declining health from a new agrarian diet are well documented, it should be emphasized that the Historic period was not the end of traditional Chumash society. It appears that continuity in traditional practices persisted for some time on the islands (see also Arnold and Graesch 2001, 2004). For example, people continued to make beads in vast quantities, and subsistence pursuits were virtually unchanged in some places. These patterns are also apparent in historic assemblages from SRI-2 on adjacent Santa Rosa Island (see Rick 2004a). Much of this is due to the relative isolation of the Channel Islands (see J. Johnson 2001), but archaeological data add to a growing body of research in North America and beyond that demonstrates considerable cultural continuity, even during the widespread colonialism and population declines that occurred during the Mission era.

7

Late Holocene Cultural and Environmental Dynamics

The Late Holocene was a time of pronounced cultural and environmental change on the northern Channel Islands, including heightened population growth, increased cultural complexity, and intensified subsistence. In this final chapter, I provide a comparative analysis of the Late Holocene San Miguel Island archaeological sites, placing these data within the context of the research issues outlined in Chapter 1. My analysis includes an examination of changes in the types and densities of artifacts associated with craft production, exchange, and subsistence, as well as faunal remains dated to the last 3,000 years. The comparison of these artifacts and faunal remains helps to reconstruct how human daily activities varied through space and time on San Miguel Island. When placed in the context of other research on the northern Channel Islands, these findings provide insight into the emergence of complexity and historical ecology among the Island Chumash in general.

One of the primary goals of this book was to examine long-term changes in human cultural and environmental dynamics. While detailed reconstructions and analyses of several sites dating to the last 3,000 years are provided, the Late Holocene represents the final portion of a long and continuous record that spans at least 13,000 calendar years (see Chapter 2). From a trans-Holocene perspective, the cultural patterns of the Late Holocene can be seen as an outgrowth of long-term cultural evolution and adaptive change. Although I focus on the last 3,000 years of prehistory, I emphasize that these developments are grounded in long-term cultural evolution. To provide this trans-Holocene context, I begin this chapter with a brief synthesis of Early and Middle Holocene precursors to the Late Holocene record of San Miguel Island. I conclude this chapter by placing this study within the broad theo-

retical realm of other research on the Channel Islands, complex hunter-gatherers, and historical ecology.

PRECURSORS TO LATE HOLOCENE CULTURAL DEVELOPMENTS ON SAN MIGUEL ISLAND

For the most part, Early Holocene peoples of the Channel Islands appear to have been fairly mobile, with relatively low population densities. Erlandson (1994) suggested that Early Holocene peoples along the California coast and Channel Islands, for example, lived in small, relatively egalitarian groups, with less formal social hierarchies or gender roles and more limited use of objects used as symbols of identity or power. Recent research at several cave and open-air sites across San Miguel Island has revolutionized our perspective on early maritime adaptations on the Channel Islands and in western North America (Table 7.1). These data suggest that early island artifact assemblages appear to contain mostly utilitarian artifacts (bone gorges, expedient stone tools, bifaces, etc.), but some sites also have a limited number of beads and ornaments, perishable cordage artifacts, and stone material types that indicate the possibility of early trade relationships with the mainland (see Connolly et al. 1995; Erlandson et al. 2005d; Vellanoweth et al. 2003; Rick et al. 2005b).

Early Holocene peoples on San Miguel Island and the broader southern California coast appear to have centered much of their economy on marine resources, including a wide variety of shellfish, nearshore fishes, and some mammals and birds (see Erlandson 1994; Erlandson et al. 1999, 2004a, 2004b, 2004c, 2005d, 2006; Kennett 2005; Rick et al. 2001a, 2006a). Most analyses of Early Holocene archaeological sites on San Miguel and the other islands reveal a focus on shellfish, supplemented by

127

Table 7.1. Major Trans-Holocene Native American Sites on San Miguel Island for which Published Data Are Available.

Site	Age	Description	References
		Terminal Pleistocene/Early Holocene	
SMI-261	11,600–8500 cal BP (9650–6550 BC)	Multicomponent cave site with a diverse early artifact assemblage, including cordage and woven artifacts, and marine faunal constituents.	Connolly et al. 1995; Erlandson et al. 1996; Rick et al. 2001a
SMI-522	10,250–8940 cal BP (8300–6990 BC)	Dense, eroding shell midden composed primarily of mussels and other rocky-shore shellfish.	Erlandson and Rick, 2002b
SMI-548	9950–8960 cal BP (8000–7010 BC)	Small shell midden dominated by mussels, owl limpets, and other rocky intertidal shellfish species.	Erlandson et al. 2004b
SMI-608	9800–8580 cal BP (7850–6630 BC)	Open-air site dominated by mussels and black abalones with a large artifact assemblage.	Braje et al. 2005a; Erlandson et al. 2005a
SMI-606	9420–8060 cal BP (7470–6110 BC)	Small, low-density shell midden dominated by rocky-shore shellfish taxa and small amounts of bone and chipped-stone artifacts.	Erlandson et al. 2004c
SMI-603	8410–7480 cal BP (6460–5530 BC)	Multicomponent cave site with a large Early Holocene artifact and faunal assemblage.	Rick et al. 2001a; Vellanoweth et al. 2002, 2003
		Middle Holocene	
SMI-1	7140–3250 cal BP (5190–1300 BC)	Interior site with multicomponent shell midden, sea mammal bones, and diverse artifact assemblage.	Erlandson 1991b; Kennett 2005; Rozaire 1978
SMI-261	6900–3540 cal BP (4950–1590 BC)	Multicomponent cave site with black abalone, mussel, top, vertebrate remains, and expedient stone tools.	Erlandson et al. 1996
SMI-603	6680–3960 cal BP (4730–2010 BC)	Multicomponent cave site with dense shellfish, fish, sea mammal, and bird remains, and expedient tools.	Vellanoweth et al. 2002, 2003
SMI-605	6740–6270 cal BP (4790–4320 BC)	Small sandstone cave with thin deposits containing shellfish and vertebrate remains and *Dentalium* artifacts.	Erlandson et al. 2005c
SMI-557	6570–5960 cal BP (4620–4010 BC)	Shell midden exposed in gully walls on south coast with dense concentration of red abalone shells.	Braje et al. 2005a; Glassow 1993a
SMI-528	5900–4800 cal BP (3950–2850 BC)	Multicomponent shell midden located in dune system on Point Bennett with faunal remains and artifacts.	Kennett 2005
SMI-396	5120–3130 cal BP (3170–1180 BC)	Large, multicomponent dune site with shellfish and vertebrate remains, expedient stone tools, and asphaltum basketry impressions.	Braje et al. 2005b
		Late Holocene	
SMI-261	3590–640 cal BP (1640 BC -AD 1310)	Multicomponent cave site with shell midden, bead-maker's artifact kit, seagrass artifacts, tarring pebbles, and dense faunal remains.	Connolly et al. 1995; Erlandson et al. 1996
SMI-525	3230–520 cal BP (1280 BC -AD 1430)	Dense eroding shell midden with several discrete strata and abundant faunal remains.	Kennett 2005; Rozaire 1978; Walker and Snethkamp 1984
SMI-503, -504	3050–1050 cal BP (1100 BC–AD 900)	Shell midden in large dune complex with evidence for stone-bowl manufacture.	Conlee 2000; Kennett and Conlee 2002; Walker and Snethkamp 1984
SMI-528	1570–1120 cal BP (AD 380–830)	Multicomponent shell midden located in dune system on Point Bennett with abundant sea mammal bones and artifacts.	Walker et al. 2002
SMI-602	540 cal BP–Historic (AD 1410–ca. 1822)	Eroding shell midden and village complex with house features and artifacts on Point Bennett rookery.	Walker et al. 2002

Note: Site descriptions are based on Rick et al. (2005b) and sources cited above. Five primary sites covered in previous chapters are not listed here. The site descriptions are for specific temporal components.

fishes, mammals, and birds (Erlandson 1991a, 1994; Erlandson et al. 1999, 2004a, 2004b, 2004c, 2006; Kennett 2005). At Daisy Cave on San Miguel Island, however, nearshore fishes appear to have been a dominant component of the diet by about 10,000 to 9,000 years ago, suggesting considerable adaptive diversity and fishing capabilities by this early time period (Rick et al. 2001a). Billfish and other deep-water species, however, appear to be largely absent from early assemblages. Erlandson et al. (2005d) have also speculated that a large assemblage of chipped-stone artifacts from SMI-608 may have been used to hunt marine mammals.

Many of the cultural patterns of the Early Holocene persist into the Middle Holocene. Although less is known about the Middle Holocene on San Miguel Island than the Early and Late Holocene, recent research provides evidence of complex and diverse human lifeways during the Middle Holocene. Several researchers have suggested that Middle Holocene cultural patterns on the Channel Islands and adjacent mainland are generally similar to those of the Early Holocene (see Erlandson and Glassow 1997), with a gradual transition toward more balanced and diversified economies. The similarities include relatively small sites, low population densities, and a focus primarily on shellfish, with most other resources serving as supplementary parts of the diet (see Erlandson and Glassow 1997; Glassow 1993b; Vellanoweth et al. 2002). Like those of the Early Holocene, artifact assemblages from many Middle Holocene contexts are fairly limited, but more diverse utilitarian and ornamental artifacts have been identified at some sites (see Erlandson and Glassow 1997; King 1990; Orr 1968; Scalise 1994). Recent XRF obsidian source characterization of Channel Islands artifacts also indicates that people on the islands were involved in large-scale exchange networks and interaction spheres since the Early and Middle Holocene (Rick et al. 2001b). At Otter Cave on San Miguel Island, Erlandson et al. (2001a) identified numerous *Dentalium* shell beads in Middle Holocene deposits, suggesting variability in the types of ornaments being produced by this early time period. Vellanoweth (2001) and others have also identified heightened exchange of *Olivella* grooved rectangle beads on the southern Channel Islands during the Middle Holocene. Interestingly, this bead type has not yet been identified on the northern Channel Islands.

Data from Cave of the Chimneys (SMI-603) also suggest diverse Middle Holocene foraging strategies focused largely on shellfish (see Vellanoweth et al. 2002). Near Otter Point, Erlandson et al. (2005c) and Vellanoweth et al. (2006) have documented relatively eclectic economies, including use of a variety of shellfish, fish, and marine mammals, at two Middle Holocene components (SMI-481, and -605) dated to ca. 6000 and 6600 cal BP (4050 and 4650 BC). On the other northern Channel Islands, Glassow (1993a, 2002b, 2005a) and Sharp (2000) illustrated human adaptations to a variety of environmental changes across the Middle Holocene at Punta Arena on Santa Cruz Island. Kennett (1998, 2004) and Perry (2004, 2005) have also demonstrated that substantial interior settlement occurred during the Middle Holocene, and Glassow (1993a, 2005a) has documented the existence of numerous red abalone middens on San Miguel, Santa Rosa, and Santa Cruz islands. Although a variety of data suggest Middle Holocene subsistence strategies and economies were transitional between Early and Late Holocene patterns, current research suggests considerable variability in Middle Holocene subsistence.

In general, the expansion of subsistence resources, exchange, and the production of a broader range of bead types (e.g., *Olivella* rectangle, barrel, clam disk, steatite) illustrate cultural diversification during the Middle Holocene (see Erlandson 1997). Increased sedentism is also indicated at some sites, but for the most part, Middle Holocene peoples appear to have remained fairly mobile and lack the complex social organization apparent during the latter half of the Late Holocene (see Erlandson 1997; Glassow 1997; Kennett 2005). Much is still to be learned about the Middle Holocene on the Channel Islands, but many of the roots of later cultural developments appear to be linked to some of the relatively complex and diverse subsistence strategies and exchange networks of the Middle Holocene.

From this trans-Holocene perspective, the cultural patterns of the Late Holocene can be seen as an outgrowth of more than 10,000 years of cultural evolution and adaptive change. About 3,500 years ago, a number of cultural changes were in place, many of which (e.g., cross-channel trade, coastal fishing and hunting, and shell-bead production) were outgrowths of Middle and Early Holocene cultural practices. The scale and intensity of cultural developments during the Late Holocene appear to increase dramatically, including new artifact forms, major demographic fluctuations, and changes in sociopolitical organization (see Erlandson and Jones 2002). During the Late Holocene, particularly the last 1,500 years, large sedentary villages, intensive craft specialization and exchange, and heightened territoriality, social hierarchy, and competition appear to be well established on the Channel Islands (see Arnold 2001b; Kennett 2005). Subsistence strategies also continued to be diversified, and there is some evidence of increased acquisition of fishes from deeper, more costly habitats (e.g., Bernard 2001, 2004; Noah 2005; Pletka 2001a). This population growth, cultural elaboration, and expansion of subsistence economies may also correlate with increased impacts on local marine environments. In the remainder of this chapter, I provide a detailed comparative analysis of the Late Holocene data from San Miguel Island, placing these data within the context of other northern Channel Islands research.

TECHNOLOGY AND CRAFT PRODUCTION

The five San Miguel archaeological sites each supply a rich assemblage of artifacts. However, the number, density, and types of artifacts from each site differ considerably. These discrepancies provide evidence of how Chumash society changed or varied through time and space. Because the nature of the artifact assemblages from each site is influenced by a number of factors not related to human behavior (e.g., surface exposures, preservation, local environmental variation, taphonomy), I focus primarily on data from the largest excavated assemblages. The size of each of the excavation units and associated samples also differ. Consequently, I rely largely on standardized densities of artifacts (per m^3) for this comparative analysis (see Arnold and Munns 1994; Kennett and Conlee 2002). In the discussions below, I refer to each dated assemblage by its calibrated age (intercept), recognizing that these dates should be treated as approximations of the age of each assemblage.

The number of artifacts represented in a site is a general reflection of how intensively, and for how long, people performed various activities. The general trend through time at the five archaeological sites is an increase in the density and diversity of artifacts recovered (Figure 7.1). This is an outgrowth of trends in the Early and Middle Holocene that also show a general increase through time in the amount and type of artifacts recovered. Although a fairly large artifact assemblage was identified during extensive surface collections at the early Late Holocene deposits at SMI-87, only about 25 to 52 formal artifacts per m^3 were recovered from the excavations (excluding bead detritus or chipped-stone debitage). These numbers are considerably lower than the 220 to 261 artifacts per m^3 from late Middle period deposits at SMI-468 and -481. Transitional period deposits at SMI-468 also have high densities, with about 958 per m^3. As mentioned in earlier chapters, relatively few Transitional components have been identified and excavated, but these data are similar to findings of Arnold (1992a; Arnold, ed. 2001) and Arnold and Graesch (2001) for Santa Cruz Island that show an increase in artifact densities, particularly shell beads, during the Transitional period. Most scholars believe that by the onset of the Late period (ca. 650 cal BP [AD 1300]), the Chumash were living in large villages or towns and had complex sociopolitical systems and exchange networks. Sites of this age often show the highest artifact densities on the Channel Islands (Arnold and Graesch 2001; Arnold et al. 2001; Kennett and Conlee 2002; Preziosi 2001; Wake 2001). This may also be a time when Chumash population was at its zenith. The data from the five archaeological sites are consistent with this trend, where the 220 cal BP (AD 1730) component at SMI-163 contains the highest number of artifacts, 2,420 per m^3. The Protohistoric component (350 cal BP [AD 1600]) at SMI-470 also contains a high value (938 per m^3) comparable to the Transitional period levels at SMI-468.

Differences in bead and other artifact style, diversity, and production also reflect changes in exchange, social organization, and personal adornment (King 1990). The densities of beads, bead detritus, and artifacts associated with their production indicate how much energy people were expending in the production of craft items, and potentially how many of these craft items were intended for trade

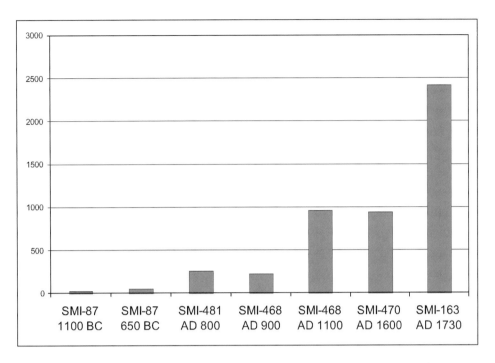

Figure 7.1. Densities of formal artifacts from Late Holocene components at five San Miguel Island archaeological sites (does not include detritus or debitage).

outside the village in which they were produced. The types of artifacts found in each of the archaeological sites vary considerably through time, reflecting these discrepancies. For example, only four different types of shell beads were found in the 3,000- to 2,500-year-old deposits at SMI-87, at least six types were found in the late Middle and Transitional deposits at SMI-468, and the highest diversity was found in Historic assemblages at SMI-163 (n = 11).

Olivella shell beads and bead detritus are among the most abundant artifacts found in Late Holocene archaeological sites on the Channel Islands, with densities of *Olivella* artifacts in some Late period sites exceeding 20,000 g per m³ (Kennett and Conlee 2002). The intensity of bead production appears to vary spatially and temporally and is related to the number of people occupying a given area and the proximity of those people to the habitat of *Olivella* and other raw materials (e.g., chert for microdrills). For Santa Cruz Island, Arnold and Munns (1994) link changes in the densities of bead-making materials and detritus, along with other variables, to the formation of craft specialization, arguing that it arose during the Transitional period. Using addi-

tional data from Santa Cruz Island, Arnold and Graesch (2001) noted a small increase in bead making during the late Middle period, followed by a great expansion during the Transitional and Late periods. Data from San Miguel and Santa Rosa islands also document an increase in bead making during the late Middle period and another increase during the Transitional period, but detritus densities vary among sites (Kennett and Conlee 2002:160).

Figure 7.2 places the densities of bead-making debris at the five San Miguel Island sites in the context of other San Miguel sites reported by Kennett and Conlee (2002). The San Miguel data illustrate a significant increase in bead making around the time of the Transitional period, with bead detritus densities three to four times higher than in Middle period deposits. Like the overall density of all artifacts, the values increase substantially in the Late period to about 5,000 to 7,000 g per m³, with the highest numbers occurring in Protohistoric/Historic deposits at SMI-602 with nearly 12,000 g per m³. Similar to data from Santa Cruz and Santa Rosa islands, the San Miguel Island data document an increase in bead making in the Transitional period (see Arnold

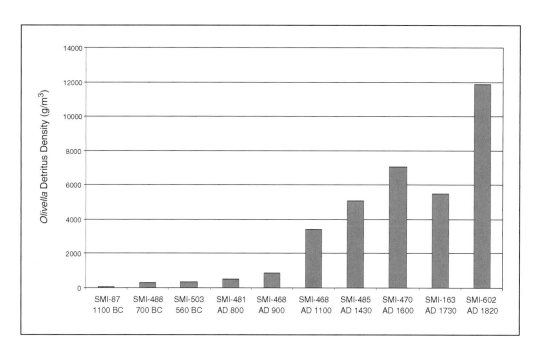

Figure 7.2. Bead detritus densities (g/m³) from Late Holocene San Miguel Island sites.

and Munns 1994; Arnold and Graesch 2001; Kennett and Conlee 2002).

King (1990) provided a bead chronology for the Santa Barbara Channel region, demonstrating that beads made from the wall portion of the *Olivella* shell are found in sites dated to the Early period and later. *Olivella* callus beads—significant because they were used as a type of currency by the Chumash—occur primarily during his Late period or the start of Arnold's (1992a; see also Arnold and Graesch 2001) Transitional period (ca. AD 1150). These trends, which have been explored and documented in detail by Arnold and Graesch (2001) and others working on Santa Cruz Island, are also apparent at the five sites I excavated. *Olivella* wall disk beads occur in four of the primary sites (SMI-481, SMI-468, SMI-163, and SMI-470), with only barrel and spire-lopped beads found in the roughly 3,000-year-old deposits at SMI-87 (Figure 7.3). In the late Middle period deposits at SMI-481, fairly high values for wall beads (96 per m³) and wall beads in production (BIP; 83 per m³) were noted. Similar quantities of BIP (122 per m³) were found in roughly the same age deposits at SMI-468. Wall bead densities then decline slightly in Transitional period deposits at SMI-468 (55 blanks, 64 beads, and 93 BIP per m³), and increase again during the

Protohistoric and Historic periods at SMI-163 (108 BIP, 167 blanks, and 67 beads per m³) and SMI-470 (125 BIP and 31 beads per m³). This rebound is similar to a trend noted by Arnold and Graesch (2001) and Kennett et al. (2000), who suggested that wall beads, particularly chipped disk or semi-ground forms, increase in abundance in postcontact assemblages. This is a time period when red abalone disk beads were also made in abundance at SMI-163 (Rick 2004c), a trend first noted by Arnold and Graesch (2001) for Santa Cruz Island.

The decline in wall beads and wall-bead production during the Late and Transitional periods, although relatively modest at the Late Holocene San Miguel sites, is associated with the appearance of beads made from the callus portion of the shell, particularly *Olivella* cup and lipped beads (Figure 7.4). Callus cup beads have long been considered diagnostic of the Late period, and in keeping with the trend noted by King (1990), *Olivella* callus beads generally occur in sites dating to the Transitional (L1) or later (see also Arnold and Graesch 2001). Modest amounts of callus BIP (26 per m³) and callus blanks (39 per m³) were present in the Transitional period deposits at SMI-468, with the highest densities found in Protohistoric deposits at SMI-470 (63 BIP, 156 blanks, and 94 beads per m³). The

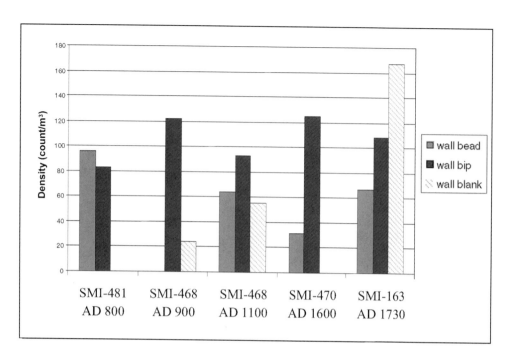

Figure 7.3. Densities (count/m^3) of *Olivella* wall beads, beads in production (BIP), and wall bead blanks in Late Holocene components at San Miguel Island sites.

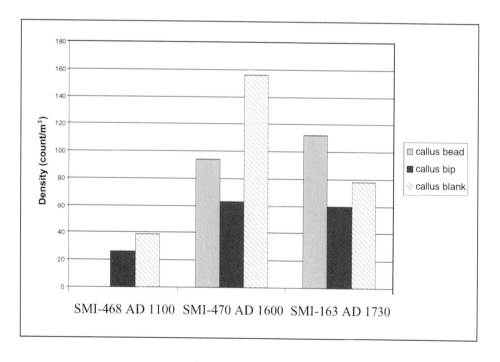

Figure 7.4. Densities (count/m^3) of *Olivella* callus beads, beads in production (BIP), and bead blanks in Late Holocene components at San Miguel Island sites.

number of callus blanks and BIP then decline slightly in the Protohistoric or Historic deposits at SMI-163. The number of finished beads, however, remains similar to previous levels. This decline in callus bead blanks and BIP occurs about the same time that people began intensifying *Olivella* wall disk and red abalone bead production.

Other than shell beads, the only artifact types to occur in great abundance are microblades and microdrills, artifacts first thought to appear during the late Middle period (Arnold 1987; Arnold et al. 2001). These artifacts were used to drill shell beads (Arnold 1987; Arnold et al. 2001; Preziosi 2001) and were identified in four of the sites I excavated (Table 7.2). Following regional trends, triangular prepared specimens generally dominate Late period assemblages, while trapezoidal and unprepared specimens dominate the earlier assemblages. Only one microblade core was identified at the sites, suggesting that microblades or microdrills were primarily being obtained through trade or were made elsewhere on the islands. The largest assemblage of microblades occurs at SMI-163, the site where bead production was also the greatest.

Subsistence-related artifacts also provide insight into Late Holocene human cultural developments. Compared with shell beads and microblades, subsistence-related artifacts are relatively rare in the excavated archaeological deposits. The most common subsistence-related artifacts include bone barbs and gorges, single-piece fishhooks, net weights, ground-stone tools, and projectile points. Although a shell fishhook dated to roughly 2500 cal BP (550 BC) was recovered from SMI-87, the use of circular shell fishhooks becomes widespread at sites dating after around 1,500 years ago (Rick et al. 2002). Bone barbs, identified at each of the sites,

suggest that spears and/or composite fishhooks were in use throughout the last 3,000 years. Finally, direct artifactual evidence for the use of boats was not identified, but faunal remains indicate the use of watercraft for subsistence and other pursuits throughout the Holocene. A slight increase in large pelagic fish (swordfish, tuna, etc.) late in time may indicate more intensive fishing in deep waters, activities that may have expanded as cross-channel voyaging and trade increased, and boats became more sophisticated during the last 2,000 to 1,000 years (see Arnold 1995; Arnold and Bernard 2005; Bernard 2001, 2004; Davenport et al. 1993; Gamble 2002). At most of the excavated sites, however, these offshore fish appear to be relatively minor constituents. I return to the artifact data at the end of this chapter to offer the broad implications of these findings for understanding emergent complexity on the islands.

SUBSISTENCE AND HISTORICAL ECOLOGY

The five archaeological sites each produced faunal assemblages with a variety of shellfish, fish, mammal, and bird remains, providing an opportunity to investigate temporal and spatial patterns in the importance of various resources and local environments. In the following section, I highlight changes through time in each of the broad animal categories, investigating differences in the human use of shellfish, fishes, mammals, and birds. I focus on overall densities of each animal category by NISP, MNI, or weight, and then examine changes in the specific taxa identified in each sample. A number of factors influence the density, abundance, and richness of faunal remains and other constituents in archaeological sites (see Chapter 3; Grayson 1984;

Table 7.2 Summary of Microblades and Microdrills by Count from the Excavated Sites.

Artifact	SMI-481 (AD 800)	SMI-468 (AD 1100)	SMI-470 (AD 1600)	SMI-163 (AD 1730)
Unprepared microblades	—	27	—	13
Unprepared microdrill	—	31	—	8
Prepared microblade	—	5	3	26
Prepared microdrill	—	10	3	54
Undiagnostic microdrill	1	4	—	—
Total	1	77	6	101

Reitz and Wing 1999), but several studies on the Channel Islands have effectively used these types of data to document changes in human subsistence (e.g., Kennett 1998; Porcasi et al. 2000; Raab et al. 1995b; Raab et al. 2002). Kirch (1997:37) also used similar methods to document human impacts on Pacific Island environments. Between 35 and 68 shellfish, fish, bird, and mammal taxa were identified in each of the components from the five sites (Table 7.3), supplying information on ecological developments, human impacts on local environments, and human responses to such ecological changes.

Shellfish and Invertebrates

The most abundant category by weight, and also the most diverse category, is that of shellfish and invertebrates. There is a general trend on the Channel Islands toward a decrease in the importance of shellfish and an increase in the importance of fish during the Late Holocene, part of a broader pattern that spans the Holocene (Glassow 1993b; Kennett 2005; Vellanoweth et al. 2002). For the most part, this trend is also present in the five Late Holocene sites I excavated (Figure 7.5). The early assemblages at SMI-87 (not including deflated levels) and SMI-481 contain relatively high densities of marine shell, followed by a decline near the end of the Middle period at SMI-468, with a slight rebound again in the Transitional component, and an increase in the Protohistoric or Historic period deposits at SMI-470 and SMI-163. The increase at SMI-163 to the highest level of any site is interesting. It seems likely that people were intensifying shellfish collecting at the site by exploiting local shellfish beds and possibly traveling to more distant regions to collect shellfish. These values correspond with the highest

fish values, suggesting that other aspects of subsistence were also being intensified.

The data from each of these sites also show interesting patterns in the importance of individual shell taxa. Because many of the shellfish taxa recovered in the samples were found in low densities, I focus primarily on eight taxa. These include California and platform mussels, black and red abalone, chitons (including *Cryptochiton*), sea urchin, *Tegula*, and owl limpet. The percentage of each of these categories as a reflection of total shell weight and MNI is displayed in Table 7.4. The combined percentage of other shellfish taxa is also presented, but for the most part these are minor or incidental contributors. The high percentage of "other shell" MNI in some of the assemblages is primarily a reflection of a large number of small limpets that were probably incidental additions to the midden.

California mussel is the dominant contributor to all the shellfish assemblages, with an average of 63 percent of the total shell weight for all components and individual values ranging from about 39 to 80 percent. When meat weights are considered, abalone, owl limpets, and other minor taxa increase slightly in some of the components. California mussel also generally dominates the shell categories by MNI, with a slightly lower average of about 52 percent and individual components ranging from 33 to 70 percent. Smaller platform mussels are also abundant in the assemblages, with an average of about 16 percent of the shell MNI, but less than about 3 percent of the average weight. In some sites (e.g., SMI-87), platform mussels contribute as much as 47 percent of the MNI, but less than 10 percent of the weight. These data suggest that platform mussels were occasionally an important part

Table 7.3. Taxonomic Richness in Late Holocene Components at Five Archaeological Sites.

Site	Age	Shellfish N[a]	Fish N[a]	Mammal N[a]	Bird N[a]	Total
SMI-87, West Unit	1100 B.C.	29	10	1	1	41
SMI-87, East Unit	650 B.C.	30	7	--	--	37
SMI-481, Stratum I	AD 800	27	17	5	4	53
SMI-468, Unit 2	AD 900	22	11	2	--	35
SMI-468, Unit 1	AD 1100	29	19	3	2	53
SMI-470, Bulk Sample	AD 1600	27	7	1	4	39
SMI-163, Unit 2	AD 1730	40	17	5	6	68

N[a] = Number of taxa (family, genus, or species) identified in each excavated sample.

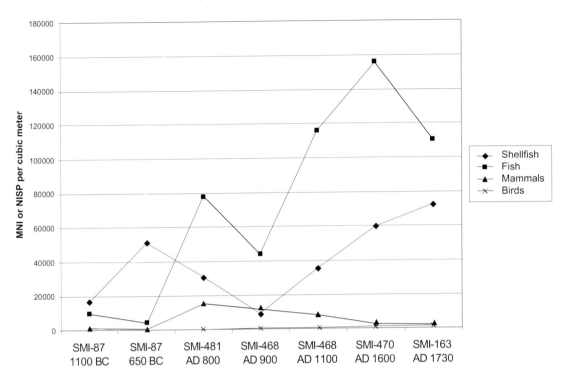

Figure 7.5. Densities of Late Holocene faunal remains (vertebrates = NISP/m^3; shellfish = MNI/m^3).

of the shellfish diet. However, there is no clear trend through time in their abundance, suggesting that variations in the importance of platform mussels are likely a result of local variability and productivity in shellfish habitats, as well as human predation on shellfish beds.

Tegula, including brown, black, and undifferentiated turbans, are the next most abundant category, with an average of about 7 percent of the weight and 8 percent of the MNI. *Tegula* never reach more than 15 percent of the MNI or 10 percent of the weight, suggesting that, like platform mussels, they were primarily supplemental. The importance of *Tegula* in the early components at SMI-87 is also comparable to low values in later components at SMI-470 and SMI-163, but there appears to be no clear pattern through time in the abundance of this resource. Red and black abalone generally contribute less than 5 percent of the shell weight or MNI, with values in the earliest components roughly the same as those in later components. Abalone is most abundant in the components from SMI-468, SMI-470, and SMI-481, where they combine to make up between 16 and 24 percent of the shell weight, but only 3 to 5 percent of the MNI, suggesting they were still a supplemental resource. Kennett

(2005:218) has suggested that human predation pressure reduced abalone populations on the Channel Islands near the end of the Middle Holocene and beginning of the Late Holocene, which may in part explain the low numbers of this resource in my Late Holocene samples (see below). However, their lower abundance in later sites could also reflect a dearth of available habitat for abalones near some sites, a greater abundance of sea otters or other abalone predators, changing environmental conditions, declines in people harvesting this resource because they focused more on fishing, or the use of abalone in fishhook and other artifact production (Glassow 1993a; Erlandson et al. 2005a; Rick et al. 2006a).

Most other shellfish taxa occur in relatively minor amounts, with only small fluctuations through time in their relative importance. Sea urchin is a minor contributor, but at SMI-87, SMI-481, and SMI-468, they make up between 5 and 7 percent of the total shell weight, a relatively high value considering how light sea urchin remains are compared with other taxa and how susceptible they are to loss through 1/8-inch screen. Erlandson et al. (2005a) recently suggested that localized abundance of sea urchin tests in Channel Islands sites may reflect local removal or reduction of sea otters and possibly

Table 7.4. Comparison of Most Abundant Shellfish Taxa as Percent of Total Shell MNI and Total Shell Weight.

Site and Age	California Mussel	Platform Mussel	Black Abalone	Red Abalone	Chiton	Sea Urchin	Tegula	Owl Limpet	Other Shell[a]
% of Total Shellfish MNI									
SMI-87 1100 BC	48.5	25.6	0.8	0.5	—	—	5.5	0.1	19.0
SMI-87 650 BC	36.2	46.9	0.7	0.6	—	—	4.8	0.1	10.7
SMI-481 AD 800	52.5	10.1	2.3	1.5	—	—	8.1	4.4	21.1
SMI-468 AD 900	33.1	3.6	3.6	1.5	—	—	15.1	6.4	36.7
SMI-468 AD 1100	58.6	12.6	2.5	0.7	—	—	9.3	2.4	13.9
SMI-470 AD 1600	62.1	3.5	2.4	0.5	—	—	9.2	2.6	19.7
SMI-163 AD 1730	69.5	8.6	0.8	0.1	—	—	4.6	0.4	16.0
Average	51.5	15.8	1.9	0.8	—	—	8.1	2.3	19.6
% of Total Shellfish Weight									
SMI-87 1100 BC	69.7	6.0	2.2	1	1.8	3	6.3	0.1	9.9
SMI-87 650 BC	65.3	7.7	2.8	1.1	2.3	5.1	5.3	0.1	10.3
SMI-481 AD 800	59.5	1.1	6.7	9.1	0.7	6.8	6.0	2.8	7.3
SMI-468 AD 900	38.5	1.5	11.5	12.5	2.6	5.0	7.7	4.6	16.1
SMI-468 AD 1100	65.3	1.5	6.3	3.1	1.2	2.5	6.7	1.7	11.7
SMI-470 AD 1600	59.1	0.3	13.3	3.0	0.5	2.7	9.8	2.2	9.1
SMI-163 AD 1730	80.1	0.9	2.9	1.1	0.6	0.5	4.7	0.4	8.8
Average	62.5	2.7	6.5	4.4	1.4	3.7	6.6	1.7	10.5

[a] Other shell is composed primarily of barnacles, small limpets, *Olivella*, and other taxa that were either not eaten, were minor contributors to the diet, or were used primarily for bead making. The high percentage of other shell in some MNI categories is a reflection of large amount of small limpets that were probably brought to the site incidentally. MNI data is not available for chitons and sea urchins.

California sheephead that prey on urchins and normally control their populations (see also Salls 1991). If Chumash hunting and fishing caused urchin populations to significantly increase, it could have led to decreased kelp forest productivity. Subsequent human predation on urchins, however, may have mediated these impacts (Erlandson et al. 2005a). Using data from a trans-Holocene sequence on San Miguel Island, Erlandson et al. (2005a:16–17) reported the percentage of urchin compared with other shellfish, with values ranging from 0.1 to 39.5 percent. The highest values may represent localized abundance of urchin and phase shifts in local kelp forest ecosystems. Although these data are preliminary in nature and may also be caused by environmental perturbations (e.g., El Niño), they provide possible evidence for the role of people in influencing the structure of kelp forests. Nevertheless, the value of sea urchin remains fairly small in most of the excavated Late Holocene sites.

To investigate potential human impact on mussel populations on San Miguel Island, Erlandson et al. (2004a) presented a trans-Holocene plot of the average shell size of California mussels through time, including measurements from some of the Late Holocene sites reported here. We assumed that as human predation pressure increases, the average size of California mussel shells should decrease. The original data set was highly variable and suggested no clear impact through time, with sizes appearing to oscillate randomly through time, possibly indicating human impact followed by periods of rebound. Another complicating factor is that shell sizes are also influenced by a variety of environmental variables, which may also influence their sizes. Recent expansion of this data set to include measurements of nearly 9,000 mussel shells from San Miguel sites shows a general trend toward size reduction through time, particularly in the Late Holocene, but with an incredible amount of variability (Figure 7.6).

We have also started measurements of black and red abalone shells to document their size profiles through time. Our analysis of black abalone measurements, which also includes historic data from nineteenth-century Chinese abalone camps, illustrates no significant change in size through the

Holocene, although the average size is considerably larger during the Historic period occupation by the Chinese (Braje et al. 2006b). The red abalone data demonstrate a decline in size during the Late Holocene. In addition to human predation, however, this size decline may be related to environmental changes associated with a reduction of red abalone in sites around the end of the Middle Holocene (Glassow 1993a). The extensive use of red abalone during the Late Holocene for technologies such as fishhooks and beads may also reduce the amount of

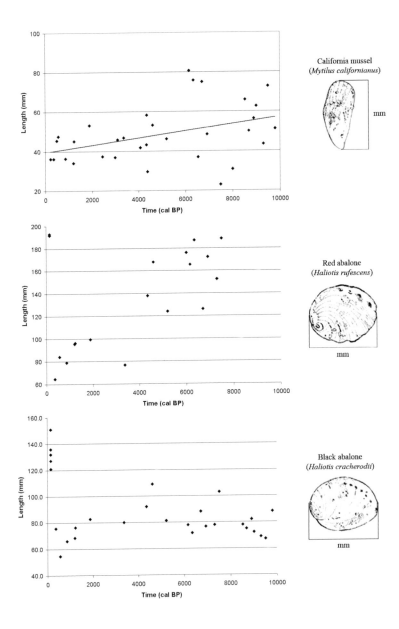

Figure 7.6. Average shell length (mm) for California mussel, black abalone, and red abalone from San Miguel Island over the last 10,000 years.

measurable shells in these deposits. Collectively, these data suggest that human predation pressure had a significant impact on San Miguel Island mussel and abalone populations, especially during the Late Holocene. Human impacts on San Miguel Island shellfish populations may have been mediated by the periodic movement of village locations, resource switching, and a general intensification of alternative resources (fish, marine mammals, etc.) through time. During the Late Holocene, these strategies became more difficult as human populations grew and the landscape became more circumscribed. Ultimately, the 10,000-year record of shellfish exploitation on San Miguel Island shows that the same species of rocky intertidal shellfish were harvested by the Chumash and their ancestors, with evidence for size reductions and predation pressure, but no clear catastrophic collapse.

Fish

Associated with the decreased significance of shellfish to Late Holocene Channel Islands economies is a dramatic increase in the importance of marine fishing (Lambert 1993; Kennett 2005). This includes an apparent pattern of fishing up the food web, where the highest trophic level fishes (swordfish, tunas, etc.) are found in sites postdating 1500 cal BP (see Bernard 2004). These increases in large, high trophic level fishes also appear to correlate with a variety of refinements in fishing technology, many of which are outgrowths of Early and Middle Holocene fishing techniques (Figure 7.7). The data from the five sites I excavated document this increase across the last 3,000 years (see Figure 7.5). The early components at SMI-87 have a low density of fish remains compared with later sites. After that the densities fluctuate somewhat, but generally increase until AD 1600, when they reach their zenith at SMI-470. The superabundance of fishes in Late period sites is similar to data recently presented for SMI-602 (Walker et al. 2002) of similar antiquity, and other data from Santa Rosa (Kennett 2005; Kennett and Kennett 2000; Rick 2004a) and Santa Cruz islands (Colten 2001; Colten and Arnold 1998; Noah 2005), indicating that this is part of a regional trend. Collectively, these data illustrate a general increase in the importance of marine fishing across the Late Holocene (see Bernard 2004; Colten 2001; Noah 2005; Paige 2000; Pletka 2001a; Rick 2004a).

Table 7.5 shows the relative importance of different fish taxa identified to family, genus, or species, as a percentage of total identified NISP. All of the sites are dominated by one of three fish taxa (rockfish, perch, and labrids). In components at SMI-87 and SMI-481, perch are most abundant (36 and 59 percent of the NISP), but most other sites have between 14 to 21 percent perch. Two components dated between about AD 900 and 1100 at SMI-468 contain large amounts of labrids (senorita or wrasse), with values between 30 and 43 percent of the identified NISP. Finally, SMI-481 contains roughly 29 percent clupeid (sardine or herring) by NISP. Some of these small fishes may be stomach contents from the large number of marine mammals at this site, but others were probably captured and eaten (see Chapter 5). Although clupeids are abundant in mainland and some Channel Islands assemblages, they have been shown to be underrepresented when residuals from mesh smaller than 1/8-inch are not analyzed. The only sample I analyzed with abundant clupeid remains also contains the highest density of marine mammal bones. All other taxa, including cabezon, mackerel, yellowtail, barracuda, billfish, and California sheephead occur in relatively low numbers.

Most of the variation in the significance of fish taxa may be a product of local variability in the abundance of fishes or habitats, the season when fishing was performed, or the types of technology people used to obtain fish. Rockfish dominate the Protohistoric and Historic period assemblages, suggesting that later people targeted these fishes, probably using single-piece shell fishhooks and other technologies. Most of the common fishes in each of the sites could have been obtained from nearshore rocky reef, kelp beds, sandy beaches, and other nearshore habitats. The general composition of fish taxa is also fairly similar to Early Holocene fish deposits at Daisy Cave, suggesting continuity in the types of fishes caught through time and human focus on the rich kelp forest and rocky-shore habitats of the Channel Islands across much of the Holocene (see Rick et al. 2001a). However, fishes from deeper-water environments (e.g., billfish) are not usually present in Early and Middle Holocene sites.

Billfishes that generally occur in deeper waters and require harpoons and watercraft to obtain are present in some of the Late Holocene sites, but generally make up less than 2 percent of the total

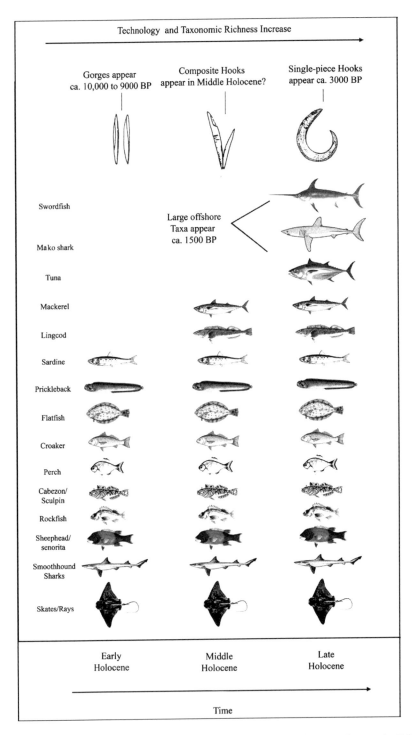

Figure 7.7. Diagram showing general increase in fish taxa through time, changes in fishing technology, and Late Holocene appearance of large, offshore taxa on the northern Channel Islands.

NISP. Most of these occur in assemblages that post-date 1150 cal BP (AD 800), after the Chumash *tomol* is thought to have come into use (Arnold 1995; Arnold and Bernard 2005; Bernard 2004; Gamble 2002), but a billfish vertebra was found on the sur-face at SMI-87, providing highly speculative evidence for the hunting of this fish as early as 3,000 years ago (see also Harrison and Harrison 1966; Rick and Glassow 1999). Davenport et al. (1993) suggested that systematic hunting of swordfish may

Table 7.5. Comparison of Most Abundant Fish Taxa as Percent of Total NISP Identified to Family, Genus, and Species.

Taxon	Rockfish	Perch	Cabezon	Clupeids	California Sheephead	Labrids	Mackerel	Other Fish
SMI-87 1100 BC	59.2	20.9	5.8	—	1.1	7.9	1.1	4.0
SMI-87 650 BC	13.8	58.8	5.0	—	—	18.8	—	3.6
SMI-481 AD 800	13.1	36.1	11.2	29.2	0.8	4.1	—	5.5
SMI-468 AD 900	36.2	15.6	5.1	5.8	3.5	29.2	1.9	2.7
SMI-468 AD 1100	28.4	15.1	2.5	4.4	1.3	43.3	1.4	3.6
SMI-470 AD 1600	68.8	17.1	5.1	0.3	—	—	—	8.7
SMI-163 AD 1730	74.5	14.3	2.9	0.8	0.6	1.5	0.4	5.0
Average	42.0	25.4	5.4	5.8	1.0	17.5	0.7	4.7

have begun roughly 2,000 years ago, but a larger data set analyzed by Bernard (2004) and Arnold and Bernard (2005) suggests that it did not become widespread until after about 1250 to 950 cal BP (AD 700 to 1000). Arnold et al. (2004:15) suggested that earlier occurrences of swordfish in archaeological sites may be from strandings. These studies demonstrate that the fishery for such large species would have required sturdy watercraft and would probably be correlated with the use of the Chumash plank canoe. The timing and origins of the plank canoe, however, remain a topic of considerable debate (see Arnold and Bernard 2005; Cassidy et al. 2004; Fagan 2004; Gamble 2002; Jones and Klar 2005).

While billfish remains were identified in most of the archaeological sites I excavated, none of the Late Holocene components suggest a focus on fishes from deeper and more costly habitats. For the most part, fishes that could have been obtained from kelp forests, rocky nearshore habitats, nearshore sandy beaches, or slightly deeper waters just beyond kelp forests, dominate the assemblages. These findings are supported by data from Santa Cruz Island presented by Colten (2001:202) who identified over 100 species of fish, but rockfish and surfperch provide over 90 percent of the fish NISP for the last 1,500 years. Some of these rockfish remains are from taxa that can inhabit deeper waters, but many are also found in nearshore habitats. Noah (2005:286) also reported the analysis of fish remains for four Historic period Chumash villages on Santa Cruz Island, noting that at all of the sites, rockfish, surfperch, sheephead, and mackerel are the most abundant fishes. Like Colten (2001),

Noah (2005) also identified a number of additional kelp forest, rocky nearshore, and other taxa, including tunas, billfish, rockfish, and mako shark.

Pletka (2001a) also presented data on fish remains from Santa Cruz Island. Although the taxa and NISP are not reported, he argues that people may have relied more systematically on deep-water and open-ocean habitats starting around the time of the Transitional period. In particular, the historic village of *Xaxas* (SCRI-240) at Prisoners Harbor produced roughly 82 billfish bones, but these still contribute just 5 percent of NISP identified to family, genus, or species (see Colten 2001:208). Additional analyses of the *Xaxas* assemblage have shown that in some of the deposits, billfishes make up about 8 to 9 percent of the total identified fish bone NISP, but nearly 20 percent by weight, making them the fourth most abundant taxon (Noah 2005: 222, 286). Similar values were reported for *Shawa* (SCRI-192), where billfishes make up about 23.7 percent of the bone weight, while at the other sites they generally make up about 5 to 6 percent of the bone weight (Noah 2005:286). Overall, the northern Channel Islands data suggest variability in human exploitation of fishes across the Late Holocene (and earlier), probably resulting from an increase in the number of people fishing, variability in the proximity and productivity of habitats (i.e., submarine canyons, kelp forests, sandy beaches) located near a given site, as well as ritualized behavior (see Hildebrandt and McGuire 2002). Increases in these offshore fishes may reflect greater cross-channel voyaging for exchange with the mainland, which would likely intensify encounter rates with these taxa.

In the only other detailed study of Late Holocene fish remains on San Miguel Island, Bowser (1993) used data from column samples excavated at Middle period deposits at SMI-504 and SMI-525 to suggest that the use of nets replaced the use of the single-piece fishhook as the primary method of capturing fishes. It is possible that the use of nets increased in some locations at the end of the Middle period, but the data from the sites I excavated suggest that hook and line was also an important fishing strategy at many locations. At some sites (e.g., SMI-468, SMI-481) netting of senorita, clupeids, perches, and other fishes may have been important, but my data show no island-wide trend toward an increased importance of netting and a decrease of hook and line fishing. Pletka (2001a: 241–242) presented similar data for Santa Cruz Island, suggesting that the use of nets may relate more to local habitats (e.g., proximity to sandy beaches) than specialized usage of nets.

Paige (2000), in one of the few studies of fish remains from Santa Rosa Island, identified over 2,000 fish bones and 21 taxa from SRI-15 and SRI-31, located on the island's west coast. SRI-15, which may be the historic Chumash village *Nimkilkil*, contains components spanning the late Middle, Transitional, and Late periods, providing an opportunity to investigate changes in fish remains during the latter half of the Late Holocene. At SRI-31, fish remains from a late Middle period component were analyzed. Similar to my assemblages, fish remains from these sites are dominated by kelp forest and nearshore taxa, particularly perch and rockfish, and appear to have been caught primarily using hook and line and nets (Paige 2000). These data are generally similar to Rick's (2004a) analysis of fish remains from SRI-2, the Chumash village of *Niaqla*, where rockfish, labrids, and perches dominate all three Late Holocene components. Although the small size of the sample may have limited the recovery of larger fish taxa, the available data suggest that Chumash peoples on San Miguel and western Santa Rosa islands largely targeted nearshore environments near the sites. This pattern appears to vary geographically, as Colten (2001), Noah (2005), and Pletka (2001a) have suggested a somewhat different pattern for some Santa Cruz Island sites.

Relying on otolith and other fish data from Late Holocene sites on Santa Cruz Island, Colten (2001) and Pletka (2001a) suggested that changes in fish species reflect paleoenvironmental developments and emergent complexity during the Transitional period. However, rather than suggesting a decrease in marine productivity during this time period, their data point to a complex array of environmental variables influencing fishing during the Transitional and other time periods, including a mix of cold and warm water taxa. Paige (2000) found an increase in the number of taxa in the Transitional period, but limited evidence for an increase in warm-water taxa, suggesting again that human fishing strategies during this time were predicated by local habitats, technology, and environmental conditions. The Transitional period component at SMI-468 also contains relatively high densities and the highest taxonomic richness of fishes in any of the five assemblages from the excavated sites.

The available data from the northern Channel Islands suggest that fishing generally increased through time and that people relied on a similar suite of fishes from nearshore environments throughout the Late Holocene. These data demonstrate substantial continuity in the types of fishes captured across the Late Holocene—except for the addition of billfish and other deep-water taxa—and probably earlier. Determining Chumash impacts on Late Holocene fishes is complicated by a variety of factors (e.g., dearth of fish-size data), but current data suggest no dramatic declines in the types of fishes being exploited. Clearly, the increase in fishing would produce greater impacts on local fisheries, but detecting these archaeologically has been problematic.

Mammals

As in many Channel Islands sites, the number of mammal taxa in the Late Holocene assemblages is small and dominated by marine mammals, reflecting the limited terrestrial fauna of the Channel Islands. Otariids and sea otters generally are the most commonly identified taxa in the deposits. Small amounts of phocid and cetacean remains were also identified, as were a few fragments that may be large terrestrial mammal bone (probably from the mainland) and small rodent bone (e.g., deer mouse). The largest assemblage of marine mammal remains by far was from SMI-481, where a suite of marine mammals was identified (see Chapter 5).

Marine mammal bone densities are generally highest in the late Middle period components (see

Figure 7.5). This is particularly true for SMI-481, where mammal densities are between four and eight times higher than at the other sites. Large increases in mammal densities at SMI-481 and SMI-468 may be primarily a result of local availability of marine mammals in the Otter Point area, where pinnipeds are common today and probably were in the past. Walker et al. (2002) and Kennett (2005) also noted that marine mammals were abundant in late Middle period deposits at SMI-528, a site occupied at roughly the same time as SMI-481. Recent research at SMI-232 on the south coast of San Miguel Island has documented dense concentrations of marine mammal remains dated to roughly AD 800 (Braje and Erlandson 2005; Braje et al. 2005a), suggesting that around 1,500 to 1,100 years ago, people were intensively hunting marine mammals. The decrease in pinniped remains in the samples after about AD 1000 is also similar to patterns described by Walker et al. (2002) for Late period assemblages at SMI-602 on Point Bennett, possibly illustrating a general decline in marine mammal abundance on San Miguel Island at this time. Colten (2001, 2002) and Noah (2005) also identified otariids, such as Guadalupe fur seal, northern fur seal, and California sea lion, as well as harbor seals, sea otters, and a variety of cetaceans in several Santa Cruz Island sites occupied over the last 1,500 years. However, at all of these sites, fish and shellfish dominate the estimated meat yields, suggesting that mammals were largely supplemental (Colten 2001; Colten and Arnold 1998).

A number of scholars have investigated patterns of ancient marine mammal hunting and ecology along the Pacific Coast of North America (e.g., Broughton 1994; Burton et al. 2002; Colten 2002; Colten and Arnold 1998; Erlandson et al. 1998; Etnier 2002, 2004; Hildebrandt and Jones 1992; Jones and Hildebrandt 1995; Jones et al. 2004; Lyman 1995; Noah 2005; Porcasi et al. 2000). Relying largely on optimal foraging theory, Hildebrandt and Jones (1992) propose a "tragedy of the commons" scenario, with the most accessible species (migratory breeders, fur seals, California sea lions, etc.) being hunted first. People then shift to harbor seals and sea otters (resident breeders), which are more difficult to acquire. Using data from San Miguel Island, Jones and Hildebrandt (1995:85) suggested that the decline in migratory breeders on the Channel Islands did not occur until after about

1,500 years ago. To Jones and Hildebrandt (1995) the islands may have remained a final respite for marine mammals despite human hunting pressure. Colten and Arnold (1998) and Colten (2002), relying largely on data from Santa Cruz Island, however, noted problems with the tragedy of the commons model. They argue that migratory breeders were most abundant in all of the Late Holocene sites they excavated, and fish and shellfish appear to dominate the diet, with much smaller contributions by marine mammals. Erlandson et al. (2004a) and Kennett (2005) also point to the dearth of pinniped remains in early sites on San Miguel Island, noting that early people focused mostly on shellfish.

Kennett (2005:222–223) recently proposed several cultural and environmental explanations for the dearth of pinnipeds in early Channel Islands sites and the increase in pinniped hunting around 1,200 years ago. Kennett (2005) suggested that pinniped haul-outs and breeding areas may have been limited to offshore rocks around the islands, making them a relatively costly resource to acquire. He also suggested that early human settlement may have been largely focused on northern Santa Rosa Island, far away from San Miguel rookeries. This implies that not until villages were established on San Miguel and technologies were improved did pinniped hunting increase. Rising sea levels and changing marine conditions may have also hindered early marine mammal populations around the islands (Kennett 2005), but Early and Middle Holocene deposits at Eel Point on San Clemente Island have produced abundant pinniped bones (Porcasi et al. 2000). Kennett's (2005) ideas about technological developments (e.g., refined watercraft) and the possibility that pinnipeds were largely on offshore rocks may help explain the dearth of marine mammals in Channel Islands sites prior to 1,500 years ago. However, numerous sites on San Miguel Island, including SMI-87, date prior to this time (see Table 7.1; Rick et al. 2005b), making his assertions about a dearth of early human settlement on San Miguel Island problematic. The available data suggest that people may have had significant impacts on San Miguel Island pinnipeds beginning around 1,500 years ago, leading to declines in pinniped abundance in island sites. Preliminary archaeological data from the Channel Islands, however, including a Late Prehistoric and possible Historic period Chumash village in the middle of the Point Bennett rookery, suggest that the large marine mammal populations noted today on San Miguel Island (see Chapter 2) are probably unprecedented for much of the Holocene. People on the mainland and islands, therefore, had an impact on the demography and structure of pinniped populations. However, there is no evidence for local extinctions of pinnipeds caused by Native Americans, and, although declines are evident, there appears to have been some degree of coexistence between humans and pinnipeds for 10,000 years. Much is to be learned about the scale of this impact and dearth of pinnipeds in earlier sites, and overgeneralizations should be avoided until larger samples of marine mammal remains from a variety of archaeological sites are available.

Birds

Bird bones are generally rare in Channel Islands archaeological sites. All of the bird taxa identified in the Late Holocene sites are residents or breeders on the Channel Islands today. These include cormorants, gulls, auklets, a grebe, a northern fulmar, and a pelican. Although bird remains are limited in the excavated samples, they were probably significant for their feathers and for making a variety of tools, including, pins, awls, tubes, and whistles.

At the five Late Holocene sites, bird remains generally contribute less than 5 percent of the total faunal sample by all measures. Bird bone densities are also relatively low in all the site components (see Figure 7.5). However, at SMI-163, bird bone densities are much higher than at any other site. This pattern may reflect local variability in the abundance of birds. Prince Island, located about 750 m northwest of SMI-163, is currently home to numerous varieties of breeding sea birds, including auklets, guillemots, and cormorants, the primary bird taxa identified at SMI-163. A high proportion of cormorant bones was also identified at *L'akayamu* (SCRI-328 and -330) on Santa Cruz Island, suggesting that this site was also located close to cormorant breeding or roosting areas (Noah 2005). The abundance of these bird remains at SMI-163 indicates the possibility of historical continuity in the presence of seabird colonies on Prince Island. One possible juvenile auklet bone from SMI-163 may support this finding, but further data are needed to confirm or deny this speculation. It is also possible that people at SMI-481 and SMI-468 took birds from nearby Castle Rock, a place where

many birds also breed today. If people were taking birds from the offshore rocks where they breed, this would have had a significant impact on bird demography, population size, and behavior. The introduction of dogs to the islands would also represent another impact on island bird populations that is difficult to detect archaeologically.

Guthrie (1980) analyzed bird remains from SMI-1, SMI-261, and SMI-525 on San Miguel Island, noting an abundance of cormorants and alcids, and other sea birds. Colten (2001) identified roughly 25 species of bird in Santa Cruz Island middens dated to the last 1,500 years, with cormorants dominating all time periods. Analysis of the four Santa Cruz Island Historic period villages by Noah (2005) also identified patterns similar to Colten's (2001), with cormorants most abundant, followed by gulls. As is the case with other types of resources, the exploitation of birds by the Chumash was probably strongly influenced by their abundance and accessibility in local site catchments, with available data indicating a focus on cormorants, alcids, and gulls.

One important difference between the Late Holocene and earlier bird assemblages is the apparent dearth of the extinct flightless goose (*Chendytes lawii*) in sites dated after the Middle Holocene (Guthrie 1980, 1993b; Rick et al. 2006a). Although the earliest dates for human arrival and the terminal dates for the extinction of pygmy mammoths may overlap (Agenbroad et al. 2005; these dates remain uncalibrated, so their precise ages remain uncertain), the flightless goose is one of the few animals known to have gone extinct during the prehistoric human era. Relatively few San Miguel or other island archaeological sites have produced flightless goose bones, however, making it unclear if humans, environmental variables, or a combination of factors led to this extinction.

LATE HOLOCENE CHANNEL ISLANDS CULTURAL DYNAMICS: SYNTHESIS AND IMPLICATIONS

Archaeological evidence of craft and other artifact production and human subsistence activities described in this book provides insight into the emergence of cultural complexity and the historical ecology of the Island Chumash. Here I provide a synthesis of these data, placing them within the context of other Channel Islands research. My summary also emphasizes the relationships and interconnections between emergent complexity and environmental developments on the Channel Islands.

About 3,000 years ago at SMI-87, people hunted marine mammals, fished in kelp forests and nearshore rocky environments, collected a variety of shellfish, and conducted other activities. Beads were made at SMI-87, but in much lower numbers than at later sites, indicating that bead making was a limited activity at this time. Most of the occupation also predates the widespread use of circular shell fishhooks, *tomols*, bow and arrows, and craft production that are characteristic of Late and Historic period Island Chumash society. Although few sites are available for comparison during this time period, the data from SMI-87 suggest that people were living in relatively large villages, probably exchanging some goods with mainlanders, and engaging in a variety of marine subsistence pursuits. The site clearly differs from classic Chumash villages, but the traits listed above suggest that antecedents of Chumash culture were in place by about 3,000 years ago or earlier (see Erlandson and Rick 2002a).

Beginning around 1,500 years ago, increases in the intensity of marine fishing are evident at SMI-481 and SMI-468. These appear to correlate with cooler sea-surface temperatures (Kennett 2005; Kennett and Kennett 2000) and a period of population growth on the Channel Islands, suggesting that people were increasing their subsistence efforts relative to growing population densities and changing environmental conditions. Such population growth must have also increased the impacts of the Chumash on Channel Islands ecosystems. Documenting these trends has been difficult, indicating complex patterns of impacts and rebound, as well ambiguities in distinguishing between changes caused by human agency versus environmental factors. Dense concentrations of marine mammal bones found at SMI-481, SMI-528, and SMI-232 suggest human hunting had a strong impact on pinniped demography, population, and behavior. Shellfish sizes also appear to decline through time, although these data illustrate temporal and spatial variability. Bead densities were still relatively low around 1,500 years ago, but are higher than in previous periods, indicating that people were intensifying exchange systems and relationships with people on other islands or the mainland.

Data from the Transitional component at SMI-468 suggest that marine mammals were less abundant, fishing increased, and the number and types of *Olivella* beads also increased substantially. These findings indicate that the cultural patterns that characterized the Late period had their origins in the Transitional and late Middle period. Human daily life was still focused on obtaining marine animals primarily from nearshore environments, but bead production and exchange became considerably more abundant. These data are comparable to some of the findings presented by Arnold (1992a, 2001a, 2001b, 2001c; Arnold and Graesch 2001) for Santa Cruz Island, but I found little or no evidence for a decrease in marine productivity at this time. In fact, the richness and density of fishes increased from earlier levels, suggesting that marine environments on San Miguel and western Santa Rosa islands continued to be productive and variable (see also Colten 2001; Erlandson and Gerber 1993; Gamble 2005; Kennett and Kennett 2000; Paige 2000; Pletka 2001a; Rick 2004a). The greater variability of fishes during the Transitional period may have also been related to increases in social complexity and fluctuating environmental conditions (Arnold 2001a, 2001b; Pletka 2001a).

New paleoenvironmental data from the Santa Barbara Channel region, presented by Kennett and Kennett (2000) and Kennett (2005), demonstrate that the last 3,000 years were a highly unstable interval and that the Transitional period may not have been a time of decreased marine productivity. The instability of Late Holocene climates and drought, particularly between about 1,500 and 700 years ago, may have promoted conflict and led to greater sociopolitical complexity (Kennett 2005; Kennett and Kennett 2000). As Bettinger (1999) suggested, however, people adapted to short-term climatic perturbations throughout the Holocene, and such events may not have led to total declines in foraging and population. Gamble (2005) also notes that the Chumash may have been fairly versatile at adapting to punctuated changes in climate, at least more so than sedentary agriculturalists. While environmental fluctuations throughout the Holocene probably influenced ancient peoples of the Channel Islands, these perturbations may have had a greater impact on densely populated groups of the last 1,500 years.

Despite these climatic fluctuations, however, similarities in the types of marine resources (California mussels, nearshore fishes, etc.) used by people across the Holocene suggest an interesting pattern of long-term continuity, interspersed by periods when new resources (e.g., offshore fishes) were acquired.

Climate change appears to have worked in concert with a variety of social factors to promote increased complexity, territoriality, craft production, and other aspects of cultural change at the end of the Middle and Transitional period (see Arnold 1992a, 2001b; Kennett 2005; Kennett and Kennett 2000). Climatic instability may have fostered some cooperation as Kennett and Kennett (2000) suggested, perhaps promoting increased exchange. J. Johnson (2000) suggested that a heterarchical exchange system increased as a mechanism to combat climatic instability of the Transitional period, illustrating another potentially cooperative response. Increases in bead production and presumably exchange at the late Middle period, Transitional period, and later sites I excavated may support this proposition (see also Arnold 1992a, 1992b). Although environmental change may have contributed to increased cultural elaboration, I emphasize that a combination of factors, including population growth and greater geographic and social circumscription, were also catalysts to the cultural patterns that emerged near the end of the Middle and beginning of the Transitional periods. For San Miguel Island, it is also possible that declines in marine mammal abundance and other resources after about 1200 cal BP (AD 750) spurred significant changes in social organization and other aspects of society.

As described in Chapter 1, changes in human health, disease, and violence during the late Middle and Transitional periods are also apparent from analyses of human skeletal remains from the Channel Islands and Santa Barbara mainland (Hollimon 1990; Lambert 1993, 1994; Lambert and Walker 1991; Walker 1986, 1989). Although the bioarchaeological data generally do not have the chronological resolution of recent archaeological studies, some general patterns are of interest. Lambert (1993), for example, documents a decline in health through time among Channel Islanders, particularly during the late Middle period when Channel Islanders became increasingly focused on fishing. This is followed by a slight rebound in human health during

the Late period (Lambert 1993). Lambert and Walker (1991) suggested that more lethal conflict occurred between about 1650 cal BP (AD 300) and 800 cal BP (AD 1150), but decreased during the Late period. To Lambert (1993, 1994) and Lambert and Walker (1991), growing population densities and greater circumscription and territoriality promoted declines in health and increased violence. When compounded with environmental perturbations, these events were important causes of cultural change and complexity. Other bioarchaeological studies from the Santa Barbara mainland and Channel Islands suggest that people living during the Transitional period suffered poorer health than people living before or after this time, and that cultural changes were probably instituted to buffer subsistence stress (Hollimon's 1990:213–214). Due to limited data on San Miguel Island skeletal populations, the extent of these patterns on San Miguel remains unclear. Walker (1986) and Lambert and Walker (1991) note that frequencies of *Cribra orbitalia*, a condition related to anemia, however, were higher on San Miguel Island than on any of the other islands or mainland, and may have been related to the dearth of freshwater and terrestrial resources on this small island. Patterns of cranial injuries in San Miguel skeletal remains were higher than on Santa Rosa Island, but less than on Santa Cruz Island (Lambert and Walker 1991; Walker 1989). The less diversified subsistence economies, including a heavy reliance on marine fishing and increased evidence for exchange at the sites I excavated after about 1,500 years ago, suggest that many of the trends inferred from other Channel Islands skeletal populations were probably also operating on San Miguel Island, but I emphasize that there is also continuity in the types of resources people were acquiring.

By the Late period, virtually all of the facets of Chumash life documented during the Historic period appear to have been in place. Populations appear to have been at their zenith, and cross-channel trade and craft production were also at their height. Late period peoples at these sites continued to focus primarily on marine fishing, supplemented by marine mammal hunting, shellfish collecting, and craft production. The density of fish remains increases substantially, corresponding with higher bead production and exchange, illustrating parallels with the Historic period Chumash. More or less, all of the aspects of Chumash culture noted by early explorers and anthropologists (sedentism and large villages, complex exchange systems, sophisticated maritime subsistence, social hierarchy, elaborate material culture, etc.) were clearly in place by the onset of the Late period. However, data from San Miguel and the other northern Channel Islands illustrate that the types of activities people conducted during this time period were still predicated by local availability of resources and proximity to other people (see Arnold, ed. 2001; Kennett 2005; Kennett and Conlee 2002; Munns and Arnold 2002). Climatic conditions may have been more stable during this time, perhaps leading to decreased violence, improved health, and increased cooperation (see Kennett 2005; Kennett and Kennett 2000; Lambert 1993; Lambert and Walker 1991).

During the Protohistoric and Historic periods, Island Chumash daily activities show substantial continuity with Late period practices, despite the potential effects of early European contact. Subsistence practices were focused on fishing, although people also appear to have intensified their use of shellfish and birds at SMI-163. Changes in cultural practices, including the appearance of glass beads, a reappearance of *Olivella* wall beads as a dominant bead type at several sites, the use of needles to drill shell beads, and increases in the production of red abalone disk beads, are also evident in the Protohistoric and Historic periods (see also Arnold and Graesch 2001; Graesch 2001, 2004; Rick 2004c). For a time, the relative isolation of the islands probably sheltered the Island Chumash from many of the demographic, economic, and social upheavals caused by the establishment of Spanish missions, presidios, and pueblos on the mainland by the end of the eighteenth century (see Arnold and Graesch 2004; J. Johnson 1999b; Walker et al. 1989). Historic disease epidemics, which greatly reduced Chumash populations (see J. Johnson 1999b; Walker and Johnson 1992), possibly led to underestimations of the Chumash population at some island villages. For instance, SMI-163 may have had larger Protohistoric or early Historic populations than baptismal records indicate (see Chapter 6). However, there is considerable continuity in the types of activities being conducted at several Historic island communities (Arnold et al. 2004; Graesch 2001, 2004; Noah 2005), indicating that this is a topic deserving considerably more research. By

about AD 1822, the last of the Island Chumash had been removed from their island homes and taken to the missions. Nonetheless, Channel Islanders had a somewhat longer period of cultural continuity and persistence than people on the mainland coast. Even after the Mission period, in fact, some groups of Island Chumash formed discrete communities on the periphery of emerging colonial towns, maintaining somewhat distinct identities and traditions through much of the nineteenth century (J. Johnson 2001:57–60; J. Johnson and Mclendon 2002).

In summary, the artifact data from San Miguel Island discussed in this book support some of the findings of Arnold (1992a, 2001b) and Kennett (2005), suggesting that bead production and exchange increased significantly around the time of the Transitional period, but are probably outgrowths of earlier increases during the late Middle period. These data illustrate that greater Chumash cultural elaboration and complexity occurred around the close of the late Middle and onset of the Transitional period. Arnold (1992a, 1992b, 2001b) has argued that data from the Transitional period on Santa Cruz Island signify the development of a simple chiefdom on the Channel Islands. My data support the fact that craft production and cultural elaboration increased at this time, but provide no clear evidence for the development of a chiefdom or ascribed status (Clark 1995; Kennett 2005). Defining such social constructs in the archaeological record is complicated by a variety of taphonomic and other biases, making these assertions tenuous for San Miguel Island, at least for now.

The Late Holocene faunal data demonstrate an increased reliance on marine fishing and decreased focus on shellfish collecting through time. However, there is continuity in the resources people were using over the last 3,000 years, including the types of fishes and shellfish that people exploited, with no evidence for catastrophic environmental conditions. A growing body of data suggests that the Chumash and their predecessors produced some significant impacts on local shellfish communities, marine mammal populations, and possibly marine birds. The Chumash affected these animals—as probably all hunters and gatherers do (Grayson 2001)—but some of these impacts were probably short-lived as people changed their village locations or turned to other resources, leading to potential rebounds. These strategies became increasingly difficult in the fairly densely populated and circumscribed landscape of the Late Holocene.

These data further illustrate the importance of San Miguel Island in the larger southern California interaction sphere and in the evolution of Chumash cultural complexity. Although it is the outermost of the northern Channel Islands and has historically been marginalized, San Miguel Islanders clearly participated in all aspects of Chumash society and were a central component of regional social and ecological developments. Many of the patterns on San Miguel Island also differ from those on adjacent Santa Rosa and Santa Cruz islands, including somewhat lower densities of *Olivella* bead-making materials, but high concentrations of bowl, red abalone bead, and fishhook production (see Conlee 2000; Kennett and Conlee 2002; Kennett 2005; Rick 2004c). The subsistence data also demonstrate that San Miguel Islanders played a key role in structuring the nature of nearshore marine ecosystems. A growing body of data points to the idea that, rather than being a peripheral part of the Chumash world, San Miguel Island was significant in the larger southern California interaction sphere.

CONCLUSIONS

The world's coastlines are remarkable environments which have played an important role in the human past. From Florida to the Northwest Coast, from Japan to California, coastal hunter-gatherers developed diverse cultural systems, and lifeways focused around the unique environments of marine and coastal settings. Coastal peoples often had dense and relatively sedentary populations, complex, long-distance exchange networks, institutional hierarchies, and sophisticated maritime technologies in the absence of widespread agriculture or domestication (Arnold 1996; Fitzhugh 2003; Lightfoot 1993; Moss and Erlandson 1995; Sassaman 2004). Even in coastal areas where agriculture emerged as the dominant mode of subsistence (e.g., Peru, Belize, and Mexico), people continued to be integrally linked to coastlines and oceans for practical and ideological purposes (Blake 1999; Moseley 1975; Stark and Voorhies 1978; see also Voorhies 2004).

This Island Chumash case study provides considerable information on the lifeways of ancient coastal peoples and human use of land and sea-

scapes, underscoring a variety of important issues for archaeologists working on the Channel Islands and in coastal areas more generally. The five archaeological sites described in this book demonstrate variability in the Late Holocene archaeological record, both in the types of fauna people exploited and the artifacts they produced and exchanged. These data suggest that there was no single path to Chumash complexity or elaboration. This is underscored by Ames' (1991:943) work on the Northwest Coast:

Social complexity and stratification on the coast has a history; it is possible that it developed more than once in time and space; it is also likely that complexity took on different guises on the coast and in the interior, sometimes through reorganizing the same social and cultural elements. Some implications of complexity may not have included stratification at all, but still exhibited a complex division of labour, specialized production, and intricate patterns of regional interaction. To be able to explain the development of social complexity on the Northwest Coast is to be able to write the history of its changes in time and space.

Such histories on the Channel Islands span at least 13,000 calendar years, with these long-term trends culminating in the Chumash that were described by early European explorers. The continued analysis of this long-term record will prove fruitful for future research on the Island Chumash and in other coastal areas around the world.

Archaeology can provide great insight into human daily activities and their relationship with larger social and cultural issues (Lightfoot et al. 1998). By reconstructing aspects of daily life, including subsistence practices and the production of beads and other artifacts, I produced a comprehensive overview of how these activities changed through time on San Miguel Island. These findings indicate that cultural developments during the early portions of the Late Holocene, and undoubtedly some during the Middle Holocene, set the stage for the relatively rapid and often punctuated changes of the last 1,000 to 1,500 years (see also Arnold 1992a; Erlandson and Rick 2002a; Gamble and Russell 2002; Kennett 2005; and others). In this sense, Island Chumash cultural elaboration was both gradual and punctuated, with a number of changes seen across the Holocene, but pronounced developments during the late Middle and Transitional periods and other times. Continued investigations of aspects of human daily life visible in the archaeological record will prove important for understanding broader changes in social and economic developments among coastal peoples.

Finally, this study illustrates the importance of historical ecological research on the Channel Islands and in other coastal areas around the world. By the Late Holocene, the Channel Islands had become an anthropogenic landscape, with people functioning as the top predator in most nearshore environments. The data presented in this study suggest that the Chumash impacted their island ecosystems, but to a much lesser degree than the numerous and profound impacts (e.g., commercial overfishing, oil spills, sea otter eradication, and sewage and agricultural runoff) of the Euroamerican period. These discrepancies may be partly a result of differing technologies, population densities, and cultural histories, but the Chumash had high population densities, an elaborate and diverse maritime technology, and an emerging regional economy by at least 1,000 to 500 years ago. People clearly played an important role in helping structure the nature of San Miguel Island marine ecosystems, probably working in concert with environmental changes to shape marine environments across the Holocene. Much is to be learned about the more than 10,000 years of cultural elaboration, population growth, and interaction of people with the marine environments of the Channel Islands. Nonetheless, trans-Holocene records from San Miguel Island suggest that the Chumash and their predecessors exploited a similar suite of shellfish, fish, marine mammals, and birds over the past 10,000 years. Quantitative and qualitative differences in archaeological and modern biological data sets have often precluded direct comparisons of these different bodies of information (see Erlandson et al. 2004a; Jackson et al. 2001), but recent research by Reitz (2004) and Morales and Roselló

(2004) have estimated trophic levels for archaeological fish assemblages that may provide a model for comparing archaeological, historical, and biological data. By building such bridges between disciplines, and placing our research in the rapidly developing field of historical ecology, we can make archaeology increasingly relevant to modern society (van der Leeuw and Redman 2002).

One of the greatest contributions archaeologists can make is to provide baseline data crucial for the restoration and remediation of marine habitats (Braje et al. 2006a). In this framework, environmental reconstructions based on archaeological faunal and other data can aid in improving management strategies for the coastal ecosystems of the Channel Islands and southern California coast, particularly when trying to establish historical baselines or targets for restoration (Jackson et al. 2001; Pauly 1995). The data presented here and in other recent San Miguel studies (e.g., Braje et al. 2006a; Erlandson et al. 2004a, 2005a, 2005b) demonstrate that archaeology provides important reconstructions of long-term changes in coastal ecosystems, underscores the deep histories of human impacts on marine environments, and ultimately yields better baseline data for managing and restoring modern coastal ecosystems.

The Channel Islands offer a productive and exciting arena for future research on coastal peoples. During the last 3,000 years, a number of changes occurred in Chumash society, spurred by growing populations, environmental changes, increased circumscription, and other variables. The Chumash and their predecessors were able to surmount a variety of environmental, health, and demographic challenges through social, political, and economic reorganization over the last 10,000 years. These changes were pronounced during the last 1,000 to 1,500 years, but had their foundation in earlier developments. Ultimately, the remarkable sequence on the Channel Islands and mainland coastal California is a testament to the innovation, resilience, and strength of the Chumash and their predecessors.

References Cited

Agenbroad, L. D.
1998   New Pygmy Mammoth (*Mammuthus exilis*) Localities and Radiocarbon Dates from San Miguel, Santa Rosa, and Santa Cruz Islands, California. In *Contributions to the Geology of the Northern Channel Islands, Southern California*, edited by P. Weigand, pp. 169–175. Bakersfield: Pacific Section of the American Association of Petroleum Geologists.

Agenbroad, L. D., J. R. Johnson, D. Morris, and T. W. Stafford, Jr.
2005   Mammoths and Humans as Late Pleistocene Contemporaries on Santa Rosa Island. In *Proceedings of the Sixth California Islands Symposium*, edited by D. Garcelon and C. Schwemm, pp. 3–7. Arcata, CA: National Park Service Technical Publication CHIS-05–01, Institute for Wildlife Studies.

Alsop, F. J. III
2001   *Birds of North America: Western Region*. New York: DK Publishing.

Ames, K. M.
1991   The Archaeology of the Longue Durée: Temporal and Spatial Scale in the Evolution of Social Complexity on the Southern Northwest Coast. *Antiquity* 65:935–945.
1994   The Northwest Coast: Complex Hunter-Gatherers, Ecology, and Social Evolution. *Annual Review of Anthropology* 23: 209–229.
2003   The Northwest Coast. *Evolutionary Anthropology* 12:19–33.

Ames, K. M., and H. D. G., Maschner
1999   *Peoples of the Northwest Coast: Their Archaeology and Prehistory*. New York: Thames and Hudson.

Anderson, R. S.
2002   Fire and Vegetation History of Santa Rosa Island, Channel Islands National Park, California. Report on file at Channel Islands National Park, Ventura.

Arnold, J. E.
1987   *Craft Specialization in the Prehistoric Channel Islands, California*. University of California Publications in Anthropology 18. Berkeley: University of California Press.
1990   An Archaeological Perspective on the Historic Settlement Pattern on Santa Cruz Island. *Journal of California and Great Basin Anthropology* 12:112–127.
1991   Transformation of a Regional Economy: Sociopolitical Evolution and the Production of Valuables in Southern California. *Antiquity* 65:953–962.
1992a   Complex Hunter-Gatherer-Fishers of Prehistoric California: Chiefs, Specialists, and Maritime Adaptations of the Channel Islands. *American Antiquity* 57:60–84.
1992b   Cultural Disruption and the Political Economy in Channel Islands Prehistory. In *Essays on the Prehistory of Maritime California*, edited by T. L. Jones, pp. 129–144. Center for Archaeological Research at Davis Publication 10. Davis: University of California.
1993   Labor and the Rise of Complex Hunter-Gatherers. *Journal of Anthropological Archaeology* 12:75–119.
1994   Studies in Prehistoric Sociopolitical Complexity in the Northern Channel Islands and Preliminary Findings from Prisoners Harbor. In *The Fourth California Islands Symposium: Update on the Status of Resources*, edited by W. Halvorsen and G. Maender, pp. 193–200. Santa Barbara: Santa Barbara Museum of Natural History.
1995   Transportation Innovation and Social Complexity among Maritime Hunter-Gatherer Societies. *American Anthropologist* 97:733–747.
1996   The Archaeology of Complex Hunter-Gatherers. *Journal of Archaeological Method and Theory* 3:77–126.
1997   Bigger Boats, Crowded Creekbanks: Environmental Stresses in Perspective. *American Antiquity* 62: 337–339.
2000   The Origins of Hierarchy and the Nature of Hierarchical Structures in Prehistoric California. In *Hierarchies in Action: Cui Bono*, edited by M. Diehl, pp. 221–240.

Center for Archaeological Investigations, Occasional Paper 27. Carbondale: Southern Illinois University.

2001a The Chumash in World and Regional Perspectives. In *The Origins of a Pacific Coast Chiefdom: The Chumash of the Channel Islands*, edited by J. E. Arnold, pp. 1–19. Salt Lake City: University of Utah Press.

2001b Social Evolution and the Political Economy in the Northern Channel Islands. In *The Origins of a Pacific Coast Chiefdom: The Chumash of the Channel Islands*, edited by J. E. Arnold, pp. 287–296. Salt Lake City: University of Utah Press.

2001c The Channel Islands Project: History, Objectives, and Methods. In *The Origins of a Pacific Coast Chiefdom: The Chumash of the Channel Islands*, edited by J. E. Arnold, pp. 21–52. Salt Lake City: University of Utah Press.

Arnold, J. E (editor)
2001 *The Origins of a Pacific Coast Chiefdom: The Chumash of the Channel Islands*. Salt Lake City: University of Utah Press.

2004 *Foundations of Chumash Complexity*. Los Angeles: UCLA Cotsen Institute of Archaeology.

Arnold, J. E., and J. Bernard
2005 Negotiating the Coasts: Status and the Evolution of Boat Technology in California. *World Archaeology* 37:109–131.

Arnold, J. E., and A. P. Graesch
2001 The Evolution of Specialized Shellworking Among the Island Chumash. In *The Origins of a Pacific Coast Chiefdom: The Chumash of the Channel Islands*, edited by J. E. Arnold, pp. 71–112. Salt Lake City: University of Utah Press.

2004 The Later Evolution of the Island Chumash. In *Foundations of Chumash Complexity*, edited by J. E. Arnold, pp. 1–16. Los Angeles: UCLA Cotsen Institute of Archaeology.

Arnold, J. E., and T. M. Green
2002 Mortuary Ambiguity: The Ventureño Chumash Case. *American Antiquity* 67:760–771.

Arnold, J. E., and A. Munns
1994 Independent or Attached Specialization: The Organization of Shell Bead Production in California. *Journal of Field Archaeology* 21: 473–489.

Arnold, J. E., and B. N. Tissot
1993 Measurement of Significant Marine Paleotemperature Variation Using Black Abalone Shells from Middens. *Quaternary Research* 39:390–394.

Arnold, J. E., R. H. Colten, and S. Pletka
1997a Contexts of Cultural Change in Insular California. *American Antiquity* 62:157–168.

Arnold, J. E., E. L. Ambos, and D. O. Larson
1997b Geophysical Surveys of Stratigraphically Complex Island California Sites: New Implications for Household Archaeology. *Antiquity* 71:157–168.

Arnold, J. E., A. M. Preziosi, and P. Shattuck
2001 Flaked Stone Craft Production and Exchange in Island Chumash Territory. In *The Origins of a Pacific Coast Chiefdom: The Chumash of the Channel Islands*, edited by J. E. Arnold, pp. 113–131. Salt Lake City: University of Utah Press.

Arnold, J. E., M. R. Walsh, and S. E. Hollimon
2004 The Archaeology of California. *Journal of Archaeological Research* 12:1–73.

Bailey, G.
1975 The Role of Shellfish in Coastal Economies: The Results of Midden Studies in Australia. *Journal of Archaeological Science* 2: 45–62.

2004 World Prehistory from the Margins: The Role of Coastlines in Human Evolution. *Journal of Interdisciplinary Studies in History and Archaeology* 1:39–50.

Bailey, G., and N. Milner
2002 Coastal Hunter-Gatherers and Social Evolution: Marginal or Central? *Before Farming: The Archaeology and Anthropology of Hunter-Gatherers (www.waspjournals. com)* 2002/3–4:1–22.

Baldwin, K. P.
1996 A History of Channel Islands Archaeology. Unpublished Master's Thesis, Department of Anthropology, California State University, Northridge.

Balée, W.
1998 Historical Ecology: Premises and Postulates. In *Advances in Historical Ecology*, edited by W. Balée, pp. 13–29. New York: Columbia University Press.

Bamforth, D. B.
1993 Stone Tools, Steel Tools: Contact Period Household Technology at Helo'. In *Ethnohistory and Archaeology: Approaches to*

Postcontact Change in the Americas, edited by J. D. Rogers and S. M. Wilson, pp. 49–72. New York: Plenum.

Bennyhoff, J. A.
1950   *California Fish Spears and Harpoons.* University of California Anthropological Records 9 (4): 295–337. Berkeley: University of California

Bennyhoff, J. A., and R. E. Hughes
1987   Shell Bead Ornament Exchange Between California and the Western Great Basin. *Anthropological Papers of the American Museum of Natural History* 64(2).

Benson, A.
1997   *The Noontide Sun: The Field Journals of the Reverend Stephen Bowers, Pioneer California Archaeologist.* Ballena Press Anthropological Papers No. 44. Menlo Park: Ballena Press.

Bernard, J. L.
2001   The Origins of Open Ocean and Large Species Fishing in the Chumash Region of Southern California. Unpublished Master's Thesis, Department of Anthropology, University of California, Los Angeles.
2004   Status and the Swordfish: The Origins of Large Species Fishing Among the Chumash. In *Foundations of Chumash Complexity*, edited by J. E. Arnold, pp. 25–51. Los Angeles: UCLA Cotsen Institute of Archaeology.

Bettinger, R. L.
1999   Comments on Environmental Imperatives Reconsidered by T. Jones et al. *Current Anthropology* 40:137–170.

Binford, L. R.
1968   Post-Pleistocene Adaptations. In *New Perspectives in Archaeology*, edited by S. R. Binford and L. R. Binford, pp. 313–341. Chicago: Aldine.

Blackburn, T. C.
1975   The Chumash Revolt of 1824: A Native Account. *Journal of California Anthropology* 2:223–227.

Blake, M. (editor)
1999   *Pacific Latin America in Prehistory: The Evolution of Archaic and Formative Cultures.* Pullman: Washington State University Press.

Bleitz, D. E.
1993   The Prehistoric Exploitation of Marine Mammals and Birds at San Nicolas Island, California. In *Third California Islands Symposium: Recent Advances in Research on the California Islands*, edited by F. G. Hochberg, pp. 519–536. Santa Barbara: Santa Barbara Museum of Natural History.

Blitz, J. H.
1988   Adoption of the Bow and Arrow in Prehistoric North America. *North American Archaeologist* 9:123–145.

Bowser, B. J.
1993   Dead Fish Tales: Analysis of Fish Remains from Two Middle Period Sites on San Miguel Island, California. In *Archaeology on the Northern Channel Islands of California: Studies of Subsistence, Economics, and Social Organization*, edited by M. A. Glassow, pp. 95–135. Archives of California Prehistory 34. Salinas: Coyote Press.

Boyd, R.
1999a   *Indians, Fire, and the Land in the Pacific Northwest*, edited by R. Boyd. Corvallis: Oregon State University Press.
1999b   *The Coming of the Spirit of Pestilence: Introduced Infectious Diseases and Population Decline Among Northwest Coast Indians, 1774–1874.* Seattle: University of Washington Press.

Brain, C. K.
1967   Bone Weathering and the Problem of Bone Pseudo Tools. *South African Journal of Science* 63(3):97–99.

Braje, T. J., and J. M. Erlandson
2005   An Archaeological Survey of the South Coast of San Miguel Island, Channel Islands National Park, California. Report on File at Channel Islands National Park, Ventura.

Braje, T. J., J. M. Erlandson, and T. C. Rick
2005a   Reassessing Human Settlement on the South Coast of San Miguel Island, California: The Use of ^{14}C Dating as a Reconnaissance Tool. *Radiocarbon* 47:11–19.

Braje, T. J., J. M. Erlandson, and J. Timbrook
2005b   An Asphaltum Coiled Basket Impression, Tarring Pebbles, and Middle Holocene water Bottles from San Miguel Island, California. *Journal of California and Great Basin Anthropology* 25:207–213.

Braje, T. J., J. M. Erlandson, D. J. Kennett, and T. C. Rick
2006a   Archaeology and Marine Conservation. *The SAA Archaeological Record* 6(1):14–19.

Braje, T. J., J. M. Erlandson, and T. C. Rick
  2006b A Historic Chinese Abalone Fishery on
         California's Northern Channel Islands.
         Historical Archaeology, in press.
Brewer, D. J.
  1992   Zooarchaeology: Method, Theory, and
         Goals. *Archaeological Method and Theory*
         4:195–244.
Broughton, J. M.
  1994   Declines in Mammalian Foraging Effi-
         ciency During the Late Holocene, San
         Francisco Bay, California. *Journal of
         Anthropological Archaeology* 13:371–401.
  1997   Widening Diet Breadth, Declining For-
         aging Efficiency, and Prehistoric Harvest
         Pressure: Ichthyofaunal Evidence from
         the Emeryville Shellmound, California.
         Antiquity 71:845–862.
  1999   *Resource Depression and Intensification Dur-
         ing the Late Holocene, San Francisco Bay:
         Evidence from the Emeryville Shellmound
         Vertebrate Fauna.* University of California
         Anthropological Records 32. Berkeley:
         University of California Press.
  2002   Pre Columbian Human Impact on Cali-
         fornia Vertebrates: Evidence from Old
         Bones and Implications for Wilderness
         Policy. In *Wilderness and Political Ecology:
         Aboriginal Influences and the Original State
         of Nature*, edited by C. E. Kay and R. T.
         Simmons, pp. 44–71. Salt Lake City:
         University of Utah Press.
Brown, A. K.
  1967   *The Aboriginal Population of the Santa Bar-
         bara Channel.* Reports of the University of
         California Archaeological Survey 69. Ber-
         keley: University of California Archaeo-
         logical Research Facility.
Burton, R. K., D. Gifford-Gonzalez, J. J. Snodgrass,
and P. L. Koch
  2002   Isotopic Tracking of Prehistoric Pinniped
         Foraging and Distribution along the
         Central California Coast: Preliminary
         Results. *International Journal of Osteoar-
         chaeology* 12:4–11.
Butler, V. L.
  1993   Natural Versus Cultural Salmonid
         Remains: Origins of The Dalles Roadcut
         Bones, Columbia River Oregon, U.S.A.
         Journal of Archaeological Science 20:1–24.
  1996   Tui Chub Taphonomy and the Importance
         of Marsh Resources in the Western Great
         Basin. *American Antiquity* 61:699–717.
  2000   Resource Depression on the Northwest
         Coast of North America. *Antiquity*
         74:649–661.
Butler, V. L., and S. K. Campbell
  2004   Resource Intensification and Resource
         Depression in the Pacific Northwest of
         North America: A Zooarchaeological
         Review. *Journal of World Prehistory*
         18:327–405.
Butzer, K. W.
  1971   *Environment and Archaeology: An Ecological
         Approach to Prehistory.* Second edition.
         Chicago: Aldine-Atherton.
  1982   *Archaeology as Human Ecology.* Cambridge:
         Cambridge University Press.
  2005   Environmental History in the Mediterra-
         nean World: Cross-Disciplinary Investi-
         gation of Cause-and-Effect for
         Degradation and Soil Erosion. *Journal of
         Archaeological Science* 32:1773-1800.
Carbone, L. A.
  1991   Early Holocene Environments and Pale-
         oecological Contexts on the Central and
         Southern California Coast. In *Hunter-
         Gatherers of Early Holocene Coastal Califor-
         nia*, edited by J. M. Erlandson and R. H.
         Colten, pp. 11–17. Los Angeles: UCLA
         Institute of Archaeology.
Carneiro, R. L.
  1981   The Chiefdom: Precursor to the State. In
         *The Transition to Statehood in the New
         World*, edited by G. Jones and R. Kautz,
         pp. 37–79. Cambridge: Cambridge Uni-
         versity Press.
Cassidy, J., L. M. Raab, and N. A. Kononenko
  2004   Boats, Bones, and Biface Bias: The Early
         Holocene Mariners of Eel Point, San
         Clemente Island, California. *American
         Antiquity* 69: 109–130.
Casteel, R. W.
  1976   *Fish Remains in Archaeology and Paleoenvi-
         ronmental Studies.* New York: Academic
         Press.
  1978   Faunal Assemblages and the
         "Wiegemethode" or Weight Method.
         Journal of Field Archaeology 5:71–77.
Castillo, E. D.
  1989   Native Response to the Colonization of
         Alta California. In *Columbian Consequences,
         Vol. 1: Archaeological and Historical Perspec-
         tives on the Spanish Borderlands West*, edited
         by D. Thomas, pp. 377–394. Washington
         DC: Smithsonian Institution.

Chartkoff, J. L., and K. K. Chartkoff
1984   *The Archaeology of California.* Stanford: Stanford University Press.

Claassen, C. A.
1998   *Shells.* Cambridge: Cambridge University Press.

Clark, J. E.
1995   Craft Specialization as an Archaeological Category. *Research in Economic Anthropology* 16:267–294.

Cole, K.L., and G. Liu.
1994   Holocene Paleoecology of an Estuary on Santa Rosa Island, California. *Quaternary Research* 41:326–335.

Colley, S. M.
1990   The Analysis and Interpretation of Archaeological Fish Remains. *Archaeological Method and Theory* 2:207–253.

Colten, R. H.
1993   *Prehistoric Subsistence, Specialization, and Economy in a Southern California Chiefdom.* Ph.D. Dissertation, University of California, Los Angeles. Ann Arbor: UMI.
2001   Ecological and Economic Analysis of Faunal Remains from Santa Cruz Island. In *The Origins of a Pacific Coast Chiefdom: The Chumash of the Channel Islands*, edited by J. E. Arnold, pp. 199–219. Salt Lake City: University of Utah Press.
2002   Prehistoric Marine Mammal Hunting in Context: Two Western North American Examples. *International Journal of Osteoarchaeology* 12:12–22.

Colten, R. H., and J. E. Arnold
1998   Prehistoric Marine Mammal Hunting on California's Northern Channel Islands. *American Antiquity* 63:679–701.

Conlee, C. A.
2000   Intensified Middle Period Ground Stone Production on San Miguel Island. *Journal of California and Great Basin Anthropology* 22:374–391.

Connolly, T. J., J. M. Erlandson, and S. E. Norris
1995   Early Holocene Basketry and Cordage from Daisy Cave, San Miguel Island, California. *American Antiquity* 60:309–318.

Cook, S. F.
1976   *The Population of California Indians, 1769–1970.* Berkeley: University of California Press.

Costello, J. G., and D. Hornbeck
1989   Alta California: An Overview. In *Columbian Consequences, Vol. 1: Archaeological and Historical Perspectives on the Spanish Borderlands West*, edited by D. Thomas, pp. 303–331. Washington DC: Smithsonian Institution.

Crumley, C. L.
1994   Historical Ecology: A Multidimensional Ecological Orientation. In *Historical Ecology: Cultural Knowledge and Changing Landscapes*, edited by C. Crumley, pp. 1–16. Santa Fe: School of American Research Press.
2001   *New Directions in Anthropology and Environment: Intersections*, edited by C. Crumley. Walnut Creek: Altamira Press.

Culleton, B. J., D. J. Kennett, B. L. Ingram, J. Erlandson, and J. Southon
2006   Intra-shell Radiocarbon Variability in Marine Mollusks. *Radiocarbon*, in press.

Dailey, M. D., J. W. Anderson, D. J. Reish, and D. S. Gorsline
1993   The California Bight: Background and Setting. In *Ecology of the Southern California Bight: A Synthesis and Interpretation*, edited by M. Dailey, D. Reish, and J. Anderson, pp. 1–18. Berkeley: University of California Press.

Davenport, D., J. R. Johnson, and J. Timbrook
1993   The Chumash and the Swordfish. *Antiquity* 67:257–272.

deFrance, S. D.
2005   Late Pleistocene Marine Birds from Southern Peru: Distinguishing Human Capture from El Niño-Induced Windfall. *Journal of Archaeological Science* 32:1131–1146.

Delaney-Rivera, C.
2001   Groundstone Tools as Indicators of Changing Subsistence and Exchange Patterns in the Coastal Chumash Region. In *The Origins of a Pacific Coast Chiefdom: The Chumash of the Channel Islands*, edited by J. E. Arnold, pp. 165–181. Salt Lake City: University of Utah Press.

DeLong, R. L., and S. R. Melin
2002   Thirty Years of Pinniped Research at San Miguel Island. In *The Fifth California Islands Symposium*, edited by D. Brown, K. Mitchell, and H. Chaney, pp. 401–406. Santa Barbara: Santa Barbara Museum of Natural History.

Dincauze, D. F.
2000   *Environmental Archaeology: Principles and Practice.* Cambridge: Cambridge University Press.

Dixon, E. J.
  1999   *Bones, Boats, and Bison: Archaeology and the First Colonization of Western North America.* Albuquerque: University of New Mexico Press.
Driver, J. C.
  1991   Identification, Classification, and Zooarchaeology. *Circaea* 9(1):35–47.
Dunnell, R. C.
  1986   Five Decades of American Archaeology. In *American Archaeology Past and Future,* edited by D. Meltzer, D. Fowler, and J. Sabloff, pp. 23–49. Washington DC: Smithsonian Institution Press.
Egan, D., and E. A. Howell (editors)
  2001   *The Historical Ecology Handbook: A Restorationist's Guide to Reference Ecosystems.* Washington DC: Island Press.
Engle, J. M.
  1993   Distribution Patterns of Rocky Subtidal Fishes Around the California Islands. In *Third California Islands Symposium: Recent Advances in Research on the California Islands,* edited by F. G. Hochberg, pp. 475–484. Santa Barbara: Santa Barbara Museum of Natural History.
Erlandson, J. M.
  1984   A Case Study in Faunalturbation: Delineating the Effects of the Burrowing Pocket Gopher on the Distribution of Archaeological Materials. *American Antiquity* 49:785–790.
  1985   Early Holocene Settlement and Subsistence in Relation to Coastal Paleogeography: Evidence from CA-SBA-1807. *Journal of California and Great Basin Anthropology* 7:103–109.
  1988a   The Role of Shellfish in Prehistoric Economies: A Protein Perspective. *American Antiquity* 52:102–109.
  1988b   Cultural Evolution and Paleogeography on the Santa Barbara Coast: A 9600-Year ^{14}C Record from Southern California. *Radiocarbon* 30:25–39.
  1991a   Shellfish and Seeds as Optimal Resources: Early Holocene Subsistence on the Santa Barbara Coast. In *Hunter-Gatherers of Early Holocene Coastal California,* edited by J. M. Erlandson and R. H. Colten, pp. 89–101. Los Angeles: UCLA Institute of Archaeology.
  1991b   The Antiquity of CA-SMI-1: A Multicomponent Site on San Miguel Island.

Journal of California and Great Basin Anthropology 13:273–279.
  1993   Summary and Conclusions. In *Archaeological Investigations at CA-SBA-1731: A Transitional Middle to Late Period Site on the Santa Barbara Channel,* edited by J. M. Erlandson and J. Gerber, pp. 187–196. Santa Barbara: Dames and Moore.
  1994   *Early Hunter-Gatherers of the California Coast.* New York: Plenum.
  1997   The Middle Holocene on the Western Santa Barbara Coast. In *Archaeology of the California Coast During the Middle Holocene,* edited by J. M. Erlandson and M. A. Glassow, pp. 91–109. Los Angeles: UCLA Institute of Archaeology.
  2001   The Archaeology of Aquatic Adaptations: Paradigms for a New Millennium. *Journal of Archaeological Research* 9:287–350.
  2002   Anatomically Modern Humans, Maritime Voyaging, and the Pleistocene Colonization of the Americas. In *The First Americans: The Pleistocene Colonization of the New World,* edited by N. Jablonski, pp. 59–92. Memoirs of the California Academy of Sciences 27. San Francisco: California Academy of Sciences.
Erlandson, J. M., and K. Bartoy
  1995   The Chumash, Cabrillo, and Old World Diseases. *Journal of California and Great Basin Anthropology* 17:153–173.
Erlandson, J. M. and S. M. Fitzpatrick
  2006   Oceans, Islands, and Coasts: Current Perspectives on the Role of the Sea in Human Prehistory. *Journal of Island and Coastal Archaeology* 1(1):5–32.
Erlandson, J. M., and J. Gerber (editors)
  1993   *Archaeological Investigations at CA-SBA-1731: A Transitional Middle-to-Late Period Site on the Santa Barbara Channel.* Santa Barbara: Dames and Moore.
Erlandson, J. M., and M. A. Glassow (editors)
  1997   *Archaeology of the California Coast During the Middle Holocene.* Los Angeles: UCLA Institute of Archaeology.
Erlandson, J. M., and T. L. Jones (editors)
  2002   *Catalysts to Complexity: Late Holocene Societies of the California Coast.* Los Angeles: UCLA Cotsen Institute of Archaeology.
Erlandson, J. M., and M. L. Moss
  1996   The Pleistocene-Holocene Transition along the Pacific Coast of North Amer-

ica. In *Humans at the End of the Ice Age: The Archaeology of the Pleistocene-Holocene Transition*, edited by L. Straus, B. Eriksen, J. Erlandson, and D. Yesner, pp. 277–302. New York: Plenum.

2001 Shellfish Feeders, Carrion Eaters, and the Archaeology of Aquatic Adaptations. *American Antiquity* 66:413–432.

Erlandson, J. M., and T. C. Rick

2002a Late Holocene Cultural Developments along the Santa Barbara Coast. In *Catalysts to Complexity: Late Holocene Societies of the California Coast*, edited by J. M. Erlandson and T. L. Jones, pp. 166–182. Los Angeles: UCLA Cotsen Institute of Archaeology.

2002b A 9700 Year Old Shell Midden on San Miguel Island, California. *Antiquity* 76: 315–316.

Erlandson, J. M. and T. K. Rockwell

1987 Radiocarbon Reversals and Stratigraphic Discontinuities: Natural Formation Processes in Coastal California Archaeological Sites. In *Natural Formation Processes of the Archaeological Record*, edited by D. Nash and M. Petraglia. BAR International Series 352:51–73.

Erlandson, J. M., T. G. Cooley, and R. Carrico

1987 A Fluted Projectile Point from the Southern California Coast: Chronology and Context at CA-SBA-1951. *Journal of California and Great Basin Anthropology* 9:120–129.

Erlandson, J. M., D. J. Kennett, B. L. Ingram, D. A. Guthrie, D. P. Morris, M. A. Tveskov, G. J. West, and P. L. Walker

1996 An Archaeological and Paleontological Chronology for Daisy Cave (CA-SMI-261), San Miguel Island, California. *Radiocarbon* 38:355–373.

Erlandson, J. M., D. J. Kennett, R. J. Behl, and I. Hough

1997 The Cico Chert Source on San Miguel Island, California. *Journal of California and Great Basin Anthropology* 19:124–130.

Erlandson, J. M., M. A. Tveskov, and R. S. Byram

1998 The Development of Maritime Adaptations on the Southern Northwest Coast of North America. *Arctic Anthropology* 35:6–22.

Erlandson, J. M., T. C. Rick, R. L. Vellanoweth, and D. J. Kennett.

1999 Marine Subsistence at a 9300 Year-Old Shell Midden on Santa Rosa Island, California. *Journal of Field Archaeology* 26:255–265.

Erlandson, J. M., R. L. Vellanoweth, A. C. Caruso, and M. R. Reid

2001a *Dentalium* Shell Artifacts from a 6600 Year Old Occupation of Otter Cave. *Pacific Coast Archaeological Society Quarterly* 37:45–55.

Erlandson, J. M., T. C. Rick, D. J. Kennett, and P. L. Walker

2001b Dates, Demography, and Disease: Cultural Contacts and Possible Evidence for Old World Epidemics Among the Island Chumash. *Pacific Coast Archaeological Society Quarterly* 37(3):11–26.

Erlandson, J. M., T. C. Rick, and R. L. Vellanoweth

2004a Human Impacts on Ancient Environments: A Case Study from California's Northern Channel Islands. In *Voyages of Discovery: The Archaeology of Islands*, edited by S. M. Fitzpatrick, pp. 51–83. Westport: Praeger Publishers.

Erlandson, J. M., T. C. Rick, R. L. Vellanoweth, and T. Largaespada

2004b CA-SMI-548: A 9500 Year Old Shell Midden at Running Springs, San Miguel Island, California. In *Emerging from the Ice Age: Early Holocene Occupations on the Central California Coast*, edited by E. Bertrando and V. Levulett. San Luis Obispo County Archaeological Society Occasional Paper 17: 81–92.

Erlandson, J. M., T. C. Rick, and M. R. Batterson

2004c Busted Balls Shell Midden (CA-SMI-606): An Early Coastal Site on San Miguel Island, California. *North American Archaeologist* 25:251–272.

Erlandson, J. M., T. C. Rick, J. A. Estes, M. H. Graham, T. J. Braje, and R. L. Vellanoweth

2005a Sea Otters, Shellfish, and Humans: 10,000 Years of Ecological Interaction on San Miguel Island, California. In *Proceedings of the Sixth California Islands Symposium*, edited by D. Garcelon and C. Schwemm, pp. 9–21. Arcata, CA: National Park Service Technical Publication CHIS-05-01, Institute for Wildlife Studies.

Erlandson, J. M., T. C. Rick, and C. Peterson

2005b A Geoarchaeological Chronology for Holocene Dune Building on San Miguel Island, California. *The Holocene* 15:1227–1235.

Erlandson, J. M., R. L. Vellanoweth, T. C. Rick, and M. R. Reid

2005c Coastal Foraging at Otter Cave: A 6600 Year Old Shell Midden on San Miguel

Island, California. *Journal of California and Great Basin Anthropology* 25:69–86.

Erlandson, J. M., T. J. Braje, T. C. Rick, and J. Peterson

2005d Beads, Bifaces, and Boats: An Early Maritime Adaptation on the South Coast of San Miguel Island, California. *American Anthropologist* 107:677–683.

Erlandson, J. M., T. C. Rick, T. L. Jones, and J. Porcasi

2006 One if By Land, Two if by Sea: Who were the First Californians? In *California Prehistory: Colonization, Culture, and Complexity*, edited by T. L. Jones. Walnut Creek: Altamira Press, in press.

Eschmeyer, W. N., E. S. Herald, and H. Hammann.

1983 *A Field Guide to Pacific Coast Fishes of North America*. Boston: Houghton Mifflin.

Etnier, M. A.

2002 *The Effects of Human Hunting on Northern Fur Seal* (Callorhinus ursinus) *Migration and Breeding Distributions in the Late Holocene*. Ph.D. Dissertation, Department of Anthropology, University of Washington. Ann Arbor: UMI.

2004 The Potential of Zooarchaeological Data to Guide Pinniped Management Decisions in Eastern North America. In *Zooarchaeology and Conservation Biology*, edited by R. L. Lyman and K. Cannon, pp. 88–102. Salt Lake City: University of Utah Press.

Fagan, B.

2004 The House of the Sea: An Essay on the Antiquity of Planked Canoes in Southern California. *American Antiquity* 69:7–16.

Fedje, D. W., and T. Christensen

1999 Modeling Paleoshorelines and Locating Early Holocene Coastal Sites in Haida Gwaii. *American Antiquity* 64:635–652.

Fedje. D. W., Q. Mackie. E. J. Dixon, and T. H. Heaton

2004 Late Wisconsin Environments and Archaeological Visibility on the Northern Northwest Coast. In *Entering America: Northeast Asia and Beringia Before the Last Glacial Maximum*, edited by D. Madsen, pp. 97–138. Salt Lake City: University of Utah Press.

Fisher, C. T., and G. M. Feinman

2005 Introduction to "Landscapes over Time." *American Anthropologist* 107:62–69.

Fitzhugh, B.

2003 *The Evolution of Complex Hunter-Gatherers: Archaeological Evidence from the North Pacific*. New York: Plenum Press.

Fladmark, K. R.

1979 Routes: Alternate Migration Corridors for Early Man in North America. *American Antiquity* 44:55–69.

Friddell, J. E., R. C. Thunnell, T. P. Guilderson, and M. Kashgarian

2003 Increased Northeast Pacific Climatic Variability During the Warm Middle Holocene. *Geophysical Research Letters* 30(11):1–4.

Gamble, L. H.

1991 *Organization of Activities at the Prehistoric Settlement Helo': A Chumash Political, Economic, and Religious Center*. Ph.D. Dissertation, Department of Anthropology, University of California, Santa Barbara. Ann Arbor: UMI.

1995 Chumash Architecture: Sweatlodges and Houses. *Journal of California and Great Basin Anthropology* 17:54–92.

2002 Archaeological Evidence for the Origin of the Plank Canoe in North America. *American Antiquity* 67:301–315.

2005 Culture and Climate: Reconsidering the Effect of Paleoclimatic Variability among Southern California Hunter-Gatherer Societies. *World Archaeology* 37:92–108.

Gamble, L. H., and G. S. Russell

2002 A View from the Mainland: Late Holocene Cultural Developments Among the Ventureño Chumash and the Tongva. In *Catalysts to Complexity: Late Holocene Societies of the California Coast*, edited by J. M. Erlandson and T. L. Jones, pp. 101–126. Los Angeles: UCLA Cotsen Institute of Archaeology.

Gamble, L. H., P. L. Walker, and G. S. Russell

2001 An Integrative Approach to Mortuary Analysis: Social and Symbolic Dimensions of Chumash Burial Practices. *American Antiquity* 66:185–212.

Gibson, R. O.

1992 An Introduction to the Study of Aboriginal Beads from California. *Pacific Coast Archaeological Society Quarterly* 28(3):1–45.

Gifford, E. W.

1940 *Californian Bone Artifacts*. Anthropological Records 3:2. Berkeley: University of California.

1947   *Californian Shell Artifacts.* Anthropological Records 9. Berkeley: University of California.

Glassow, M. A.

1977   *An Archaeological Overview of the Northern Channel Islands, California.* Tucson: National Park Service, Western Archaeological Center.

1982   Archaeological Investigations on Eastern San Miguel Island, Channel Islands National Park, California. Report on File at the Central Coast Information Center, University of California, Santa Barbara.

1993a   The Occurrence of Red Abalone Shells in Northern Channel Island Archaeological Middens. In *Third California Islands Symposium: Recent Advances in Research on the California Islands,* edited by F. G. Hochberg, pp. 567–576. Santa Barbara: Santa Barbara Museum of Natural History.

1993b   Changes in Subsistence on Marine Resources through 7,000 years of Prehistory on Santa Cruz Island. In *Archaeology on the Northern Channel Islands of California: Studies of Subsistence, Economics, and Social Organization,* edited by M. A. Glassow, pp. 75–94. Archives of California Prehistory 34. Salinas: Coyote Press.

1996   *Purismeño Chumash Prehistory: Maritime Adaptations Along the Southern California Coast.* Fort Worth: Harcourt Brace College Publishers.

1997   Middle Holocene Cultural Developments in the Central Santa Barbara Channel Region. In *Archaeology of the California Coast During the Middle Holocene,* edited by J. M. Erlandson and M. A. Glassow, pp. 73–90. Los Angeles: UCLA Institute of Archaeology.

1999   Measurement of Population Growth and Decline During California Prehistory. *Journal of California and Great Basin Anthropology* 21:45–66.

2000   Weighing vs. Counting Shellfish Remains: A Comment on Mason, Peterson, and Tiffany. *American Antiquity* 65:407–414.

2002a   Late Holocene Prehistory of the Vandenberg Region. In *Catalysts to Complexity: Late Holocene Societies of the California Coast,* edited by J. M. Erlandson and T. L. Jones, pp. 183–204. Los Angeles: UCLA Cotsen Institute of Archaeology.

2002b   Prehistoric Chronology and Environmental Change at the Punta Arena Site, Santa Cruz Island, California. In *Proceedings of the Fifth California Islands Symposium,* edited by D. Browne, K. Mitchell, and H. Chaney, pp. 555–562. Santa Barbara: Santa Barbara Museum of Natural History.

2002c   The Value of Ethnographic Collections in Museums. *ACPAC Newsletter,* November 2002 Issue, pp. 1–2.

2005a   Variation in Marine Fauna Utilization by Middle Holocene Occupants of Santa Cruz Island. In *Proceedings of the Sixth California Islands Symposium,* edited by D. Garcelon and C. Schwemm, pp. 23–34. Arcata, CA: National Park Service Technical Publication CHIS-05–01, Institute for Wildlife Studies.

2005b   Prehistoric Dolphin Hunting on Santa Cruz Island, California. In *The Exploitation and Cultural Importance of Sea Mammals,* edited by G. Monks, pp. 107–120. Oxford: Oxbow Books.

Glassow, M. A., and L. R. Wilcoxon

1988   Coastal Adaptations Near Point Conception, California, with Particular Regard to Shellfish Exploitation. *American Antiquity* 53:36–51.

Glassow, M. A., L. R. Wilcoxon, and J. Erlandson

1988   Cultural and Environmental Change During the Early Period of Santa Barbara Channel Prehistory. In *The Archaeology of Prehistoric Coastlines,* edited by G. Bailey and J. Parkington, pp. 64–77. New York: Cambridge University Press.

Glassow, M. A., D. J. Kennett, J. P. Kennett, and L. R. Wilcoxon

1994   Confirmation of Middle Holocene Ocean Cooling Inferred from Stable Isotopic Analysis of Prehistoric Shells from Santa Cruz Island, California. In *The Fourth California Islands Symposium: Update on the Status of Resources,* edited by W. Halvorson and G. Maender, pp. 223–232. Santa Barbara: Santa Barbara Museum of Natural History.

Gobalet, K. W.

1997   Fish Remains from the Early 19th Century Native Alaskan Habitation at Fort Ross. In *The Native Alaskan Neighborhood: A Multiethnic Community at Colony Ross,* edited by K. Lightfoot, A. Schiff, and T. Wake, pp.

319–327. Contributions of the Archaeological Research Facility 55. Berkeley: University of California.

2001 A Critique of Faunal Analysis; Inconsistency among Experts in Blind Tests. *Journal of Archaeological Science* 28:377–386.

Graesch, A. P.
2000 Chumash Houses, Households and Economy: Post-Contact Production and Exchange on Santa Cruz Island. Unpublished Master's Thesis, University of California, Los Angeles.

2001 Culture Contact on the Channel Islands: Historic-Era Production and Exchange Systems. In *The Origins of a Pacific Coast Chiefdom: The Chumash of the Channel Islands*, edited by J. E. Arnold, pp. 261–285. Salt Lake City: University of Utah Press.

2004 Specialized Bead Making Among Island Chumash Households: Community Labor Organization During the Historic Period. In *Foundations of Chumash Complexity*, edited by J. E. Arnold, pp. 133–171. Los Angeles: UCLA Cotsen Institute of Archaeology.

Gragson, T. L.
2005 Time in Service to Historical Ecology. *Ecological and Environmental Anthropology* 1:2–9.

Graham, M. H., P. K. Dayton, and J. M. Erlandson
2003 Ice-Ages and Ecological Transitions on Temperate Coasts. *Trends in Ecology and Evolution* 18:33-40.

Grayson, D. K.
1984 *Quantitative Zooarchaeology: Topics in the Analysis of Archaeological Faunas.* New York: Academic Press.

2001 The Archaeological Record of Human Impact on Animal Populations. *Journal of World Prehistory* 15:1–68.

Greenwood, R. S.
1978 Archaeological Survey and Investigation, Channel Islands National Monument, California. Volumes I and II. Report on file at the Central Coast Information Center, University of California, Santa Barbara.

1982 Archaeological Survey on San Miguel Island, Channel Islands National Park, California. Volumes I and II. Report on file at the Central Coast Information Center, University of California, Santa Barbara.

Guthrie, D. A.
1980 Analysis of Avifaunal and Bat Remains from Midden Sites on San Miguel Island. In *The California Islands: Proceedings of a Multidisciplinary Symposium*, edited by D. Power, pp. 689–702. Santa Barbara: Santa Barbara Museum of Natural History.

1993a Listen to the Birds? The Use of Avian Remains in Channel Islands Archaeology. In *Archaeology on the Northern Channel Islands, California*, edited by M. A. Glassow, pp. 153–167. Archives of California Prehistory 34. Salinas: Coyote Press.

1993b New Information on the Prehistoric Fauna of San Miguel Island, California. In *Third California Islands Symposium: Recent Advances in Research on the California Islands*, edited by F. G. Hochberg, pp. 405–416. Santa Barbara: Santa Barbara Museum of Natural History.

Habu, J.
2002 *Subsistence-Settlement Systems and Intersite Variability in the Moroiso Phase of the Early Jomon Period of Japan.* Ann Arbor: International Monographs in Prehistory 14.

2004 *Ancient Jomon of Japan.* Cambridge: Cambridge University Press.

Halvorson, W. L.
1994 Ecosystem Restoration on the California Channel Islands. In *The Fourth California Islands Symposium: Update on the Status of Resources*, edited by W. L. Halvorson and G. J. Maender, pp. 485–490. Santa Barbara: Santa Barbara Museum of Natural History.

Harrison, W. M.
1964 *Prehistory of the Santa Barbara Coast, California.* Ph.D. Dissertation, Department of Anthropology, University of Arizona. Ann Arbor: UMI.

Harrison, W. M., and E. S. Harrison
1966 An Archaeological Sequence for the Hunting People of Santa Barbara, California. *University of California Archaeological Survey Annual Report* 8:1–89. Los Angeles: University of California.

Hayashida, F. M.
2005 Archaeology, Ecological History, and Conservation. *Annual Review of Anthropology* 34:43–65.

Hayden, B.
1995 Pathways to Power: Principles for Creating Socioeconomic Inequalities. In *Foundations of Social Inequality*, edited by T. D.

Price, and G. Feinman, pp. 15–86. New York: Plenum.

1998 Observations on the Prehistoric Social and Economic Structure of the North American Plateau. *World Archaeology* 29:242–261.

Hegmon, M.

2003 Setting Theoretical Egos Aside: Issues and Theory in North American Archaeology. *American Antiquity* 68:213–243.

Henshilwood, C. S., J. C. Sealy, R. Yates, K. Cruz-Uribe, P. Goldberg, F. E. Grine, R. G. Klein, C. Poggenpoel, K. van Niekerk, and I. Watts

2001 Blombos Cave, Southern Cape, South Africa: Preliminary Report on the 1992–1999 Excavations of the Middle Stone Age Levels. *Journal of Archaeological Science* 28:421–448.

Heusser, L. E.

1978 Pollen in Santa Barbara Basin, California: A 12,000 Year Record. *Geological Society of America Bulletin* 89:673–678.

Heye, G. G.

1921 *Certain Artifacts from San Miguel Island, California*. Indian Notes and Monographs 7(4). New York: Museum of the American Indian, Heye Foundation.

Higham, C. F. W.

1996 A Review of Archaeology in Mainland Southeast Asia. *Journal of Archaeological Research* 4:3–49.

Higham, C. F. W., and R. Thosarat

1994 *Khok Phanom Di: Prehistoric Adaptation to the World's Richest Habitat*. Fort Worth: Harcourt Brace.

Hildebrandt, W. R., and T. L. Jones

1992 Evolution of Marine Mammal Hunting: A View from the California and Oregon Coasts. *Journal of Anthropological Archaeology* 11:360–401.

Hildebrandt, W. R., and K. R. McGuire

2002 The Ascendance of Hunting During the California Middle Archaic: An Evolutionary Perspective. *American Antiquity* 67:231–256.

Hollimon, S. E.

1990 *Division of Labor and Gender Roles in Santa Barbara Channel Prehistory*. Ph.D. Dissertation, Department of Anthropology, University of California, Santa Barbara. Ann Arbor: UMI.

Hudson, T., and T. C. Blackburn

1982 *The Material Culture of the Chumash Interaction Sphere. Vol. 1: Food Procurement and Transportation*. Ballena Press Anthropological Papers No. 25. Los Altos and Santa Barbara: Ballena Press and Santa Barbara Museum of Natural History.

Hudson, T., J. Timbrook, and M. Rempe

1978 *Tomol: Chumash Watercraft as Described in the Ethnographic Notes of John P. Harrington*. Ballena Press Anthropological Papers 9. Los Altos and Santa Barbara: Ballena Press and Santa Barbara Museum of Natural History.

Inman, D. L.

1983 Application of Coastal Dynamics to the Reconstruction of Paleocoastlines in the Vicinity of La Jolla, California. In *Quaternary Coastlines and Marine Archaeology*, edited by P. Masters and N. Flemming, pp. 1–49. New York: Academic Press.

Jackson, J. B. C., M. X. Kirby, W. H. Berger, K. A. Bjorndal, L. W. Botsford, B. J. Bourque, R. H. Bradbury, R. Cooke, J. Erlandson, J. A. Estes, T. P. Hughes, S. Kidwell, C. B. Lange, H. S. Lenihan, J. M. Pandolfi, C. H. Peterson, R. S. Steneck, M. J. Tegner, and R. R. Warner

2001 Historical Overfishing and the Recent Collapse of Coastal Ecosystems. *Science* 293:629–637.

Jenkins, D. L., and J. M. Erlandson

1996 *Olivella* Grooved Rectangle Beads from a Middle Holocene Site in the Fort Rock Valley, Northern Great Basin. *Journal of California and Great Basin Anthropology* 18:296–306.

Johnson, A. W., and T. Earle

1987 *The Evolution of Human Societies: From Foraging Group to Agrarian State*. Stanford: Stanford University Press.

Johnson, D. L.

1972 *Landscape Evolution on San Miguel Island, California*. Ph.D. Dissertation, Department of Geography, University of Kansas. Ann Arbor: UMI.

1980 Episodic Vegetation Stripping, Soil Erosion, and Landscape Modification in Prehistoric and Recent Historic Time, San Miguel Island, California. In *The California Islands: Proceedings of a Multidisciplinary Symposium*, edited by D. Power, pp. 103–121. Santa Barbara: Santa Barbara Museum of Natural History.

1983 The California Continental Borderland: Landbridges, Watergaps, and Biotic Dispersals. In *Quaternary Coastlines and Marine Archaeology*, edited by P. Masters and N. Flemming, pp. 482–527. New York: Academic Press.

1989 Subsurface Stone Lines, Stone Zones, Artifact-Manuport Layers, and Biomantles Produced by Bioturbation via Pocket Gophers (*Thomomys bottae*). *American Antiquity* 54:370–389.

Johnson, J. R.

1982 An Ethnohistoric Study of the Island Chumash. Unpublished Master's Thesis, Department of Anthropology, University of California, Santa Barbara.

1988 *Chumash Social Organization: An Ethnohistorical Perspective*. Ph.D. Dissertation, Department of Anthropology, University of California, Santa Barbara. Ann Arbor: UMI.

1989 The Chumash and the Missions. In *Columbian Consequences, Vol. 1: Archaeological and Historical Perspectives on the Spanish Borderlands West*, edited by D. Thomas, pp. 365–375. Washington DC: Smithsonian Institution.

1993 A Geographic Analysis of Island Chumash Marriage Networks. In *Archaeology on the Northern Channel Islands of California: Studies of Subsistence, Economics, and Social Organization*, edited by M. A. Glassow, p. 19–46. Archives of California Prehistory 34. Salinas: Coyote Press.

1999a The Chumash Sociopolitical Groups on the Channel Islands. In Cultural Affiliation and Lineal Descent of Chumash Peoples in the Channel Islands and Santa Monica Mountains, edited by S. McLendon and J. Johnson, pp. 51–66. Report on file at the Archaeology and Ethnography Program, National Park Service, Washington, DC

1999b Chumash Population History. In Cultural Affiliation and Lineal Descent of Chumash Peoples in the Channel Islands and Santa Monica Mountains, edited by S. McLendon and J. Johnson, pp. 93–130. Report on file at the Archaeology and Ethnography Program, National Park Service, Washington, DC

2000 Social Responses to Climate Change Among the Chumash Indians of South-Central California. In *The Way the Wind Blows: Climate, History, and Human Action*, edited by R. McIntosh, J. Tainter, and S. McIntosh, pp. 301–327. New York: Columbia University Press.

2001 Ethnohistoric Reflections of Cruzeño Chumash Society. In *The Origins of a Pacific Coast Chiefdom: The Chumash of the Channel Islands*, edited by J. E. Arnold, pp. 53–70. Salt Lake City: University of Utah Press.

Johnson, J. R., and S. McLendon

1999a The Nature of Chumash Sociopolitical Groups. In Cultural Affiliation and Lineal Descent of Chumash Peoples in the Channel Islands and Santa Monica Mountains, edited by S. McLendon and J. Johnson, pp. 51–66. Report on file at the Archaeology and Ethnography Program, National Park Service, Washington, DC

1999b Chumash Social History After Mission Secularization. In Cultural Affiliation and Lineal Descent of Chumash Peoples in the Channel Islands and Santa Monica Mountains, edited by S. McLendon and J. Johnson, pp. 131–178. Report on file at the Archaeology and Ethnography Program, National Park Service, Washington, DC

2002 The Social History of Native Islanders Following Missionization. In *Proceedings of the Fifth California Islands Symposium*, edited by D. Brown, K. Mitchell, and H. Chaney, pp. 646–653. Santa Barbara: Santa Barbara Museum of Natural History.

Johnson, J. R., T. W. Stafford, Jr., H. O. Ajie, D. P. Morris

2002 Arlington Springs Revisited. In *Proceedings of the Fifth California Islands Symposium*, edited by D. Browne, K. Mitchell, and H. Chaney, pp. 541–545. Santa Barbara: Santa Barbara Museum of Natural History.

Jones, T. L.

1991 Marine Resource Value and the Priority of Coastal Settlement: A California Perspective. *American Antiquity* 56:419–443.

2003 *Prehistoric Human Ecology of the Big Sur Coast, California*. Contributions of the University of California Archaeological Research Facility 61.

Jones, T. L., and W. R. Hildebrandt

1995 Reasserting a Prehistoric Tragedy of the Commons: Reply to Lyman. *Journal of Anthropological Archaeology* 14:78–98.

Jones, T. L., and K. A. Klar

2005 Diffusionism Reconsidered: Linguistic and Archaeological Evidence for Prehistoric Polynesian Contact with Southern California. *American Antiquity* 70:457–484.

Jones, T. L., and G. Waugh
   1995   *Central California Coastal Prehistory: A View from Little Pico Creek.* Los Angeles: UCLA Institute of Archaeology.

Jones, T., L., G. M. Brown, L. M. Raab, J. L. McVickar, W. G. Spaulding, D. J. Kennett, A. York, and P. L. Walker
   1999   Environmental Imperatives Reconsidered: Demographic Crises in Western North America During the Medieval Climatic Anomaly. *Current Anthropology* 40:137–170.

Jones, T. L., R. T. Fitzgerald, D. J. Kennett, C. H. Miksicek, J. L. Fagan, J. Sharp, and J. Erlandson
   2002   The Cross Creek Site (CA-SLO-1797) and Its Implications for New World Colonization. *American Antiquity* 67:213–230.

Jones, T. L., W. R. Hildebrandt, D. J. Kennett, and J. F. Porcasi
   2004   Prehistoric Marine Mammal Overkill. *Journal of California and Great Basin Anthropology* 24:69–80.

Junak, S., T. Ayers, R. Scott, D. Wilken, and D. Young
   1995   *A Flora of Santa Cruz Island.* Santa Barbara: Santa Barbara Botanic Garden.

Justice, N. D.
   2002   *Stone Age Spear and Arrow Points of California and the Great Basin.* Bloomington: Indiana University Press.

Kay, C. E.
   2002   Are Ecosystems Structured from the Top Down or Bottom Up?: A New Look at an Old Debate. In *Wilderness and Political Ecology: Aboriginal Influences and the Original State of Nature*, edited by C. E. Kay and R. T. Simmons, pp. 215–237. Salt Lake City: University of Utah Press.

Kay, C. E., and R. T. Simmons (editors)
   2002   *Wilderness and Political Ecology: Aboriginal Influences and the Original State of Nature.* Salt Lake City: University of Utah Press.

Keefer, D. K., S. D. deFrance, M. E. Moseley, J. B. Richardson III, D. R. Satterlee, and A. Day-Lewis.
   1998   Early Maritime Economy and El Niño Events at Quebrada Tacahuay, Peru. *Science* 281:1833–1835.

Kelsey, H.
   1985   European Impact on the California Indians, 1530–1830. *The Americas* 41:494–511.

   1986   *Juan Rodriguez Cabrillo.* San Marino: Huntington Library.

Kennett, D. J.
   1998   *Behavioral Ecology and Hunter-Gatherer Societies of the Northern Channel Islands, California.* Ph.D. Dissertation, Department of Anthropology, University of California, Santa Barbara. Ann Arbor: UMI.

   2005   *The Island Chumash: Behavioral Ecology of a Maritime Society.* Berkeley: University of California Press.

Kennett, D. J., and C. A. Conlee
   2002   Emergence of Late Holocene Sociopolitical Complexity on Santa Rosa and San Miguel Islands. In *Catalysts to Complexity: Late Holocene Societies of the California Coast*, edited by J. M. Erlandson and T. L. Jones, 147–165. Los Angeles: UCLA Cotsen Institute of Archaeology.

Kennett, D. J., and J. P. Kennett
   2000   Competitive and Cooperative Responses to Climatic Instability in Coastal Southern California. *American Antiquity* 65:379–396.

Kennett, D. J., B. L. Ingram, J. M. Erlandson, and P. L. Walker.
   1997   Evidence for Temporal Fluctuations in Marine Radiocarbon Reservoir Ages in the Santa Barbara Channel, Southern California. *Journal of Archaeological Science* 24:1051–1059.

Kennett, D., J. R. Johnson, T. C. Rick, D. P. Morris, and J. Christy
   2000   Historic Chumash Settlement on Eastern Santa Cruz Island, Southern California. *Journal of California and Great Basin Anthropology* 22:212–222.

Kennett, J. P., and B. L. Ingram
   1995   A 20,000 Year Record of Ocean Circulation and Climate Change from the Santa Barbara Basin. *Nature* 377:510–514.

King, C. D.
   1971   Chumash Inter-Village Economic Exchange. *Indian Historian* 4(1):30–43.

   1990   *Evolution of Chumash Society: A Comparative Study of Artifacts Used for Social System Maintenance in the Santa Barbara Channel Region Before a.d. 1804.* New York: Garland Publishing.

King, L. B.
   1982   *Medea Creek Cemetery: Late Inland Patterns of Chumash Social Organization, Exchange, and Warfare.* Ph.D. Dissertation, Department of Anthropology,

University of California, Los Angeles. Ann Arbor: UMI.

Kinlan, B. P., M. H. Graham, and J. M. Erlandson
2005   Late Quaternary Changes in the Size and Shape of the California Channel Islands: Implications for Marine Subsidies to Terrestrial Communities. In *Proceedings of the Sixth California Islands Symposium*, edited by D. Garcelon and C. Schwemm, pp. 131–142. Arcata, CA: National Park Service Technical Publication CHIS-05-01, Institute for Wildlife Studies.

Kirch, P. V.
1997   Microcosmic Histories: Island Perspectives on "Global" Change. *American Anthropologist* 99:30–42.

2004   Oceanic Islands: Microcosms of "Global Change." In *The Archaeology of Global Change: The Impact of Humans on their Environment*, edited by C. Redman, S. James, P. Fish, and J. D. Rogers, pp. 13–27. Washington DC: Smithsonian Institution Press.

Kirch, P. V., and T. L. Hunt (editors)
1997   *Historical Ecology in the Pacific Islands: Prehistoric Environmental and Landscape Change.* New Haven: Yale University Press.

Kirch, P. V., J. R. Flenley, D. W. Steadman, F. Lamont, and S. Dawson
1992   Ancient Environmental Degradation. *National Geographic Research and Exploration* 8:166–179.

Klein, R. G.
1999   *The Human Career: Human Biological and Cultural Evolution.* Chicago: University of Chicago Press.

Klein, R. G., and K. Cruz-Uribe
1984   *The Analysis of Animal Bones from Archaeological Sites.* Chicago: University of Chicago Press.

Klein, R.G., G. Avery, K. Cruz-Uribe, D. Halkett, J. E. Parkington, T. Steele, T. P. Volman, and R.Yates
2004   The Yserfontein 1 Middle Stone Age Site, South Africa, and Early Human Exploitation of Coastal Resources. *Proceedings of the National Academy of Sciences* 101:5708–5715.

Koerper, H. C., C. Prior, R. E. Taylor, and R. O. Gibson
1995   Additional Accelerator Mass Spectrometry (AMS) Radiocarbon Assays on *Haliotis* Fishhooks from CA-ORA-378. *Journal of*

California and Great Basin Anthropology 17:273–279.

Kolb, M. J., and J. E. Snead
1997   It's a Small World After All: Comparative Analyses of Community Organization in Archaeology. *American Antiquity* 62:609–628.

Koloseike, A.
1969   On Calculating the Prehistoric Food Resource Value of Molluscs. *Archaeological Survey Annual Report* 11:143–162. Los Angeles: University of California.

Koyama, S., and D. H. Thomas (editors)
1981   *Affluent Foragers: Pacific Coasts East and West.* Senri Ethnological Studies 9.

Krech, S., III
1999   *The Ecological Indian: Myth and History.* New York: W.W. Norton and Company.

Kroeber, A. L.
1925   *Handbook of the Indians of California.* Bureau of American Ethnology Bulletin 78. Washington DC: Smithsonian Institution.

Kuhn, T. S.
1977   *The Essential Tension: Selected Studies in Scientific Traditions and Change.* Chicago: University of Chicago Press.

Lambert, P. M.
1993   Health in Prehistoric Populations of the Santa Barbara Channel Islands. *American Antiquity* 58:509–522.

1994   *War and Peace on the Western Front: A Study of Violent Conflict and Its Correlates in Prehistoric Hunter-Gatherer Societies of Coastal Southern California.* Ph.D. Dissertation, Department of Anthropology, University of California, Santa Barbara. Ann Arbor: UMI.

Lambert, P. M., and P. L. Walker
1991   Physical Anthropological Evidence for the Evolution of Social Complexity in Coastal Southern California. *Antiquity* 65:963–973.

Landberg, L. C.W.
1965   *The Chumash Indians of Southern California.* Southwest Museum Papers 19. Los Angeles: Southwest Museum.

1975   Fishing Effort in the Aboriginal Fisheries of the Santa Barbara Region, California: An Ethnohistorical Appraisal. In *Maritime Adaptations of the Pacific*, edited by R. W. Casteel and G. I. Quimby, pp. 145–170. The Hague: Mouton and Co.

Larson, D. O., J. R. Johnson, and J. C. Michaelsen
1994 Missionization among the Coastal Chumash of Central California: A Study of Risk Minimization Strategies. *American Anthropologist* 96:263–299.

Le Boeuf, D. J., and M. L. Bonnell
1980 Pinnipeds of the California Islands: Abundance and Distribution. In *The California Islands: Proceedings of a Multidisciplinary Symposium*, edited by D. Power, pp. 475–493. Santa Barbara: Santa Barbara Museum of Natural History.

Lee, R. B., and I. Devore (editors)
1968 *Man the Hunter.* Chicago: Aldine.

Lightfoot, K. G.
1993 Long-Term Developments in Complex Hunter-Gatherer Societies: Recent Perspectives from the Pacific Coast of North America. *Journal of Archaeological Research* 1:167–201.

2005 *Indians, Missionaries, and Merchants: The Legacy of Colonial Encounters on the California Frontier.* Berkeley: University of California Press.

Lightfoot, K. G., and W. S. Simmons
1998 Culture Contact in Protohistoric California: Social Context of Native and European Encounters. *Journal of California and Great Basin Anthropology* 20(2):138–170.

Lightfoot, K. G., A. Martinez, and A. M. Schiff
1998 Daily Practice and Material Culture in Pluralistic Social Settings: An Archaeological Study of Culture Change and Persistence from Fort Ross, California. *American Antiquity* 63:199–222.

Littleton, J.
1999 The Taphonomy of Aboriginal Burials, Western New South Whales. In *Taphonomy: The Analysis of Processes from Phytoliths to Megafauna*, edited by M. Mountain and D. Bowdery, pp. 69–78. Research Papers in Archeology and Natural History 30. Canberra: The Australian National University.

Love, M.
1996 *Probably More Than You Wanted to Know About the Fishes of the Pacific Coast.* Santa Barbara: Really Big Press.

Lyman, R. L.
1994 *Vertebrate Taphonomy.* Cambridge: Cambridge University Press.

1995 On the Evolution of Marine Mammal Hunting on the West Coast of North America. *Journal of Anthropological Archaeology* 14:45–77.

1996 Applied Zooarchaeology: The Relevance of Faunal Analysis to Wildlife Management. *World Archaeology* 28:110–125.

2002 Taxonomic Identifications of Zooarchaeological Remains. *The Review of Archaeology* 23:13–20.

Lyman, R. L., and K. P. Cannon, editors
2004 *Zooarchaeology and Conservation Biology.* Salt Lake City: University of Utah Press.

McCawley, W.
1996 *The First Angelinos: The Gabrielino Indians of Los Angeles.* Banning and Novato: Malki Museum Press/Ballena Press.

McGuire, R. H.
1996 Why Complexity is Too Simple. In *Debating Complexity*, edited by D. Meyer, P. Dawson, and D. Hanna, pp. 23–29. Alberta: The Archaeological Association of the University of Calgary.

McLendon, S.
1999 Introduction. In Cultural Affiliation and Lineal Descent of Chumash Peoples in the Channel Islands and Santa Monica Mountains, edited by S. McLendon and J. Johnson, pp. 1–19. Report on file at the Archaeology and Ethnography Program, National Park Service, Washington, DC

McLendon, S., and J. R. Johnson
1999 Cultural Affiliation and Lineal Descent of Chumash Peoples in the Channel Islands and Santa Monica Mountains. Report on file at the Archaeology and Ethnography Program, National Park Service, Washington, DC

Marquardt, W. H.
1988 Politics and Production Among the Calusa of South Florida. In *Hunters and Gatherers, Volume 1, History, Evolution, and Social Change*, edited by T. Ingold, D. Riches, and J. Woodburn, pp. 161–188. Oxford: Berg Publishers.

1992a The Calusa Domain: An Introduction. In *Culture and Environment in the Domain of the Calusa*, edited by W. Marquardt, pp. 1–7. Gainesville: University of Florida Institute of Archaeology and Paleoenvironmental Studies Monograph 1.

1992b Calusa Culture and Environment: What Have We Learned? In *Culture and Environment in the Domain of the Calusa*, edited by W. Marquardt, pp. 423–436. Gainesville: University of Florida Institute of Archaeology and Paleoenvironmental Studies Monograph 1.

1994   The Role of Archaeology in Raising Environmental Consciousness: An Example from Southwest Florida. In *Historical Ecology: Cultural Knowledge and Changing Landscapes*, edited by C. Crumley, pp. 203–221. Santa Fe: School of American Research Press.

1995   Four Discoveries: Environmental Archaeology in Southwest Florida. In *Case Studies in Environmental Archaeology*, edited by E. J. Reitz, L. A. Newsom, and S. J. Scudder, pp. 17–32. New York: Plenum.

2001   The Emergence and Demise of the Calusa. In *Societies in Eclipse: Eastern North America at the Dawn of European Colonization*, AD 1400–1700, edited by D. Brose, R. Mainfort, and C. Cowan, pp. 151–171. Washington DC: Smithsonian Institution Press.

Martin, S. L., and V. S. Popper
2001   Paleobotanical Investigations of Archaeological Sites on Santa Cruz Island. In *The Origins of a Pacific Coast Chiefdom: The Chumash of the Channel Islands*, edited by J. E. Arnold, pp. 245–259. Salt Lake City: University of Utah Press.

Martz, P. C.
1992   Status Distinctions Reflected in Chumash Mortuary Populations in the Santa Monica Mountains Region. In *Essays on the Prehistory of Maritime California*, edited by T. L. Jones, pp. 145–156. Center for Archaeological Research at Davis Publication 10. Davis: University of California.

Mason, R. D., M. L. Peterson, and J. A. Tifffany
1998   Weighing vs. Counting: Measurement Reliability and the California School of Midden Analysis. *American Antiquity* 63:303–324.

Matson, R. G., and G. Coupland
1995   *The Prehistory of the Northwest Coast*. San Diego: Academic Press.

Miller, D. J., and R. N. Lea.
1972   Guide to the Coastal Marine Fishes of California. *California Department of Fish and Game Bulletin* 157.

Morales, A., and E. Roselló
2004   Fishing Down the Food Web in Iberian Prehistory? A New Look at the Fishes

from Cueva de Nerja (Malaga, Spain). In *Pettis Animaux Et Societes Humaines Du Complement Alimentaire Aux Ressources Utilitaires XXIV*, edited by J. Brugal and J. Desse, pp. 111–123. Antibes: APDCA.

Moratto, M. J.
1984   *California Archaeology*. New York: Academic Press.

Moriarty, J. R. III
1967   Transitional Pre-Desert Phase in San Diego County, California. *Science* 155:553–556.

Morris, P. A.
1974   *A Field Guide to Pacific Coast Shells*. Boston: Houghton Mifflin.

Morris, R. H., D. P. Abbott, and E. C. Haderlie
1980   *Intertidal Invertebrates of California*. Stanford: Stanford University Press.

Morwood, M. J., P. O'Sullivan, F. Aziz, and A. Raza
1998   Fission Track Age of Stone Tools and Fossils on the East Indonesian Island of Flores. *Nature* 392:173–176.

Morwood, M. J., F. Aziz, P. O'Sullivan, P. Nasruddin, D. Hobbs, and A. Raza
1999   Archaeological and Paleontological Research in Central Flores, East Indonesia: Results of Fieldwork 1997–1998. *Antiquity* 73:273–286.

Moseley, M. E.
1975   *The Maritime Foundations of Andean Civilization*. Menlo Park: Cummings.

Moss, M. L.
1989   *Cultural Ecology of the Prehistoric Angoon Tlingit*. Ph.D. Dissertation, Department of Anthropology, University of California, Santa Barbara. Ann Arbor: UMI.

Moss, M. L., and J. M. Erlandson
1995   Reflections on North American Pacific Coast Prehistory. *Journal of World Prehistory* 9:1–45.

Munns, A. M., and J. E. Arnold
2002   Late Holocene Santa Cruz Island: Patterns in Continuity and Change. In *Catalysts to Complexity: Late Holocene Societies of the California Coast*, edited by J. M. Erlandson and T. L. Jones, 127–146. Los Angeles: UCLA Cotsen Institute of Archaeology.

Noah, A. C.
2005   *Household Economies: The Role of Animals in a Historic Period Chiefdom on the California Coast*. Ph.D. Dissertation, Department of Anthropology, University of California, Los Angeles. Ann Arbor: UMI.

Olson, R. L.
1930   Chumash Prehistory. *University of Califor-nia Publications in American Archaeology and Ethnology* 28:1–21.

Orr, P. C.
1968   *Prehistory of Santa Rosa Island.* Santa Bar-bara: Santa Barbara Museum of Natural History.

Osborn, A. J.
1977   Strandloopers, Mermaids, and Other Fairy Tales: Ecological Determinants of Marine Resource Utilization-the Peru-vian Case. In *For Theory Building in Archaeology*, edited by L. R. Binford, pp. 157–205. New York: Academic Press.

Paige, P.
2000   Archaeological Fish Remains as Indica-tors of Paleoenvironmental Change: An Ichthyofaunal Analysis of Two Multi-component Sites on Western Santa Rosa Island. Unpublished Master's Paper, Department of Anthropology, University of California, Santa Barbara.

Parkington, J. E.
2003   Middens and Moderns: Shellfishing and the Middle Stone Age of the Western Cape, South Africa. *South African Journal of Science* 99: 243–247.

Pauketat, T. R.
2001   Practice and History in Archaeology: An Emerging Paradigm. *Anthropological The-ory* 1:73–98.

2003   Materiality and the Immaterial in Histor-ical-Processual Archaeology. In *Essential Tensions in Archaeological Method and The-ory*, edited by T. L. VanPool and C. S. VanPool, pp. 41–53. Salt Lake City: Uni-versity of Utah Press.

Pauly, D.
1995   Anecdotes and the Shifting Baselines Syndrome of Fisheries. *Trends in Ecology and Evolution* 10(10):430.

Pearsall, D. M.
2000   *Paleoethnobotany: A Handbook of Procedures.* Second edition. San Diego: Academic Press.

Perlman, S. M.
1980   An Optimum Diet Model, Coastal Vari-ability, and Hunter-Gatherer Behavior. *Advances in Archaeological Method and The-ory* 3:257–310.

Perry, J. E.
2003   *Changes in Prehistoric Land and Resource Use Among Complex Hunter-Gatherer-Fishers on Eastern Santa Cruz Island, Cali-fornia.* Ph.D. Dissertation, Department of Anthropology, University of California, Santa Barbara. Ann Arbor: UMI.

2004   Quarries and Microblades: Trends in Pre-historic Land and Resource Use on Santa Cruz Island. In *Foundations of Chumash Complexity*, edited by J. E. Arnold, pp. 113–132. Los Angeles: UCLA Cotsen Institute of Archaeology.

2005   Early Period Resource Use on Eastern Santa Cruz Island. In *Proceedings of the Sixth California Islands Symposium*, edited by D. Garcelon and C. Schwemm, pp. 43–53. Arcata, CA: National Park Service Technical Publication CHIS-05-01, Institute for Wildlife Studies.

Pletka, S. M.
2001a   The Economics of Island Chumash Fish-ing Practices. In *The Origins of a Pacific Coast Chiefdom: The Chumash of the Chan-nel Islands*, edited by J. E. Arnold, pp. 221–244. Salt Lake City: University of Utah Press.

2001b   Bifaces and the Institutionalization of Exchange Relationships in the Chumash Sphere. In *The Origins of a Pacific Coast Chiefdom: The Chumash of the Channel Islands*, edited by J. E. Arnold, pp. 133–149. Salt Lake City: University of Utah Press.

Pisias, N. G.
1978   Paleooceanography of the Santa Barbara Basin During the Last 8000 Years. *Qua-ternary Research* 11:366–384.

Porcasi, J. F.
1999   Prehistoric Exploitation of Albatross on the Southern California Channel Islands. *Journal of California and Great Basin Anthropology* 21:94–112.

Porcasi, J. F., and S. L. Andrews
2001   Evidence for a Prehistoric *Mola mola* industry on the Southern California Coast. *Journal of California and Great Basin Anthropology* 23:51–66.

Porcasi, J. F., and H. Fujita
2000   The Dolphin Hunters: A Specialized Pre-historic Maritime Adaptation in the Southern California Channel Islands and Baja California. *American Antiquity* 65:543–566.

Porcasi, J. F., T. L. Jones, and L. M. Raab
2000   Trans-Holocene Marine Mammal Exploitation on San Clemente Island: A

Tragedy of the Commons Revisited. *Journal of Anthropological Archaeology* 19:200–220.

Porcasi, P., J. F. Porcasi, and C. O'Neill
1999   Early Holocene Coastlines of the California Bight: The Channel Islands as First Visited by Humans. *Pacific Coast Archaeological Society Quarterly* 35 (2 & 3):1–24.

Power, D. M.
1980   Introduction. In *The California Islands: Proceedings of a Multidisciplinary Symposium*, edited by D. M. Power, pp. 1–4. Santa Barbara: Santa Barbara Museum of Natural History.

Prentiss, W. C., and I. Kuijt (editors)
2004   *Complex Hunter-Gatherers: Evolution and Organization of Prehistoric Communities on the Plateau of Northwestern North America.* Salt Lake City: University of Utah Press.

Preston, W.
1996   Serpent in Eden: Dispersal of Foreign Diseases into Pre-Mission California. *Journal of California and Great Basin Anthropology* 18:2–37.

1998   Serpent in the Garden: Environmental Change in Colonial California. In *Contested Eden: California Before the Gold Rush*, edited by R. A. Gutierrez and R. J. Orsi, pp. 260–298. Berkeley: University of California Press.

2002   Portents of Plague from California's Protohistoric Period. *Ethnohistory* 49:69–121.

Preziosi, A. M.
2001   Standardization and Specialization: The Island Chumash Microdrill Industry. In *The Origins of a Pacific Coast Chiefdom: The Chumash of the Channel Islands*, edited by J. E. Arnold, pp. 151–163. Salt Lake City: University of Utah Press.

Price, T. D., and J. A. Brown (editors)
1985   *Prehistoric Hunter-Gatherers: The Emergence of Cultural Complexity.* Orlando: Academic Press.

Quilter, J., and T. Stocker
1983   Subsistence Economies and the Origins of Andean Complex Societies. *American Anthropologist* 85:545–562.

Raab, L. M.
1996   Debating Prehistory in Coastal Southern California: Resource Intensification Versus Political Economy. *Journal of California and Great Basin Anthropology* 18:64–80.

Raab, L. M., and K. Bradford
1997   Making Nature Answer to Interpretivism: Response to J. E. Arnold, R. H. Colten, and S. Pletka. *American Antiquity* 62:340–341.

Raab, L. M., and W. J. Howard
2002   Modeling Cultural Connections Between the Southern Channel Islands and Western United States: The Middle Holocene Distribution of *Olivella* Grooved Rectangle Beads. In *Proceedings of the Fifth California Islands Symposium*, edited by D. Browne, K. Mitchell, and H. Chaney, pp. 590–597. Santa Barbara: Santa Barbara Museum of Natural History.

Raab, L. M., and D. O. Larson
1997   Medieval Climatic Anomaly and Punctuated Cultural Evolution in Coastal Southern California. *American Antiquity* 62:319–336.

Raab, L. M., J. F. Porcasi, K. Bradford, and A. Yatsko
1995a   Debating Cultural Evolution: Regional Implications of Fishing Intensification at Eel Point, San Clemente Island. *Pacific Coast Archaeological Society Quarterly* 31(3):3–27.

Raab, L. M., K. Bradford, J. F. Porcasi, and W. J. Howard
1995b   Return to Little Harbor, Santa Catalina Island, California: A Critique of the Marine Paleotemperature Model. *American Antiquity* 60:287–308.

Raab, L. M., A. Yatsko, T. S. Garlinghouse, J. F. Porcasi, and K. Bradford
2002   Late Holocene San Clemente Island: Notes on Comparative Social Complexity in Coastal Southern California. In *Catalysts to Complexity: Late Holocene Societies of the California Coast*, edited by J. M. Erlandson and T. L. Jones, pp. 13–26. Los Angeles: UCLA Cotsen Institute of Archaeology.

Ramenofsky, A. F.
1987   *Vectors of Death: The Archaeology of European Contact.* Albuquerque: University of New Mexico.

Raymond, S.
1981   The Maritime Foundation of Andean Civilization: A Reconsideration of the Evidence. *American Antiquity* 46:806–821.

Redman, C. L.
1999   *Human Impact on Ancient Environments.* Tucson: University of Arizona Press.

Redman, C. L., S. R. James, P. R. Fish, and J. D. Rogers (editors)
2004 *The Archaeology of Global Change: The Impact of Humans on their Environment.* Washington DC: Smithsonian Institution Press.

Reitz, E. J.
2004 "Fishing Down the Food Web": A Case Study from St. Augustine, Florida, U.S.A. *American Antiquity* 69:63–83.

Reitz, E. J., and E. S. Wing
1999 *Zooarchaeology.* Cambridge: Cambridge University Press.

Rick, J. W.
1987 Dates as Data: An Examination of the Peruvian Preceramic Radiocarbon Record. *American Antiquity* 52:55–73.

Rick, T. C.
2002 Eolian Processes, Ground Cover, and the Archaeology of Coastal Dunes: A Taphonomic Case Study from San Miguel Island, California, U.S.A. *Geoarchaeology* 17:811–833.

2004a *Daily Activities, Community Dynamics, and Historical Ecology on California's Northern Channel Islands.* Ph.D. Dissertation, Department of Anthropology, University of Oregon. Ann Arbor: UMI.

2004b Social and Economic Dynamics on Late Holocene San Miguel Island, California. In *Foundations of Chumash Complexity,* edited by J. E. Arnold, pp. 97–112. Los Angeles: UCLA Cotsen Institute of Archaeology.

2004c Red Abalone Bead Production and Exchange on California's Northern Channel Islands. *North American Archaeologist* 24:213–237.

Rick, T. C., and J. M. Erlandson
2000 Early Holocene Fishing Strategies on the California Coast: Evidence from CA-SBA-2057. *Journal of Archaeological Science* 27:621–633.

2001 Late Holocene Subsistence Strategies on the South Coast of Santa Barbara Island, California. *Journal of California and Great Basin Anthropology* 23:297–307.

2003 Archeology, Ancient Human Impacts on the Environment, and Cultural Resource Management on Channel Islands National Park, California. *CRM: The Journal of Heritage Stewardship* 1:86–89.

2004 Archaeological Site Assessments on San Miguel and Santa Rosa Islands, Channel Islands National Park, California. Report on file at Channel Islands National Park, Ventura.

Rick, T. C., and M. A. Glassow
1999 Middle Holocene Fisheries of the Central Santa Barbara Channel Region, California: Investigations at CA-SBA-53. *Journal of California and Great Basin Anthropology* 21:236–256.

Rick, T. C., J. M. Erlandson, and R. L. Vellanoweth
2001a Paleocoastal Marine Fishing on the Pacific Coast of the Americas: Perspectives from Daisy Cave, California. *American Antiquity* 66:595–613.

Rick, T. C., C. E. Skinner, J. M. Erlandson, and R. L. Vellanoweth
2001b Obsidian Source Characterization and Human Exchange Systems on California's Channel Islands. *Pacific Coast Archaeological Society Quarterly* 37(3):27–44.

Rick, T. C., R. L. Vellanoweth, J. M. Erlandson, and D. J. Kennett
2002 On the Antiquity of the Single-Piece Fishhook: AMS Radiocarbon Evidence from the Southern California Coast. *Journal of Archaeological Science* 29:933–942.

Rick, T. C., D. J. Kennett, and J. M. Erlandson
2005a Preliminary Report on the Archaeology and Paleoecology of the Abalone Rocks Estuary, Santa Rosa Island, California. In *Proceedings of the Sixth California Islands Symposium,* edited by D. Garcelon and C. Schwemm, pp. 55–63. Arcata, CA: National Park Service Technical Publication CHIS-05–01, Institute for Wildlife Studies.

Rick, T. C., J. M, Erlandson, R. L. Vellanoweth, and T. J. Braje
2005b From Pleistocene Mariners to Complex Hunter-Gatherers: The Archaeology of the California Channel Islands. *Journal of World Prehistory* 19:169-228.

Rick, T. C., J. M. Erlandson, T. J. Braje, J. A. Estes, M. H. Graham, and R. L. Vellanoweth
2006a Historical Ecology and Human Impacts on Coastal Ecosystems of the Santa Barbara Channel, California. In *Ancient Human Impacts on Marine Environments: A Global Perspective,* edited by T. C. Rick and J. M. Erlandson. Berkeley: University of California Press, in press.

Rick, T. C., J. M, Erlandson, and R. L. Vellanoweth
2006b   Taphonomy and Site Formation on California's Channel Islands. *Geoarchaeology* 21:567–589.

Ricketts, E. F., J. Calvin, and J. W. Hedgpeth
1985   *Between Pacific Tides.* Fifth edition. Stanford: Stanford University Press.

Riedman, M.
1990   *The Pinnipeds: Seals, Sea Lions, and Walruses.* Berkeley: University of California Press.

Roberts, L. J.
1991   *San Miguel Island: Santa Barbara's Fourth Island West.* Carmel, CA: Cal Rim Books.

Roberts, N.
1998   *The Holocene: An Environmental History.* Second Edition. Oxford: Blackwell Publishers

Rogers, D. B.
1929   *Prehistoric Man on the Santa Barbara Coast.* Santa Barbara: Santa Barbara Museum of Natural History.

Rowley-Conwy, P.
2001   Time, Change, and the Archaeology of Hunter-Gatherers: How Original is the "Original Affluent Society"? In *Hunter-Gatherers: An Interdisciplinary Perspective,* edited by C. Panter-Brick, L. H. Layton, and P. Rowley-Conwy, pp. 39–72. Cambridge: Cambridge University Press.

Rozaire, C. E.
1978   A Report of the Archaeological Investigations of Three California Channel Islands: Santa Barbara, Anacapa, and San Miguel. Report on file at the Central Coast Information Center, University of California, Santa Barabra.

Salls, R. A.
1988   *Prehistoric Fisheries of the California Bight.* Ph.D. Dissertation, Department of Anthropology, University of California, Los Angeles. Ann Arbor: UMI.

1991   Early Holocene Maritime Adaptation at Eel Point, San Clemente Island. In *Hunter-Gatherers of Early Holocene Coastal California,* edited by J. M. Erlandson and R. H. Colten, pp. 63–80. Los Angeles: UCLA Institute of Archaeology.

Sandweiss, D. H., H. McInnis, R. L. Burger, A. Cano, B. Ojeda, R. Paredes, M. C. Sandweiss, and M. D. Glascock.
1998   Quebrada Jaguay: Early South American Maritime Adaptations. *Science* 281:1830–1833.

Sassaman, K. E.
2004   Complex Hunter-Gatherers in Evolution and History: A North American Perspective. *Journal of Archaeological Research* 12:227–280.

Scalise, J. L.
1994   *San Clemente Island's Social and Exchange Networks: A Diachronic View of Interaction among the Maritime Adapted Southern and Northern Channel Islands, California.* Ph.D. Dissertation, Department of Anthropology, University of California, Los Angeles. Ann Arbor: UMI.

Schiffer, M. B.
1986   Radiocarbon Dating and the "Old Wood" Problem: The Case of the Hohokam Chronology. *Journal of Archaeological Science* 13:13–30.

1987   *Formation Processes and the Archaeological Record.* Albuquerque: University of New Mexico Press.

2000   Social Theory in Archaeology: Building Bridges. In *Social Theory in Archaeology,* edited by M. B. Schiffer, pp. 1–13. Salt Lake City: University of Utah Press.

Schoenherr, A. A.
1992   *A Natural History of California.* Berkeley: University of California Press.

Schoenherr, A. A., C. R. Feldmeth, and M. J. Emerson
1999   *Natural History of the Islands of California.* Berkeley: University of California Press.

Sharp, J. T.
2000   Shellfish Analysis from the Punta Arena Site, a Middle Holocene Red Abalone Midden on Santa Cruz Island, California. Unpublished Master's Thesis, Cultural Resources Management, Sonoma State University.

Silliman, S. W.
2001   Theoretical Perspectives on Labor and Colonialism: Reconsidering the California Missions. *Journal of Anthropological Archaeology* 20:379–407.

2004   *Lost Laborers in Colonial California: Native Americans and the Archaeology of Rancho Petaluma.* Tucson: University of Arizona Press.

Simmons, I. G.
2001   *An Environmental History of Great Britain: From 10,000 Years Ago to the Present.* Edinburgh: Edinburgh University Press.

Smith, C. F.
1998 *A Flora of the Santa Barbara Region, California*. Second Edition. Santa Barbara: Santa Barbara Botanic Garden and Capra Press.

Soil Survey Staff
2003 *Keys to Soil Taxonomy* (Ninth Edition). United States Department of Agriculture.

Stannard, D. E.
1992 *American Holocaust: Columbus and the Conquest of the New World*. Oxford: Oxford University Press.

Stark, B. L., and B. Voorhies (editors)
1978 *Prehistoric Coastal Adaptations: The Economy and Ecology of Maritime Middle America*. New York: Academic Press.

Stein, J. K.
1992 The Analysis of Shell Middens. In *Deciphering a Shell Midden*, edited by J. Stein, pp. 1–24. New York: Academic Press.
2001 A Review of Site Formation Processes and Their Relevance to Geoarchaeology. In *Earth Sciences and Archaeology*, edited by P. Goldberg, V. Holliday, and C. Ferring, pp. 37–54. New York: Kluwer Academic/Plenum Publishers.

Stein, J. K., and W. R. Farrand (editors)
2001 *Sediments in Archaeological Context*. Salt Lake City: University of Utah Press.

Steneck, R. S., M. H. Graham, B. J. Bourque, D. Corbett, J. M. Erlandson, J. A. Estes, and M. J. Tegner
2002 Kelp Forest Ecosystems: Biodiversity, Stability, Resilience and Future. *Environmental Conservation* 29:436-459.

Stewart, B. S., and P. K. Yochem
2002 Community Ecology of California Channel Islands Pinnipeds. In *Proceedings of the Fifth California Islands Symposium*, edited by D. Brown, K. Mitchell, and H. Chaney, pp. 413–420. Santa Barbara: Santa Barbara Museum of Natural History.

Stiner, M. C.
1994 *Honor Among Thieves: A Zooarchaeological Study of Neandertal Ecology*. Princeton: Princeton University Press.

Stuiver, M., and P. J. Reimer
1993 Extended ^{14}C Data Base and Revised Calib 3.0 ^{14}C Age Calibration Program. *Radiocarbon* 35: 215–230.
2000 *Calib 4.3 Radiocarbon Calibration Program 2000*. Quaternary Isotope Lab, University of Washington.

Tainter, J. A.
1977 Population Dynamics on the Santa Barbara Coast. *Pacific Coast Archaeological Society Quarterly* 13(3):33–54.

Tartaglia, L. J.
1976 *Prehistoric Maritime Adaptations in Southern California*. Ph.D. dissertation, Department of Anthropology, University of California, Los Angeles. Ann Arbor: UMI.

Thomas, D. H. (editor)
1989 *Columbian Consequences, Vol. 1: Archaeological and Historical Perspectives on the Spanish Borderlands West*. Washington DC: Smithsonian Institution.
1990 *Columbian Consequences, Vol. 2: Archaeological and Historical Perspectives on the Spanish Borderlands East*. Washington DC: Smithsonian Institution.
1991 *Columbian Consequences, Vol. 3: The Spanish Borderlands in Pan-American Perspective*. Washington DC: Smithsonian Institution.

Timbrook, J.
1990 Ethnobotany of the Chumash Indians, California, Based on the Ethnographic Notes of John P. Harrington. *Economic Botany* 44:236–253.
1993 Island Chumash Ethnobotany. In *Archaeology on the Northern Channel Islands, California: Archaeology on the Northern Channel Islands of California: Studies of Subsistence, Economics, and Social Organization*, edited by M. A. Glassow, pp. 47–62. Archives of California Prehistory 34. Salinas: Coyote Press.

Timbrook, J., J. R. Johnson, and D. D. Earle
1982 Vegetation Burning by the Chumash. *Journal of California and Great Basin Anthropology* 4:163–186.

van der Leeuw, S., and C. L. Redman
2002 Placing Archaeology at the Center of Socionatural Studies. *American Antiquity* 67:597–605.

VanPool, C. S., and T. L. VanPool
2003 Introduction: Method, Theory, and the Essential Tension. In *Essential Tensions in Archaeological Method and Theory*, edited by T. L. VanPool and C. S. VanPool, pp. 1–4. Salt Lake City: University of Utah Press.

Vellanoweth, R. L.
2001 AMS Radiocarbon Dating and Shell Bead Chronologies: Middle Holocene Exchange and Interaction in Western North America. *Journal of Archaeological Science* 28:941–950.

Vellanoweth, R. L., and J. M. Erlandson
  1999   Middle Holocene Fishing and Maritime
          Adaptations at CA-SNI-161, San Nicolas
          Island, California. *Journal of California
          and Great Basin Anthropology* 21(2): 257–
          274.
Vellanoweth, R. L., and D. R. Grenda
  2002   Paradise or Purgatory: Environments
          Past and Present. In *Islanders and Main-
          landers: Prehistoric Context for the Southern
          California Bight*, edited by J. Altschul and
          D. Grenda, pp. 67–84. Tucson: SRI Press.
Vellanoweth, R. L., T. C. Rick, and J. M. Erlandson
  2002   Middle and Late Holocene Maritime
          Adaptations on Northeastern San Miguel
          Island, California. In *Proceedings of the Fifth
          California Islands Symposium*, edited by D.
          Browne, K. Mitchell, and H. Chaney, pp.
          607–614. Santa Barbara: Santa Barbara
          Museum of Natural History.
Vellanoweth, R. L., M. R. Lambright, J. M. Erlandson, and T. C. Rick
  2003   Early New World Maritime Technolo-
          gies: Sea Grass Cordage, Shell Beads, and
          a Bone Tool from Cave of the Chimneys,
          San Miguel Island, California. *Journal of
          Archaeological Science* 30:1161–1173.
Vellanoweth, R. L., T. C. Rick, J. M. Erlandson, and
G. Reynolds
  2006   A 6000 Year Old Red Abalone Midden on
          San Miguel Island, California. *North
          American Archaeologist*, in press.
Villa, P.
  1982   Conjoinable Pieces and Site Formation
          Processes. *American Antiquity* 47:276–290.
Voorhies, B.
  2004   *Coastal Collectors in the Holocene: The
          Chantuto People of Southwest Mexico.*
          Gainesville: University Press of Florida.
Wagner, H. R.
  1929   *Spanish Voyages to the Northwest Coast of
          North America in the Sixteenth Century.* San
          Francisco: California Historical Society.
Wake, T. A.
  2001   Bone Tool Technology on Santa Cruz
          Island and Implications for Exchange. In
          *The Origins of a Pacific Coast Chiefdom: The
          Chumash of the Channel Islands*, edited by
          J. E. Arnold, pp. 183–197. Salt Lake City:
          University of Utah Press.
Walker, P. L.
  1986   Porotic Hyperostosis in a Marine-
          Dependent California Indian Popula-

          tion. *American Journal of Physical Anthro-
          pology* 69:345-354.
  1989   Cranial Injuries as Evidence of Violence
          in Prehistoric Southern California. *Amer-
          ican Journal of Physical Anthropology*
          80:313-323.
Walker, P. L., and J. M. Erlandson
  1986   Dental Evidence for Prehistoric Dietary
          Change on the Northern Channel
          Islands, California. *American Antiquity*
          51:375–383.
Walker, P. L., and J. R. Johnson
  1992   The Effects of Contact on the Chumash
          Indians. In *Disease and Demography in the
          Americas*, edited J. Verano and D.
          Ubelaker, pp. 127–139. Washington DC:
          Smithsonian Institution Press.
Walker, P. L., and P. E. Snethkamp
  1984   Archaeological Investigations on San
          Miguel Island—1982: Prehistoric Adap-
          tations to the Marine Environment.
          Report on file at the Central Coast Infor-
          mation Center, University of California,
          Santa Barbara.
Walker, P. L., P. Lambert, and M. J. DeNiro
  1989   The Effects of European Contact on the
          Health of Alta Californians. In *Columbian
          Consequences, Vol. 1: Archaeological and His-
          torical Perspectives on the Spanish Border-
          lands West*, edited by D. Thomas, pp.
          349–364. Washington DC: Smithsonian
          Institution.
Walker, P. L., D. J. Kennett, T. L. Jones, and R. L.
Delong
  2002   Archaeological Investigations of the
          Point Bennett Pinniped Rookery on San
          Miguel Island. In *Proceedings of the Fifth
          California Islands Symposium*, edited by D.
          Brown, K. Mitchell, and H. Chaney, pp.
          628–632. Santa Barbara: Santa Barbara
          Museum of Natural History.
Wallace, W.
  1955   A Suggested Chronology for Southern
          California Coastal Archaeology. *Southwest
          Journal of Anthropology* 11:214–230.
Warren, C. N.
  1967   The Southern California Millingstone
          Horizon: Some Comments. *American
          Antiquity* 32:233–236.
  1968   Cultural Tradition and Ecological Adap-
          tation on the Southern California Coast.
          *Eastern New Mexico University Contribu-
          tions to Anthropology* 1(3):1–14.

Waselkov, G. A.
1987   Shellfish Gathering and Shell Midden Archaeology. *Advances in Archaeolgoical Method and Theory* 10:93–210.

Wason, P. K.
1994   *The Archaeology of Rank*. New York: Cambridge University Press.

Weaver, D. W.
1969   General Geology of the Region. In *Geology of the Northern Channel Islands*, edited by D. Weaver, D. Doerner, and B. Nolf, pp. 9–10. American Association of Petroleum Geologists and Society of Economic Paleontologists and Mineralogists Pacific Section Special Publication.

Wheeler, A., and A. K. G. Jones.
1989   *Fishes*. Cambridge: Cambridge University Press.

Whitlock, C. and M. A. Knox
2002   Prehistoric Burning in the Pacific Northwest. In *Fire, Native Peoples, and the Natural Landscape*, edited by T. R. Vale, pp. 195–231. Washington DC: Island Press.

Wilson, D. J.
1981   Of Maize and Men: A Critique of the Maritime Hypothesis of State Origins on the Coast of Peru. *American Anthropologist* 85:93–120.

Wood, W. R., and D. L. Johnson
1978   A Survey of Disturbance Processes in Archaeological Site Formation. *Advances in Archaeological Method and Theory* 1:315–381.

Yatsko, A.
2000   *Late Holocene Paleoclimatic Stress and Prehistoric Human Occupation on San Clemente Island*. Ph.D. Dissertation, Department of Anthropology, University of California, Los Angeles. Ann Arbor: UMI.

Yesner, D. R.
1980   Maritime Hunter-Gatherers: Ecology and Prehistory. *Current Anthropology* 21:727–750.

1987   Life in the Garden of Eden: Causes and Consequences of the Adoption of Marine Diets by Human Societies. In *Food and Evolution*, edited by M. Harris and E. Ross, pp. 285–310. Philadelphia: Temple University Press.

Ziegler, A. C.
1975   Recovery and Significance of Unmodified Faunal Remains. In *Field Methods in Archaeology*, edited by T. Hester, R. Heizer, and J. Graham, pp. 183–205. Palo Alto: Mayfield Publishing.

Zohar, I., and M. Belmaker
2005   Size Does Matter: Methodological Comments on Sieve Size and Species Richness in Fish Bone Assemblages. *Journal of Archaeological Science* 32:635–641.

Index